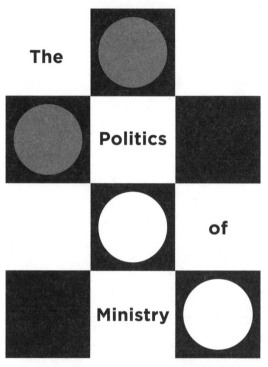

The Politics of Ministry

Bob Burns,
Tasha D. Chapman
& Donald C. Guthrie
Foreword by Steven Garber

Navigating
Power Dynamics
and Negotiating
Interests

IVP Books

An imprint of InterVarsity Press
Downers Grove, Illinois

InterVarsity Press
P.O. Box 1400, Downers Grove, IL 60515-1426
ivpress.com
email@ivpress.com

InterVarsity Press® is the book-publishing division of InterVarsity Christian Fellowship/USA®, a movement of students and faculty active on campus at hundreds of universities, colleges, and schools of nursing in the United States of America, and a member movement of the International Fellowship of Evangelical Students. For information about local and regional activities, visit intervarsity.org.

Scripture quotations, unless otherwise noted, are from The Holy Bible, English Standard Version, copyright © 2001 by Crossway Bibles, a division of Good News Publishers. Used by permission. All rights reserved.

While any stories in this book are true, some names and identifying information may have been changed to protect the privacy of individuals.

Cover design: David Fassett
Interior design: Daniel van Loon
Images: © Nadine Westveer / EyeEm / Getty Images

ISBN 978-0-8308-4150-9 (print)
ISBN 978-0-8308-7380-7 (digital)

Printed in the United States of America ♾

InterVarsity Press is committed to ecological stewardship and to the conservation of natural resources in all our operations. This book was printed using sustainably sourced paper.

Library of Congress Cataloging-in-Publication Data
A catalog record for this book is available from the Library of Congress.

P	25	24	23	22	21	20	19	18	17	16	15	14	13	12	11	10	9	8	7	6	5	4	3	2	1
Y	38	37	36	35	34	33	32	31	30	29	28	27	26	25	24	23	22	21	20	19					

"I once spoke with a six-term US Congressman who told me, 'I once considered the ministry, but thought it was just too political!' Needless to say, I howled. For anyone in, thinking about, or trying to penetrate the mysterious politics of church life, this book will function like an ecclesial MRI revealing subtle layers of how decisions are made, who stays and who goes, and much that goes on under the surface of ministry. Burns, Chapman, and Guthrie nail it. The light they shed from current research illuminates what is for most of us a dark and often dangerous landscape."

Tom Pfizenmaier, Gordon-Conwell Theological Seminary

"It's only a matter of time until we leaders realize we're not really as good at working with people as we thought, and we're not sure what to do about it. Through relatable stories, practical tools, and helpful new language, this book provides essential training in how to work with and through God's people, in ways that honor him and increase our self-awareness as leaders."

Leela Murty, thirty-year campus staff member and former northeast regional director with Cru

"Burns, Chapman, and Guthrie present rich substance, timely practical resources and case studies for applying biblical theology into the challenges of daily ministry.... This book will help us in seminaries to more effectively prepare pastors and leaders to face future challenges in ministry with realistic hope. It will also be a tool to sustain them as they grow in wise stewardship of people, power, interests, and negotiation wherever God calls them."

Mark L. Dalbey, president and associate professor of applied theology at Covenant Theological Seminary

"Politics? Ministry? The two words on the surface appear incongruous, even disconcerting. Yet more often than we may know, the derail-er of a pastor or ministry leader is not their own moral failing or lack of competence, but rather the invisible yet powerful systems at work in the context they have entered.... The resources and tools provided in this important book will help a ministry leader (or any leader) navigate contextual waters that may seem calm on the surface but often have a powerful undertow."

Lisa Pratt Slayton, CEO, Pittsburgh Leadership Foundation

"Those called to lead the church quickly learn they must not only read the Bible well, they must also read the room well. Utilizing a scholarly bent with practitioner flair, a persuasive case is made that the longevity and fruitfulness of Christian leadership is in good part due to a growing competency in navigating the inevitable political realities any faith community presents. For all who are called to the enterprise of church leadership, *The Politics of Ministry* is an invaluable guide down the path of greater effectiveness and influence. I highly recommend it."

Tom Nelson, senior pastor of Christ Community Church in Kansas City, president of Made to Flourish, author of *The Economics of Neighborly Love*

"Drawing on years of teaching and ministry experience, Bob Burns, Tasha Chapman, and Donald Guthrie have provided readers with a wise, thoughtful, helpful, and insightful guide regarding ministry and church relationships. Addressing issues of power, interests, and negotiation, our authors point readers toward opportunities for redemption and resilience in both relationships and structures for the good of the gospel and the edification of the church. Drawing on case studies and providing direction for personal or group reflection, the book is focused on authentic application for those new to ministry, for those with a long tenure in ministry, as well as for those who have experienced pain, setback, and disappointment in ministry."

David S. Dockery, president of Trinity International University and Trinity Evangelical Divinity School

"This book addresses political issues in ministry with honesty and clarity, illustrated with rich examples from real-life stories. The conceptual frameworks provided—interests, power, negotiation, and ethical considerations—are extremely helpful to understand the phenomena and to explore redemptive approaches in various situations. This is a must-read for all who are involved in various types of church and parachurch ministry."

Sutrisna Harjanto, Bandung Theological Seminary, Bandung, Indonesia

"People often enter a new ministry with great energy and hope only to discover they have been thrust into a bewildering set of expectations, conflicting demands, and unspoken rules. After a while they may even feel jaded about Christian ministry and quietly begin looking for another job. A key benefit of this book is that it names and encourages us to be honest about the social dynamics that occur in any church or organization. The authors point the way to a more healthy, human, and informed way of living the good news of Jesus in community."

John F. Thomas, senior director for training, Redeemer City to City

"*The Politics of Ministry* is an excellent and one-of-a-kind toolkit for anyone involved in Christian ministry around the world and committed to redeeming the messiness in ministry. As scholar-practitioners, Bob Burns, Tasha Chapman, and Donald Guthrie, with real-life examples and thought-provoking questions, facilitate how to navigate different power dynamics and how to negotiate interests."

Ebenezer G. P. Perinbaraj and **Esther T. Rajamani,** founders and coexecutive directors of Rabah Network, Chennai, India

"Politics is a dirty word in the church of Jesus Christ and increasingly in our American culture. People are sick of leaders focused only their own interests who use power for personal agendas. Many sincere leaders are naive about power; but Jesus challenges us to be shrewd as snakes as well as innocent as a dove. Here is a book with the beauty of a snake and the ethics of a dove."

Richard G. Thompson, Great Lakes district superintendent, Evangelical Free Church of America

Contents

Foreword

Steven Garber

Just politics.

A long time ago now, I spent years teaching on Capitol Hill, year by year drawing very motivated students into the corridors of the glory and shame that is Washington, DC. We asked a lot of them, pressing them into an intellectual and moral seriousness, about what they believed and why they believed it, particularly focused on the nature of public responsibility in a pluralizing, secularizing, and globalizing world.

The first essay I wrote in my tenure there as a senior member of the faculty was simply titled "Just Politics." Playing off of the cynical view that many have of political life—"That's just politics!"—thereby distancing themselves from any relationship with and responsibility for the question at hand. I reflected on our propensity to see the sorrows and strains of the Washington, DCs, of history as windows into the corruption that is inherent in politics. *Why care?* Of course we shouldn't, because it is always and only "just politics" after all.

But that didn't seem enough for me. During my boyhood summers, when I traveled the mountain passes of Colorado with my grandfather, whose lifelong work was cattle buying, he would quiz me, expecting me to know about our nation and world. In my undergraduate years, the faculty of my college gave me the award for "the student most committed to political responsibility." So, from earliest days, I have believed that somehow, difficult as it often is, impossible as it sometimes feels, politics matters—that vocations in the public squares of history are worthy of our hopes and dreams because the hard work of politics is finally our work together for the flourishing of all. Even when we know that making peace with proximate justice must be done if we are to keep on keeping on as citizens. We yearn for things to be as they ought to be, in our very bones dissatisfied with the lies and deceptions, the greed and malice that too often marks what we know as "politics." Simply said, to believe in and work for just politics is an ambition that should draw all of us together because our common good depends on it.

That is as true of public life in the push and shove of politics—local, national, global—as it is of congregational life in the church. Politics then becomes something that is ours together, a way of thinking and living that accounts for the demands of a common life. In this very good book, *The Politics of Ministry*, the authors argue that "politics is the art of getting things done with others." To see it that way is to return to the older, wiser, deeper understanding of the *polis* and what it means for who we are and how we live. We are in this together, human beings that we are.

In the inimitable words of author and cultural critic Wendell Berry, offered through the colloquial wisdom of his character Burley Coulter, "The way we are, we are members of each other. All of us. Everything. The difference ain't in who is a member and who is not, but in who knows it and who don't." That is as true of our membership in communities like Berry's Port William as it is of the cities and states of our lives—and of the communities and churches that make us, us. We are members of each other.

And yet, so very often we don't feel like it; perhaps sometimes we don't want to be "members of each other." For most of us the more we know of the world, the harder it is to love the world; and the more we know of each other, the harder it is to love each other. We would rather not, for a thousand different reasons. Psychologically and sociologically, we stumble over our humanness, longing for intimacy but afraid of intimacy, hoping for community but afraid of community. In the remarkably prescient words of Sherry Turkle, professor at MIT whose work focuses on the social ecology of our technological society, we are "alone together," connected to everyone everywhere. But because of the fears implicit in being known by each other and knowing more of each other, we choose our aloneness instead, feeling overwhelmed by the responsibility of knowledge.

It is here where the authors offer rare insight, skilled physicians of the soul of the church that they are, inviting us to learn over their shoulders and through their hearts from their practiced insights into why we often stumble over each other—and why that is not inevitable. Complex and comprehensive, wise and nuanced, together they represent years of experience in organizations and institutions that are necessarily political, where "getting things done together" is the name of the game. Rather than the despair of "that's just (the politics of) the church!," their life together has brought them into a common calling of caring for the health of the church.

There is nothing romanticized here. They have each spent too long in the church, too long embedded in more communal and corporate life, to offer anything other than a holy *realecclesiastik* for all with ears to hear. Written into their study are the realities of power, interests, negotiation, and ethics, four dynamics woven into every family, every church, every business, every school, every seminary, and every state. But if we are to find our way to the redemption of the necessarily political character of our common life, we have to understand them—power, interests, negotiation, and the ethical implications—and we must steward them for the sake of all. We destroy ourselves, and each other when we pretend that we are anything other than "members of each other" with responsibilities for each other.

In Stanley Hauerwas's essay "The Story-Formed Community," a playfully profound study of the novel *Watership Down*, he theologically reflects on the ways that stories shape us, especially the ways that they shape us in and through our communities. After stating his ten theses for the reform of Christian social ethics, then developing a fascinating study of the moral complexities of the rabbit communities whose story it is—full of fractiousness and contention, hope and longing—he concludes hopefully, "We could form our lives together by trusting in truth and love to banish the fears that create enmity and discord." *Who are we? How will we live?* The questions and the answers are so basic to a good life and to a good society. Hauerwas's long interest in character as central to our identity is communally embodied in the common life of rabbits, which might seem to be so different, and yet so it is so similar to ours, human beings that we are.

What is given to us in *The Politics of Ministry* is a way forward, moving beyond the worn-down cynicism born of our life together in the church. With the wisdom of hard-won scholarship about organizational life and leadership, twined together with pastoral hearts long offered to God and his people, Bob Burns, Tasha Chapman, and Don Guthrie are teachers to us all, at least to anyone who has been burdened by the weight of one more experience of "that's just politics!"—feeling as if faith and hope and love are words emptied of any existential meaning, words without flesh. Instead, they have labored in love together for our sake, for the church's sake, for Christ's sake, believing that the redemption of the politics of ministry is both possible and plausible. May it be so.

Introduction

Politics and *ministry*. The two words are rarely used together, especially these days. However, ministry means working with people. And people have conflicting interests. These interests lead people to act in certain ways. So, whenever people get together, they will be negotiating their interests. Traditional hymns or contemporary choruses? Children in service or in children's church? Immersion or sprinkling? Group meetings early morning or evening?

In this book we look at politics from a wider and more neutral perspective than the partisan haggling on Capitol Hill. Here, *politics is the art of getting things done with others*. We believe whenever people work, play, or just hang out together, politics happens. Because—consciously or unconsciously, ethically or unethically—people are constantly negotiating for their interests. Therefore, ministry is political.

That's what this book is about. We weave real-life stories of people in ministry through a discussion of four themes that construct the political experience: power, interests, negotiation, and ethical challenges. Added to these themes are the ensuing relationship dynamics involved whenever people negotiate interests with available power. The stories are real, but we have changed settings and names to honor confidences.

Bob and Donald were first introduced to these themes while studying with Ron Cervero at the University of Georgia. Ron has written extensively on the political experience of those involved in adult education. At first, perhaps like you, we were turned off by the term *politics*. But as we listened and learned, we quickly related his ideas to the events of our lives and work in ministry.

We realized that we were constantly engaged in the ethical and relational challenges of negotiating interests with others: with family members, people at church, work colleagues, and friends. Then we began to see these same dynamics played out in Scripture as the gospel affected people in their social contexts. Eventually we both ended up teaching about educational ministry and leadership, together with our colleague Tasha Chapman, who added to our shared understanding and continuing research of politics in life and in ministry.

After years of researching and testing these ideas in classrooms, leadership seminars, ministry consultations, and our own churches, we now share them with you. We have learned much from those who have worked on the ideas with us and from our own successes and failures as we have sought to apply them in our own lives.

As we wrote this book, we were thinking about four types of readers.

- Foremost in our minds was anyone involved in Christian ministry, whether as a volunteer or employee, in a church or a parachurch context. We had those who serve in the name of Jesus as our focus.

- At the same time, we were concerned that people who have been confused or injured in ministry contexts might gain new, helpful perspectives on their experiences for healing and future fruitfulness.

- We also desired to share what we've learned with those who are just starting out in vocational ministry. We are concerned for those who might be going naively into ministry leadership assuming that people in their ministry will understand each other and get along. We have logged enough years in ministry to know that the joys of serving Jesus are always mingled with disagreements and uncertainty, if not bitter and painful disappointments and conflicts.

- Finally, while the focus of this book is on the context of ministry, we believe all aspects of life involve politics. So we pray that anyone reading this book will consider its applicability beyond explicit ministry contexts to every sphere of life.

An ounce of reflection can lead to a pound of learning. Therefore, throughout each chapter we include sets of questions worth pondering. These questions can be used in many ways. One idea is personal reflection. Consider writing journal entries in response to these questions, as well as jotting down other thoughts and feelings that this book raises. Another strategy is to work through the book with others. The questions can serve as discussion guides. Take time to make new concepts your own by adding stories and insights from your own experiences to the stories in the book.

Chapter ① 1

Three Ministry Stories

Ministry work is people work, and people work is messy. We begin with three true stories from different contexts. These stories are unique to those who were involved, yet they have the capacity to change those of us who will hear and seek to understand.

Brian's Story

Brian was dazed. He sat in his office chair, his head in his hands. *What have I gotten myself into?* he asked himself. *This isn't the way it's supposed to be!*

Roughly two months earlier, Brian had graduated from a theological seminary. During his last term he had explored opportunities to serve as an assistant pastor. He figured that he needed to start his ministerial life working under the mentorship of a more experienced pastor. After submitting his name and résumé to a number of churches, he finally found an opportunity at Trinity Church that seemed to have everything he was looking for.

Brian had a series of lengthy phone conversations with Trinity's search committee. Then he and his wife, Sarah, visited the church over a long weekend. He met with the pastor, the search committee, and the governing board. The church extended an official call to employment, and Brian accepted. Just two weeks after graduation, Brian and Sarah moved into an apartment near the church, and Brian began his new job as a pastor.

Funny thing about that official call: Brian was offered the position of *associate* pastor rather than assistant pastor. This may sound like a trivial difference. But in Brian's denominational world it was a big deal. The "associate" title was usually considered a promotion given pastors after they served as an assistant for a number of years. With that title came the responsibility to serve as a voting member of the church governing board.

Brian wondered why he was offered this higher status. He was confident that his references had put in a good word for him, and he had done well in his classwork. Maybe one of his professors had said something that brought this honor, or he had he impressed the search committee so much that they thought he had earned it. Unfortunately, he would soon discover a troubling reason for being made a voting member on the board.

Brian's first two months were filled with typical adjustments to a new job: learning policies and procedures, getting to know people, meeting with committees, and even preaching in the morning service. He particularly appreciated the personal times he had with Joe, the senior pastor. Joe had been an ordained pastor for twenty-seven years. He enjoyed sharing with Brian lessons he had learned, and began coaching Brian on leading worship and administering the sacraments.

However, the most significant job responsibility on Brian's schedule for those first two months was preparing for his ordination exams. In Brian's denomination the ordination process was like running the gauntlet: written exams, an oral exam before a committee, and then another oral examination before selected pastors and board members in the region. After much study and preparation, Brian passed. The ceremony for his ordination and installation took place at Trinity's Sunday evening service. His parents attended, so did his college friends. Sarah was so proud. It was a night Brian had dreamed of for years.

What Brian did not know was that a group of influential board members at Trinity had also been waiting for this time. Monday morning after Brian's ordination, two board members invited the senior pastor, Joe, to lunch at the local country club. There they "asked" him to resign and offered him a generous severance if he did. If he would not, they were prepared to call a congregational meeting to publicly state his failures and demand his termination. Joe agreed to resign. Later that afternoon the entire board—without Brian—met at the church to receive the resignation. By that evening Joe had removed everything from his office.

Tuesday morning Brian drove to church for his first work day after his ordination. His day was to start with a regularly scheduled meeting with Joe. This morning, however, a board member met Brian at the church office. In a brief conversation, Brian was informed that Joe had resigned and that he, Brian, was now the interim senior pastor. This meant he was now responsible for worship planning, preaching, pastoral care, and moderating the board meetings. And wasn't it convenient that he was already a voting member of the board and could immediately assume those responsibilities? Then the board member left. Brian sat in shock.

Reflections on Brian's Story

Years later Brian shared how naive he was when he took his first pastoral position. Although he had been involved in church ministry as a lay leader, he had not experienced anything particularly hurtful before. He expected church work to be pleasant, with people getting along well together. "I was blind to the facts," he lamented.

Only in hindsight did Brian realize why the board had called him to be an associate pastor. It was not because of his sterling attributes. "They had planned to eliminate the senior pastor long before they ever talked with me," he sighed. "And from an organizational standpoint, they needed someone to manage the crisis and hold the congregation together until they could call a new senior pastor."

For the next year at the church, Brian was flying by the seat of his pants. As he put it, "I was scared to death. That was a critical time for me. For the first time I saw how precarious the pastor's position can be. It was a wake-up call to be more aware. And probably to be a lot less trusting." Brian stuck it out at Trinity until a new senior pastor was hired. Then, as Brian described it, he "escaped" by accepting the next available call to a different church.

When Brian left the church, he and his wife were fearful of church board leaders and much less trusting of people in general. They started to assume ministry leadership would be risky and emotionally challenging. Pastor Joe, his family, and most of the congregants were equally blindsided by the abrupt termination. The board's actions resulted in painful conflicts and broken trust between congregants and the board members. The situation affected the broader community as well. Rumors and gossip about the church spread for months afterward.

Questions to Ponder

1. How did you respond as you read Brian's story?

2. Does your reaction to this story feel similar to something you've experienced? How so? What events does it remind you of?

3. Make a list of words, images, and feelings that come to mind when you consider the word *politics*.

4. In what ways do you associate any of the items on your list with ministry activity?

5. In light of the list, note some desires you have for your own leadership work involving other people.

Ministry as Messy Work

Brian's experience was rather extreme. However, it is not unusual for pastors to change churches every four to five years.[1] The important work of Dean Hoge and Jacqueline Wenger found many reasons for such fast transitions in the pastorate, but conflicting viewpoints and opinions—and the way they are managed—is one primary factor.[2]

We need to get honest about just how messy it is to work with people in ministry. The process of managing differences of thought and expectations between people is complicated, unpredictable, and emotionally taxing. It is often full of conflict. How can everyone's ideas, values, and goals align to move the same direction? It helps to name this messy but redemptive work. The term that wakes us up to this challenge is *politics*.[3] To many it might sound like a swear word, never to be applied to ministry. People often associate *politics* with lies, deceit, underhanded backroom deals, and mudslinging campaigns.

> Politics is what happens between people when they try to get something done together.

Consider what happened to Brian. Would you describe that as political? Brian's later self-description of being naive was spot on. He may have studied the brokenness of humanity while in seminary, but he had not translated it into his expectations of working with people. His naivety prevented him from being prepared to deal with the politics of ministry contexts. Being involved in ministry—or any place where we are working with people—means facing disagreements that result in conflictual actions. Therefore, when people try to accomplish something together, they are inevitably involved in the complicated process that this book explores in detail. That process is called *politics*, a term we will define more fully in chapter two.

One reason the people work of politics is so challenging is that we all have *interests*. Our interests usually reflect the way we think the world should function. Interests can be described as deep-seated values, goals, and beliefs. Often, interests sit in the back of our consciousness, strongly yet secretly influencing our opinions and decisions. They steer us like the rudder of a ship. At other times our interests propel us like the noisy motor of a speedboat, leaving large wakes that rock everyone around us.

We often do whatever we can to get the world—or at least our little corner of it—to operate in a way that reflects our interests. Interests are not necessarily selfish. Our beliefs and values, coupled with our sense of responsibility, can be quite honorable and good. Yet interests can ignite the resistance of others who perceive the situation differently.

We can see where Brian's interests were in conflict with the Trinity Church leadership. He wanted to minister to God's people in peaceful harmony. He wanted to learn from Pastor Joe by working alongside him. He wanted to think that his job was secure. And he wanted to believe the leadership thought he was special because they hired him as an associate pastor.

Some of the Trinity board members' interests were quite opposite to Brian's. They had an idea of what their church should be like, and Joe did not fit into the picture. So they wanted him out of the picture as quickly and as quietly as possible. But if necessary, they were also willing to create a public spectacle to make it happen. They also wanted the church to maintain some semblance of leadership consistency after Joe's departure. So they made sure Brian was in place with the required pastoral position before they ousted Joe.

> **Interests are deep-seated values, goals, and beliefs that reflect the way we think the world should function.**

But what about the interests of Sarah, Brian's wife? Of Joe and his family? Of the individual congregants of the church? Or even the interests of God? How do they fit into what happened? We explore these dynamics in later chapters. But in every story, all participants have interests. And for good or ill, people act on the basis of their interests. Let's see how this works out in a story from Jesus' ministry.

Jesus' Story

According to the first two chapters of Mark, Jesus began his public ministry with three activities. He proclaimed the good news of God's coming kingdom with unusual power and authority.[4] He called disciples.[5] And he healed many sick people.[6]

In the midst of this activity, Jesus entered a Capernaum synagogue on the Sabbath (Mark 3:1-6). There was a man in the synagogue with a withered hand. We do not know if this man came on his own or if he was planted there by Jesus' opponents as bait for a trap. What we do know is that there were people in the synagogue who "watched Jesus, to see whether he would heal him on the Sabbath, so that they might accuse him" of breaking the Sabbath laws (v. 2).

Jesus was well aware of the situation. He knew there were people who wanted to indict him for breaking the Sabbath. He brought the conflict into the open to engage his critics by asking the disabled man to come forward in front of everyone. He invited his critics to discuss and to learn with him. Jesus asked, "Is it lawful on the Sabbath to do good or to do harm, to save life or to kill?" (v. 4).

How would these opponents respond? Would they debate Jesus directly in front of the worshipers? Would they delay making any comments? Perhaps they would enlist the support of others? Would they ask Jesus counterquestions to clarify their understanding? Or would they avoid confrontation altogether? The Bible says they selected this final option, refusing to respond to Jesus' question at all.

How do you feel when you are trying to speak with others who refuse to talk to you? What is it like to try to have a conversation with someone and all you get are vague words or stone-cold silence?

When Jesus' opponents refused to talk, he looked around the synagogue. Perhaps he used the silence as a way to focus the attention of the crowd. The Bible says he was angry at the religious leaders, grieved at their hardness of heart. But he did not strike out against his accusers. He chose to use his anger and grief in a positive, constructive manner, to help all those watching learn both the answer to his question and the type of power he spoke with. He turned to the invalid and commanded, "Stretch out your hand" (v. 5). The man stretched it out and was fully restored.

What was Jesus' opponents' response to this miraculous healing? Did they wonder where he received such power and authority? Were they thankful that a man's withered hand suddenly became whole? Did they praise God for the healing? Did they exclaim, like those in Capernaum who had recently seen Jesus make a paralytic walk, "We never saw anything like this"?

There were representatives of two opposing Jewish sects in the synagogue: Pharisees and Herodians. These two groups held opposite views on many civil, theological, and religious issues. Under normal circumstances, they despised each other. But in this case, they found a common enemy, a shared interest. So the Pharisees and Herodians left the synagogue and held a conference on how to destroy Jesus.

It's fascinating to read through the Gospels and discover that a vast majority of the conversations Jesus had were conflicts. Sometimes the conflicts were rather mild, such as when Jesus challenged a rich young man to sell everything he had, give it to the poor, and follow him. That man walked away sorrowful (Mark 10:17-22). Yet often the conflicts were intense, with potentially enormous consequences, such as the time leaders sent spies to get Jesus in trouble with the Roman government by asking him whether it was lawful to pay taxes to Caesar (Luke 20:19-26).

Different interests lead to diverse opinions, actions, and disputes. Sometimes the stakes of the conflicts are very high, and the results are significant for many people. But before we assume every shared ministry experience ends in harmful conflict, let's look at one more story.

Questions to Ponder

1. What interests of the Pharisees and Herodians did Jesus challenge?

2. What seem to be some of Jesus' interests in this story?

3. What risks was Jesus taking in promoting his interests?

Mia and Caroline's Story

Mia and Caroline were marketplace professionals and active laypersons in their nine-year-old church. They had been involved in the church since its earliest days and had always appreciated the warm, close-knit relationships in the congregation. However, as the church grew, the comfort of being known and knowing most everyone could not be sustained. To help build community, various programs were started. But Mia and Caroline both felt that more needed to happen.

"What can we do?" they wondered, and "How will the church leadership respond to our ideas?" Then they learned of a local artist who led painting parties—an opportunity for groups to try their hand with brush and colors on canvas. Mia and Caroline asked the artist how she facilitated these parties, how many could participate, and what it would cost. With this information in hand, they set up an appointment with their pastor and pitched the idea: "What if we provided an opportunity where our women could sign up to paint together for an evening? They would have fun and get to know one another better."

After talking through some of the details, their pastor gave Mia and Caroline wholehearted approval. As a result, so many women signed up for the event that two classes were arranged. New friendships began, old relationships reconnected, neighbors participated, and people built trust together as they created "masterpieces" on canvas.

The stories of Brian and Jesus were filled with conflict. In stark contrast, Mia and Caroline's story sounds straightforward and seamless, as people worked with common interests. Yet in all three stories, similar processes were taking place. We study these common processes in this book and will explore these and other stories more fully. But first we must grapple with the dreaded word *politics* and see how it can serve as a fitting and useful name for all that takes place between people as they try to get something done together in ministry.

Questions to Ponder

1. How do the experiences of Mia and Caroline compare with those of Brian and of Jesus?

2. What are some of the possible reasons why they had an easy time getting their idea approved by their pastor?

3. Consider a recent, simple decision you have made with others. What interests did you have? What might have been the interests of the others? How were these interests communicated, discussed, and acted on?

4. In what ways do you consider working with people to be messy? How do you contribute to the messiness?

Chapter 2

The Four Dynamics
of Politics

When we ask friends what comes to mind when they hear the word *politics*, their responses are not surprising:

"*Politics* is when someone is willing to manipulate to get their desired outcome."

"*Politics* means doing anything you need to do to get what you want."

"*Politics* means using subterfuge, sound bites, and popular media to gain power."

Our friends reflect a typical view of what politics is, seeing it as the opposite of how Christians should live in this world. Viewed this way, the term *politics* refers to harmful actions of deceit and domination. One pastor told us, "What really wears me out in the ministry is all the political stuff . . . all the crap!"

However, *politics* in its broader and more neutral sense is different. In this book we assume that all of life is political—incorporating the themes of power, interests, negotiation, and ethics. Every day, people are using their power to negotiate their interests in relationships with other people, always with ethical implications, in order to get things done. We are always being political. The only way to avoid it is by being a complete hermit.

People have different interests, which move them to act in different ways, especially when confronted with decisions. Their interests might be good and honorable or selfish and destructive. Either way, the higher the stakes (the potential for gain or loss), the more

> All of life is political, since people daily use their power to negotiate their interests in relationships with other people, always with ethical implications, in order to get things done.

fervently people act to promote and protect their interests.[1] Whenever people actively advance their interests, they have entered the realm of politics.

Politics is the art of getting things done with others. Political activity can be positive and fruitful. As Cornell professor of city planning John Forester suggests, it involves our shared actions of choosing among conflicting (or merely diverse) wants and interests, developing trust, locating support and opposition, developing sensitivity to timing, knowing the relational and formal organizational expectations, and following both the obvious and hidden cultural rules of interaction.[2] Re-read that sentence again. It describes day-to-day experiences of dealing with people—what it takes to get along and accomplish work in almost every sphere of life. The process of politics goes on even when we are in agreement with others.

All ministry involves politics. This is not a problem, just a fact when using our definition of politics. It's helpful to name it this way in order to observe the process and learn to engage it redemptively. Our interests are part of being human, part of bearing the image of God. Politics is a necessary part of our service to and with others. The political process can be respectful, unifying, and fruitful, just as much as it can be competitive, selfish, and destructive. When people work together, they are inevitably involved in politics. When teaching on conflict, Jesus could also have said, "Whenever two or three are gathered together, there is politics."

We find the research of authors Ronald Cervero and Arthur Wilson very helpful in naming the political process. We summarize their material by stating that redemptive political work involves the four shared activities of perceiving the dynamics of *power* among people, understanding differences between the *interests* of people, engaging explicitly in *negotiation* between the people involved, and considering the *ethical implications* of actions, decisions, and resulting consequences.[3]

> Political work involves the four shared activities of perceiving the dynamics of *power* among people, understanding differences between the *interests* of people, engaging explicitly in *negotiation* between the people involved, and considering the *ethical implications* of actions, decisions, and resulting consequences

These four activities are interdependent and result in consequences that will impact people working together, often in unpredictable ways. The purpose of this chapter is to introduce each of these four political activities. Later chapters explore the skills involved in working with these concepts concretely.

Questions to Ponder

1. Pick an event in your life when you came together with others to accomplish something. List all the shared activities involved in accomplishing your goal.

2. How does your list compare to this book's description of politics?

3. Label each item of your activities list with one or more of the four political actions listed. As you label them, you may think of more activities you could add to your list.

Power

Power, in its most basic sense, is the capacity to act and to influence others. Power is a gift from our Creator, granted to us as his image bearers for the stewardship and dominion of his creation. Power is derivative; we did not create it ourselves. Using the term *power* this way reminds us that everyone—from the most influential to the most helpless—has some power, some capacity to act or to influence. This description of power also helps us notice differences in power and how others use the power they have. And the word *capacity* accounts for a person's unique talents and abilities. Finally, this definition reminds us that power is essentially a relational dynamic. For example, even the infant in the grocery line has power in its capacity to smile and to influence those nearby to smile and wave back.

Most activities—whether in ministry, sports, business, or marriage—involve working with people. Life happens among relationships. And the relationships people have are largely defined by the way they act and react to each other over time. The histories and dynamics of our relationships define and limit our behaviors. In other words, our *relationships shape our power*—our capacity to act and to influence. The amount of power people have is largely based on the history, trust, and understanding they have developed with others.

> *Power*, in its most basic sense, is the capacity to act and to influence others.

To explore the concept of power, let's expand on a story mentioned in our earlier book, *Resilient Ministry*.[4] A conflict arose among a church's board members over how many pastors the church should have. One group strongly believed that laypersons should run the church. They stated that pastors should equip the laity to do the ministry, citing Ephesians 4:12 to support their view. These leaders reasoned, "We don't need more pastors. If the ones we have were training our people better, we would have more mature members and less of a need to hire more pastors."

Other board members countered, "The expectations of this congregation are for high-quality activities. That chapter in Ephesians also says that God gives leaders to the church. You can't expect laypersons—who have full-time jobs, families, and personal lives—to have the time, energy, or expertise to lead ministries of quality. We need more staff."

How does our description of power—the capacity to act and to influence others—help us better interpret the board's disagreement regarding the number of pastors needed for their church? The answer begins with an investigation of their relational histories. Most of the board members who were against hiring more pastors had been in the church for over twenty years. Many came to faith in Christ and to membership in the church through a thriving ministry that emphasized laypersons taking responsibilities. Therefore, due to their own experiences, these older board members thought their views were foundational for ministry practice. In addition, they had served together over many years leading Bible studies, sitting on committees, and raising children. Now many lived near each other in retirement. Over the years the congregation venerated them as fathers in the faith, thus increasing their power. They had supported each other through the years, and they now expected support from each other when in conflict with other board members. That's politics. That's power.

The younger board members wanted to hire more pastors. What were their relevant histories? Many had grown up as children in this same church. They especially appreciated having had the leadership of a youth pastor and other ministry staff when they were growing up. (The older board members had agreed to hire these staff years ago since they did not have the time or ability to work with the young people.) Other prohiring board members were newer to the congregation. They had come to faith through various campus ministries with vocational ministry staff teams.

They shared a value for ministry leadership provided by trained leaders. Some had participated together in the same college ministry. Since joining the church after college, most had bonded in community groups, where they shared the experiences of starting families and establishing careers.

Considering power as the capacity to act and to influence others, which board members have more power to lead in this congregation? Where does their power come from? Both groups draw power from their positions on the board and from their own constituencies, founded in the relational histories and commitments they have formed together.

Broadly speaking, there are two types of power: formal and relational. Formal power is the exercise of power legitimated by recognized social structures or organizations. It is usually indicated by an official title, assigned to a person for a particular responsibility. In our example, members of both groups had gone through leadership training and had been voted in by their congregation to serve on the church board. Technically, all these leaders seem to have the same formal power. Each board member has the right to speak and a vote at the meetings.

> **Two Types of Power**
> 1. **Formal power is the exercise of power that has been legitimated by recognized social structures or organizations.**
> 2. **Relational power comes from the interpersonal associations one has in a community and the place one's subgroup holds within the community.**

However, the length of time one holds a formal position often increases the amount of formal power associated with it. So, the older board members have more formal power on the board because most of them have served on it much longer than the younger group. Their voice and vote carries more weight.

The second type of power is relational. It comes from the interpersonal associations one has in a community and the place one's subgroup holds within the community. Therefore, in addition to formal power, each board member also has a unique level of relational power within the congregation and within its subgroups. In this case, one would expect the older board members to have more relational power among their peers, and the younger members to have relational power within their community groups and peers.

To make the situation more interesting, let's inject Mrs. Jones into this story. Mrs. Jones has been in the church for over forty years—longer than most of the older board members! She has taught third grade Sunday school throughout these years. This means she taught some of the board members (young and old alike) when they were in third grade. In addition, she taught all of the older leaders' children, and currently teaches many children of the younger leaders. And Mrs. Jones is good friends with many of the other younger leaders because she consciously chose to participate in their community group. She says she likes the group because, "They keep me young." It also helps her build trusting relationships with people she might otherwise not know.

Mrs. Jones is loved and respected in the congregation. Over the past forty years people have come to her to share their burdens and to seek her wisdom. It is not unusual for pastors or other leaders to seek her out when faced with personal or congregational issues. So, when the question of hiring more pastors comes up, numerous people ask for her opinion.

Given this situation, who has more power in the church to influence the hiring dilemma? Most likely, it is Mrs. Jones. As we saw earlier, both age-related groups on the board have the formal power of their office. And each has relational power among their friends and peers. Then there is Mrs. Jones. She has never held a position of formal power in the congregation beyond being the third grade Sunday school teacher. But her relational power in the congregation is enormous. An appraisal of church decisions during the past ten years would show that most of the significant changes aligned with the opinions of Mrs. Jones.

Formal power plays an important role in accomplishing God's purposes. However, over time, relational power almost always surpasses formal power. This may be hard for some to believe. After all, if you have served in a hierarchical context where your leaders are overbearing, you may feel that formal power will trump relational power at every point. Formal power can easily appear supreme. And it can be, for a short or even intermediate time.

However, over the long haul, relational power will usually transcend formal power. Formal power depends on the loyal cooperation of group members, without whom nothing would get done or change. Over time, the personal needs, values, and priorities of people will outweigh that organizational loyalty. Therefore, formal leaders (including those at the top of the organizational chart or group's hierarchy) must focus on developing healthy, trusting relationships if they want to gain more influence to get things accomplished.

We agree with a pastor friend who concluded, "Formal power runs out quickly. Ultimately, all power devolves down to a level of relationship. And if I haven't developed trust with people, I can only get so far."

Questions to Ponder

1. When hearing the word *power*, many people think of Lord Acton's quote, "Power tends to corrupt, and absolute power corrupts absolutely." Thus, they assume power is inherently bad. How do you respond to the idea that power is the capacity to act and to influence others? How does this definition compare with Lord Acton's quote?

2. We have stated that power is largely based on the history, strength, and relational health in a group of people. How does this understanding compare to your previous ideas about power?

3. In what ways have you recently seen formal and relational power expressed in your organization? Describe the influence in your organization of a "Mr. or Mrs. Jones," a person without a significant formal position but who has great relational power.

Unlike formal power, relationship power builds over time into a primary power resource often called *relationship capital*. This difference is critical to understanding power. Most organizations need financial capital to grow and mature. Leaders understand this. However, they often do not realize that trust and healthy relationships among people, or relationship capital, is just as important an asset for their organization to develop. Relationship capital is an organization's resources located within the relationships among employees, clients, constituents, providers, congregants, and other relevant people.

On a personal level, relationship capital is the strength of trust and respect that a relationship has built over time. One has to exercise risk and vulnerability with another to build it. Relationship capital includes the amount of positive feelings, goodwill, grace, and ready forgiveness that one possesses for another. The amount of relationship capital people have is usually based on the history, strength, and health of their personal connections. This mutual capacity to trust within relationships allows each person to give the other the benefit of the doubt and to risk honesty.

One can imagine having a trust savings account with each person in one's organization. Full trust accounts lead to more productive and healthy groups. A wise leader will intentionally build relationship capital with others so there is "money in the bank" when circumstances occur that require withdrawals. For example, when leaders give positive feedback and listen carefully to others, they build up trust in those accounts. When leaders bring more challenges and changes to others, they withdraw relationship capital from the accounts with those people. The process of working through differing power and priorities always requires that trust withdrawals be made by everyone involved. However, when a final decision is reached with honesty and respect, the trust built between people who have worked through the issue often exceeds that which was expended in the process.

> Relationship capital in an organization is its resources within the relationships among employees, clients, constituents, providers, congregants, and other relevant people. Relationship capital on a personal level is the strength of trust and respect that a relationship has built over time.

Relationship capital should be built out of sincere care for the other and not out of selfish gain. Unhealthy relationship capital is built on fear, domination, and awe of formal power. This counterfeit relationship capital is highly unreliable. It can disappear in a moment of truthful insight on the part of those with less power.

In Mark 3, Jesus confronted Jewish leaders who held a legalistic view of the Sabbath and were callous toward the man with a withered hand. What was the response of the Jewish leaders to Jesus' rebuke? The text says that they wanted to destroy Jesus. So why didn't they simply have him arrested, taken to trial, and killed? After all, they had all the formal power. Jesus had no title of formal recognition in the Jewish religious system of the day. The reason given again and again in the Gospels for their lack of action is that Jesus was popular among the people (e.g., Luke 6:17-18; 19:47-48).[5] They were drawn to Jesus because of his sincere care for them, his miraculous healings, his truthful and authoritative teaching, and his godly character and lifestyle. Relationship capital gave Jesus the power to continue in public ministry for about three years despite opposition from the religious authorities.

Questions to Ponder

1. Describe the relationship capital you have with people in your various groups, organizations, and family. What conversations and experiences built this capital over time?

2. Consider a time when you had to spend relationship capital by acting in a way that was against the desires and opinions of another. What were the results? How did the relationship change?

Interests

Human interests are the priority preferences we have at a given time.[6] Interests stem from many possible sources: personal or organizational goals and investments, values, beliefs, desires, expectations, predispositions, experiences, identity, or sense of worthiness.[7] In short, interests are what we care about. Whenever we are involved with others, especially when we are making plans, we bring our interests to the activity. Jonathan Edwards, a famous mid-eighteenth-century pastor, once said that the human will always chooses according to its strongest inclination at the moment.[8]

> Human interests are specific priority preferences at a given time. Interests stem from many possible sources: personal or organizational goals and investments, values, beliefs, desires, expectations, predispositions, experiences, identity, or sense of worthiness.

In chapter one we saw interests at work in the stories of Brian, Jesus, and Mia and Caroline. These people put their interests into action. Brian eagerly pursued an assistant pastorate where he could learn ministry under the guidance of a seasoned senior pastor. When the Pharisees and Herodians came to hear Jesus in the synagogue, they clearly wanted to catch Jesus breaking their laws. Mark 3:2 says, "They watched Jesus to see whether he would heal [the man with a withered hand] on the Sabbath." Mia and Caroline wanted to strengthen friendships among the women of their congregation; their pastor shared that desire and approved their plan.

To explore the concept of interests, let's revisit the conflict among a church's board members over how many pastors the church should have. Remember that one group strongly believed laypersons should run the church. On the other side of the conflict, board members countered with arguments for hiring more staff.

Both groups had passions and beliefs behind their interests. Both groups were convinced they knew the correct priority. And both groups cited the Bible as an authority to legitimize their interests. The board members needed to take time to more fully understand each other's interests and the interests of the congregation. Conflicting interests are worked out in relationships. How could their differing interests be resolved in such a way that they could build trust and understanding between each other? How could they come to a wise decision that would preserve the unity of the church while also furthering good change? Chapters eight and nine on negotiation explore these questions in depth.

Let's bring together the political concepts we've discussed so far. People bring *interests* to any planning and change process. For example, Mia and Caroline used their *relational power* to bring their *interests* to their pastor in the hope of being able to lead a painting party. They had no formal *power* or title in the church. Their relationship capital with the pastor provided the *power* to help them gain his support for their endeavor. The pastor had similar *interests*, desiring to see the church's fellowship deepen. He believed the women's plan would help. With his *formal power* and his trust in the women's ability to host this event, he gave them the *formal power* to conduct the new event.

Questions to Ponder

1. Consider the event you chose in the last set of questions. What were two to three interests that influenced the activity? Who represented those interests? How were those interests communicated?

2. Think about a recent conflict you had with a colleague. What were some of your interests in this conflict? How did you represent your interests? Why were these interests important to you?

Negotiation

Negotiation is the process when two or more persons with common or conflicting interests work toward reaching an agreement.[9] In negotiation people use their power—the capacity to act and to influence others—to further their interests. People will promote their interests, or the interests of those they are representing, using whatever power is available to them.

The negotiation process can take minutes or years. It is usually not a single conversation. During the negotiation, four unique activities take place. People bring their own specific interests to the process, they promote their interests between each other, and they use the power available to them to promote their interests. Finally, people affect the ongoing interests and power of those involved by their actions during and after the negotiation.

> **Negotiation involves four unique activities:**
>
> 1. **People bring their own specific interests to the process.**
> 2. **People promote their interests between each other.**
> 3. **People use the power available to them to promote their interests.**
> 4. **People affect the ongoing interests and power of those involved by their actions during and after the negotiation.**

To illustrate these four activities, we return to the story of Mia and Caroline. From the last chapter we saw that the two women went to their pastor to propose an event where the women in the church could enjoy getting to know one another better. After asking questions about goals, timing, costs, and promotion, the pastor approved wholeheartedly.

Mia and Caroline did not simply want to hold a painting party. Their deeper interest was to strengthen an area they perceived as weak in the church—the level of authentic relationships among the women. Holding this church event was a vehicle to attain their deeper interest. If the painting evening was a success, they were planning to leverage that positive result to promote future relationship-building events. As for their pastor, he had also noticed how relationship bonds in the church had been weakening. He had been praying and pondering about this same concern when Mia and Caroline asked to meet with him. While their program proposal did not address all of his concerns, it was a step toward his interests. He saw it as one piece of a bigger puzzle for meeting new needs in the church.

Here we see the four aspects of negotiation. First, they each brought their expressed and hidden interests to the negotiation conversation. Second, a negotiation was initiated between Mia, Caroline, and their pastor. Third, they negotiated with their available power. Mia and Caroline had power from their longstanding involvement and relationships in the congregation, their detailed plans for the event, and their trusting, healthy relationships with the pastor. In response, the pastor enthusiastically approved the activity, accepting risk for the new event because of his trust in Mia and Caroline.

The fourth aspect of negotiation resulted in Mia and Caroline increasing in power because their interests (hosting new events to promote relationships) were now understood and highly valued by the pastor. In fact, their event drew so much positive response that they needed to hold two sessions to accommodate everyone. This success increased their relational capital and thus their relational power in the church. It also enhanced their capacity to further pursue women's ministry. The pastor's and the women's respect and trust for Mia and Caroline's values and abilities were strengthened. As a result, Mia and Caroline were able to initiate a number of other ministry gatherings.

Questions to Ponder

Review a recent negotiation in which you were involved.

1. Who were you negotiating with?

2. What interests were being negotiated?

3. What power was available to those in the negotiation? How was this power used?

4. In what ways did the negotiation maintain, strengthen, or diminish the interests of those involved? And how did it change the power of those involved?

Ethical Implications

Inevitably, when ministry leaders discuss issues of interests, power, relationships, and negotiation, they raise concerns about ethics (the principles of moral behavior). "What is the difference between negotiation and manipulation?" Or "If I think my opinion is correct, is it right for me to push for it?" Or "How do I know if I am using my power in a way that honors God and serves others?"

Jesus calls us to pursue leadership that is radical in its servant-oriented, grace-based, and kingdom-focused manner. This type of leadership should neither attempt to control others nor abdicate responsibility. In light of these limits, how can healthy leadership occur when multiple power and interest differences collide in the decision-making process? The answer centers on identifying who the interested parties (or stakeholders) are, how they are represented, and how the negotiation process is managed in light of biblical principles.

Stakeholders are all those who have something to gain or to lose as a result of the decisions and actions being considered by the participants in active negotiation. Put more simply, those with vested interests are stakeholders. When stakeholders have conflicting interests, they bring more anxiety and fear of potential loss to the negotiation process. Depending on the nature of a ministry decision, relevant stakeholders could include ministry staff, officers, members, regular attenders, children, youth, visitors, and even those in the wider community. We could even consider God

> **Stakeholders are all those who have something to gain or to lose as a result of the decisions and actions being considered by the participants in active negotiation.**

as the ultimate stakeholder over all activities in his church or even in the whole of his creation.

Ministry program planners exercise power by making ethical decisions about whose interests matter and which needs their programs should address.[10] In every ministry decision, those negotiating the decision will address some interests while consciously or unconsciously neglecting other interests. Therefore, planners need to take time to consider the interests of *all* stakeholders involved in the ministry. Planners should also consciously review how their own interests are influencing their actions and decisions, and consider how their plans will reflect kingdom priorities. *What* and *how* decisions are made and *how* resources are used to accomplish work determine the direction of the ministry and affects everyone involved.

In Brian's experience at Trinity Church many stakeholders had something to gain or to lose as a result of the situation (though not all were involved in the negotiation process). First, there was Brian and his wife, Sarah. Then there was Senior Pastor Joe and his family. The elders and their families made up another stakeholder group. Add to these the members of the search committee that worked with and nominated Brian, the broader membership of the congregation, the people in the city where the church was located, and Brian's friends and family who attended his ordination. Of course, it is also helpful to consider God as a stakeholder.

Ministry leaders have biblical principles to consider when wielding the power of influence over others. The apostle Paul exhorts the church in Philippi, "Do nothing from selfish ambition or conceit, but in humility count others more significant than yourselves. Let each of you look not only to his own interests, but also to the interests of others" (Philippians 2:3-4). He then proceeds to describe Jesus as the ultimate example of a servant leader. A few verses later, Paul commends his apprentice Timothy to the Philippian church. He uses a likely hyperbole to compare Timothy to other selfish believers: "I hope in the Lord Jesus to send Timothy to you soon, so that I too may be cheered by news of you. For I have no one like him, who will be genuinely concerned for your welfare. For they all seek their own interests, not those of Jesus Christ" (Philippians 2:19-21). Therefore, we do well to reflect on the extent to which we are promoting our own interests over those of Jesus Christ when negotiating.

> Planners need to take time to consider the interests of all stakeholders involved in the ministry, review how their own interests are influencing their decisions, and consider how their plans will reflect kingdom priorities.

Four simple yet provocative questions help to define the key ethical issues of ministry politics. Every ministry leader must reflect on these questions.

1. Who are the stakeholders in this situation?

2. What are the probable interests of each stakeholder?

3. How will those interests be represented during the negotiation process?

4. To what degree are we serving the welfare of God's church and the redemption of his world over our selfish interests?

Thoughtful answers to these questions will illuminate the direction to go in order to provide healthy leadership for the political process. As we seek to lead God's people, we need to honestly answer these ethical questions and help others with power in the negotiation process to consider them as well. As one pastor friend of ours commented about these questions: "There are times when I think sinful interests do need to be strategically worked around. Other times there are often valid interests that are differing to my own. Am I manipulating things so those interests can't be considered? We leaders have to be discerning about these things."

These distinctions are not easy to make. However, we will proceed much more wisely by prayerfully asking the questions and reflecting on the motivations behind our interests, our use of power, the relational dynamics involved, our methods of negotiating, and relevant biblical principles. This ethical reflection work will help to broaden our options and to generate strategies on how to proceed. When we learn to reflect on our leadership this way, we can invite others involved in the negotiation process to join us in asking these important ethical questions.

Questions to Ponder

1. Consider a recent time when you felt neglected, manipulated, or disregarded by someone else during the planning process. What actions led to these feelings? What relevant decisions were being made? Who was directly involved in the negotiation and decision-making process?

2. Reflect on a recent decision you made that resulted in surprising and unintended consequences for others. What reasons can you list for why this might have happened? Consider your answers in light of the ethical questions above and relevant biblical principles.

3. Describe a time when you felt that people misaligned their own interests with those of Jesus Christ.

Conclusion

In this chapter we have explored each aspect of our definition of ministry politics: power (including relationship capital), interests, negotiation, and ethical implications. We considered four key ethical questions to ask in the political process: Who are the stakeholders? What are their interests? How are the stakeholders represented during negotiation? To what degree are we serving the welfare of Jesus' church and the redemption of his world over our selfish interests? Those involved in ministry are always experiencing the politics of negotiation. Sometimes politics happens in quiet consensus. At other times it occurs in the midst of uncertainty, anxiety, and conflict. Regardless of context, stakeholders will press their interests forward with their available power. Because of this, politics is unavoidable in ministry.

Chapter ③

Power in Ministry Politics

Jesus described the Christian life as an uneasy tension between humility and shrewdness in working with people. In Matthew 10 Jesus sent his disciples out to minister in the nearby towns and gave them the message that "The kingdom of heaven is at hand" (v. 7). He supported his message with miraculous power to "heal the sick, raise the dead, cleanse lepers, cast out demons" (v. 8) But he and his disciples would not always be well received. This amazing work came with Jesus' dire warning of persecution. "Behold, I am sending you out as sheep in the midst of wolves, so be wise as serpents and innocent as doves" (v. 16). So, we approach the topic of power in the politics of ministry with an honest recognition of our need for God's wisdom and compassion.

There are many different beliefs about power—what it is, why you need it, how you get it, how you should use it, and how you can lose it. In addition, many people use the term *power* synonymously with *authority* or make various distinctions between the two words. In both modern English and New Testament Greek, *power* and *authority* have multiple possible meanings that overlap extensively. To avoid confusing semantics and yet be able to deal with the complexities of these abstract concepts, we focus this study using only the term *power*. Power, in its most basic sense, is the capacity to act and to influence others. Chapter ten is on ethics and there we will explore the morality of using power. Here we describe the most helpful ways we have learned to think about power for the sake of healthier ministry. We begin with a short story to illustrate several issues concerning the use of power.

Sue's Story

That's odd, thought Sue. *My announcement for the new depression support group isn't here. It was here last week.* Sue was reading the Sunday morning bulletin announcements before the worship service began. After the service, she noticed that a poster announcing the depression support group was gone. She had personally put it up ten days before. She became concerned and started looking for the other posters she had placed around the church. Most of them had also been removed. Now Sue was mad! *How dare someone mess with my publicity!*

Sue had been the director of Christian education at Grace Church ever since graduating from seminary a year earlier. Prior to seminary, she had served as a staff ministry leader in two small, fairly new churches. Grace was a larger, well-established church with several pastors and other ministry leaders on full-time staff.

Sue reported to Assistant Pastor Dan. She liked working with him, and they shared a similar vision for Christian education. Sue was confident that Dan represented her well at the weekly pastors' meetings. Dan also gave Sue advice on who to go to for assistance. He seemed to know his way around the staff jungle. He also trusted Sue, so she felt confident in freely pursuing her work.

She was careful, however, to always get the approval for new initiatives from the church's Christian education committee. Because she knew that there were many views on counseling and depression, Sue had been extra careful to speak with all the committee members about this new support group ministry. The committee had given official approval for this much-needed program at their last meeting.

Organizing this new ministry had taken lots of time. Sue knew that several people were counting on it to help get through the upcoming holidays. The groups were going to meet for twelve weeks—November through January—and complete a workbook on depression that had been chosen by the counseling pastor. This pastor had originally alerted Sue to the needs of many adult members struggling with depression. Most of these members had kept their difficulties to themselves and felt alone. This new ministry would show respect and care from the church and would provide a place for mutual encouragement. This pastor also helped Sue recruit qualified people to lead the sessions.

Sue was determined to find out who had messed with her publicity. On Monday morning she called the volunteer in charge of bulletin announcements. The volunteer responded calmly, "Oh, Mike (another pastor on staff) cancelled that announcement earlier last week. I don't think the senior pastor believes in depression." Sue had never even spoken to pastor Mike or to the senior pastor about this ministry! As she pondered this news, Sue received a call from the bookstore. "Your case of workbooks is in," she was told. Then the phone rang again. One of the support group leaders she had recruited asked eagerly, "When will the next planning meeting be?"

> The capacity to communicate with others depends on the strength and health of the relevant relationships. Assessing communication patterns usually illuminates the power differences between people.

We leave Sue's story open-ended at this point, with Sue facing a huge dilemma of how to respond. What would you do if you were in her shoes? We will provide more details of her story throughout the book. Already, her story illustrates many issues we need to learn to observe about power in ministry.

Power and Communication

We can understand the frustration and confusion Sue must have felt. She thought she had all the power she needed to launch the new support groups. After all, the original idea came from the counseling pastor. It had been affirmed by Dan, her supervisor. And the Christian education committee had given official approval. What went wrong?

What Sue experienced was a painful introduction to power in the politics of ministry. In chapter two we saw that ministry happens in the context of relationships. The histories and current status of these relationships affects our ability to get things done. Ministry also happens in the context of power differences, which also greatly influence our ability to accomplish goals.

Notice how in each case story discussed so far, the capacity to communicate well with others depends on the strength and health of the relevant relationships. Assessing communication patterns usually illuminates the power differences between people. Like Brian's experience at Trinity Church, Sue was still a relative newcomer at her church. She lacked a long history of relationships in the system. While she had worked at developing a good partnership with Dan and the members of the Christian education committee, she was clearly not in communication with either Pastor Mike or the senior pastor.

We saw earlier how Brian was kept out of the loop regarding the termination of Senior Pastor Joe. Brian had little capacity to intervene or influence the situation. In a similar way, Sue was not informed about the removal of her posters or bulletin announcement. In both stories, the lack of healthy communication reflected their lack of power to act.

In sharp contrast there is the fruitful experience of Mia and Caroline, who wanted to host a women's relationship-building activity. These women had a long-standing friendship with their pastor, and they all trusted and respected each other. This made a significant difference as they presented their pastor with plans for a new event. Communication was honest and oriented toward collaborative problem solving. The women were able to influence the pastor's thinking. In return, the pastor empowered them to launch the new ministry.

Because power is the capacity to act and influence, communication is a major expression of power. Our ability to communicate and be understood is usually a direct representation of our power. If we are not fluent in the dominant language and culture of the people in our organization, then we will feel significantly less powerful than others, despite any formal titles or position we may have. Our diversity of cultures, languages, generations, socioeconomics, and gender add real barriers to trust-building communication. Sue was new to a big church culture and was one of the few female ministry leaders on staff. This added to her lack of power and to limited capacity to advocate for her new initiative.

More than the content of what we communicate, the *manner* in which we communicate with each other has enormous potential either to build up or tear down relationship capital. For example, we have the incredible challenge *not* to erode trust with our use of digital media to communicate. Emails and texts lose much meaning because they have no

> More than the content of what we communicate, the *manner* in which we communicate with each other has enormous potential either to build up or tear down relationship capital.

tone of voice or body language conveyed with the content and because responses are delayed.

It is easy to misunderstand each other. Missionary and distinguished professor of mission and anthropology Paul Hiebert summarized the challenge well when he wrote,

> Two of the greatest problems faced by missionaries entering new cultures are misunderstandings and premature judgments. These are particularly damaging because we are generally unaware of them. As individuals we have strong convictions about reality. Rarely do we stop to ask whether others see it as we do, since it seems so obvious that things are as we see them.[1]

On a microlevel, we all enter new cultures to varying degrees when we work with others. We need to use our power to further healthy communication and to withhold snap evaluations, whether we are working with people overseas or with people across the hall.

Other Capacities of Power in Ministry

People most commonly associate the concept of human power with the actions of using force, making decisions, and owning resources. We also tend to assume that the more power one person possesses, the less power is available to others. Therefore, the dominant or more powerful person prevails over the subordinates. Sue jumped to this assumption in guessing that the bulletin volunteer merely obeyed the senior pastor because he had more power than Sue did. Therefore, Sue assumed that the senior pastor ordered the publicity to stop, that he had more power and so got his way, and that Sue's initiative had to cease. He obviously had more formal capacity to act than Sue did, but Sue made huge assumptions on very little known facts.

> People most commonly associate the concept of human power with the actions of using force, making decisions, and owning resources. However, power is much more complex than the use of force or domination. There are many dimensions of our ability to act or to influence people.

However, power is much more complex than the use of force or domination. There are many dimensions of our ability to act or to influence people. For example, even though Sue seems to have much less power, she still has some capacity to act and to influence others in her church. Sue could have taken a number of actions in response to the situation.

The week after the publicity disappeared, she could have attempted to meet with Pastor Mike or the senior pastor to inquire into their interests and actions and to explain her own. She could have taken her concerns back to Pastor Dan and to the Christian education committee, who had approved her program. She could have gone over the head of the senior pastor and appealed directly to the church board. She could have continued to move the ministry forward without churchwide publicity. Or, on the extreme end, she could have used her power to resign.

Another common use of power is more sophisticated than direct action or communication. Power can be increased through "managing the meaning" of an act, idea, or circumstance. In Sue's story, critical questions become: Who gets to define the legitimacy of depression? What will be done about it? Did the senior pastor cancel Sue's publicity in order to manage the meaning and significance of depression at Grace Church? If so, did he feel this was necessary to maintain his credibility and thus his influence and power in the church? If she had not used the term *depression* in her publicity, would someone still have removed it? These questions show that the management of meaning and word choice makes a huge difference in many arguments. Again, communication is at the heart of the use of power.

One further aspect of power is worth our attention. Faith-and-culture expert Andy Crouch expresses this idea well in his book *Playing God: Redeeming the Gift of Power*. Crouch makes this concluding summary in a chapter on institutions:

> Ultimately, every member of any human institution bears some power and some responsibility for [the institution's] flourishing. Our best leaders and our most admired celebrities, along with our most feared tyrants and despots, only have their unequal power as long as the image bearers in their institutions grant it to them.[2]

In other words, both the sports star and the dictator have more power because other people in their organizational contexts give power to them. This draws us back to a point we've previously stressed: ministry (and all of life) takes place in complicated systems of human relationships. And these relationships set the framework for power dynamics in ministry.

Clearly, Sue was involved in a complicated relational situation. She thought that she was doing everything correctly, following all the church's decision-making rules. However, she was shocked by the sudden removal of her publicity. This undermined her trust in the explicit rules of how to get work done, her trust in Dan, and her trust in the committee overseeing her ministry. They seemed to have failed to provide her with the necessary power to act that she thought they had given her.

Sue's story illustrates how power is intricately involved in the people work of ministry. The amount of power a person has largely depends on that individual's relational context. This is particularly true for those who serve in ministry, where special access is often granted into other's lives during crucial times such as weddings and funerals. Therefore, it is necessary to expand our description of power as the capacity to act and to influence others as a result of socially structured relationships.[3]

> An expanded description of power is the capacity to act and to influence others as a result of socially structured relationships.

Ministry relationships fall on a wide spectrum. They move from associations that exist only on a professional basis to friendships that are highly personal and trusted, sometimes even closer than biological family. The relationship Sue had with the senior pastor of Grace Church was purely professional. She had never met with him on a friendship basis and did not even have a professional line of communication with him. In the other case story, Brian had quickly developed a growing trust with Pastor Joe. While more professional in nature, their relationship might have blossomed into a much closer, informal friendship had Joe not been forced to resign. And years before Mia and Caroline asked to sponsor a new church activity, they had developed a highly trusted relationship with their pastor. The three of them talked with each other on a first name basis and considered each other more like family.

Every ministry context—whether in the family, a church, or another organization—has a complicated structure of relationships. The capacity to act and to influence others is largely a result of the history, strength, and health of these social webs. Adding to this complexity, these affiliations between people develop in both formal and informal ways, leading to distinct types of power.

Questions to Ponder

1. What are possible reasons why no one communicated with Sue when her publicity was removed?

2. In the church where you worship or the organization where you work, name some relationships you consider more professional and some that are more personal. What are the differences in levels of trust that you experience in these relationships?

3. Think of three social groups in your life. Describe the power structure in each group. How does the use of power relate to what the group accomplishes?

Formal Power

Let's look again at formal power in distinction to relational power, which we introduced in chapter two. Formal power is a person's capacity to act and to influence others through socially constructed relationships due to a position. The position usually comes with accompanying responsibilities, a written job description, and a title, all set by an organization. People gain formal power when they accept an official position. In the marketplace, these positions could be chief executive officer, manager, professor, or many other roles. In a church these official positions might be pastor, elder, board member, director, deacon, committee member, or small group leader. In parachurch groups positions may be area director, president, coordinator, or team leader. Note that in ministry, those with formal power are not necessarily paid employees.

We cannot create formal power for ourselves out of thin air. Authorized people in organizations give formal power to other people in their organization. In other words, formal power is made legitimate by the social system within which the power is exercised. The members of an organization authorize the formal power of another in three ways: they provide the opportunity to use the power; they confer the formal power (often through a ritual); and they publicly

> Every ministry context—whether in the family, a church, or another organization—has a complicated structure of relationships. The capacity to act and to influence others is largely a result of the history, strength, and health of these social webs.

recognize the person with the formal power.[4] Cultural rules, both of the broader society and of the organization, largely determine what it looks like to authorize formal power in these ways.

The Pharisees, for example, were primarily merchants and tradespeople and not trained in school. However, much like a union, they were a closed community. Admission into the order was strictly regulated by current members. Therefore, a new recruit would have to be recognized and invited by members to join. A candidate must then agree to obey all of the detailed rules of the Pharisaic tradition and enter a probation period. If he completed the trial season

> Formal power is a person's capacity to act and to influence others through socially constructed relationships due to a position. The members of an organization authorize the formal power of another in three ways: they provide the opportunity to use the power; they confer the formal power (often through a ritual); and they publicly recognize the person with the formal power.

successfully, he was then institutionally conferred a Pharisee, with all the accompanying privileges and responsibilities.[5] Because of their intense dedication to and observance of the Jewish law in Jesus' day, Pharisees held great influence with the masses and other Jewish leaders. In other words, their formal power was publicly recognized. Today we have much the same process for granting formal power to people in ministry.

People can assert formal power based solely on their official position. Often, this power is a capacity they would *not* have apart from the formal title. For example, after Joe resigned as pastor of Trinity Church, Brian was responsible to moderate the church board meetings. Usually persons in their mid-twenties would not have such a position of power. Brian told us, "This older board member went ballistic at the meeting. I mean, he really went on a tirade. And I called him down. He'd never been called down before. And to his credit, he apologized to me as moderator, using that term. And it never happened again while I was there." Brian exercised his formal power of being board moderator. Even though he was new to the church and the youngest person at the board meeting, Brian successfully used formal power to correct a much older board member.

Bill, another friend of ours, became pastor of a church at age twenty-six. The week after he was installed as pastor, a seventy-year-old man asked him out to lunch. His message to Bill was as clear as it was concise: "Don't let anybody intimidate you; your position here is not because of your age." In the majority (white male) culture of the United States, such a young man would not generally have this much capacity to lead and to influence. But this church gave him the titles of pastor and moderator, which came with a great amount of formal power.

We have heard many stories about people causing great harm to their ministry organizations upon suddenly gaining a formal title and formal power. At one church a couple of highly dissatisfied congregants remained silent about their interests until they were elected to the church board. Only after they had been selected, trained, and installed as church officers did they assert their critical viewpoints. At the next board meeting they abruptly attempted to fire the pastor. Their sudden change in behavior left others feeling deceived, and the church exploded in conflict as a result.

On the flip side, exercising formal power can be strategic and beneficial for the organization, particularly in times of instability or crisis. One memorable example concerns Sue's senior pastor on the morning of 9/11, just after terrorists flew planes into the Twin Towers in New York City. That morning, the church building was full of women in small group Bible studies, children in nursery and childcare, and teachers and students in the fourteen-room elementary school. The senior pastor calmly gathered the church staff and the women's small group Bible studies, told them what the news media was reporting, prayed with them, and sent them home to be with and comfort their families and friends. Then he called the whole school together and did much the same. These quick and decisive actions helped keep people from panicking and causing more chaos.

A friend named Eric exercised formal power when he became the pastor of a church already in deep conflict and turmoil. The conflict was spearheaded by Doug, who had previously served on the church board. From the beginning of Eric's ministry, Doug stood against everything Eric introduced. Doug was due to be reelected to the board soon after Eric became pastor. But because of Doug's harsh, critical attitude, Eric used his formal power to prevent the regularly scheduled election of board members. In the role of pastor, Eric also began having conversations with currently serving board members about Doug's public behavior and the impact of Doug's actions on the health of the church. In these conversations it soon became evident that Doug had a long history of undermining others' initiatives in the church. Eventually, the board concluded that while Doug affirmed the church's theology, he did not exhibit the character traits the Bible expected of leaders (e.g., 1 Timothy 3:1-7; Titus 1:5-9). Nor was he in agreement with the church's ministry philosophy. Postponing the election gave Eric and the church leaders time to evaluate Doug's qualifications for serving on the board.

In a later conversation, Eric shared the importance of utilizing formal power at strategic times. "It is important for pastors to take a strong hand in the empowering role of developing church leadership. Who is involved in leadership is just about the whole game. Because out of that flows the culture of the church." Another pastor expressed the same sentiment when he described how he intentionally used his formal power to create processes to prevent others from initiating sudden changes: "I will create barriers from leadership and influence. I do that consciously, very consciously. If the wrong people get in the wrong positions at the wrong time exerting the wrong influence, pretty soon the church is ripped apart."

Formal power has boundaries. First, specifically focused responsibilities come with a formal role. In other words, one person cannot be doing everyone else's job. Second, people are limited in their use of formal power by the bounded context of their organization. Rarely will other people accept or expect the use of formal power outside its context. For example, people do not expect or allow Tasha, one of the authors of this book, to direct the educational ministries of her church just because she has this formal role at the nearby seminary.

The broader society determines cultural rules that set the limits of formal power outside the organization. In this way, the people are actually (though not necessarily consciously) choosing to what extent they will place themselves under formal power. For example, when visiting the United States, a Hungarian friend who is a pastor rarely refers to a title or seeks to influence others as a pastor. She observes that pastors are not well respected by US society. In Hungary, however, the cultural boundaries for the formal power of the pastorate are quite different. A striking example of this occurred when she was standing in line to purchase cheese at a Budapest market. An elderly man at the front of the line was being rude to and angry with the salesclerk. Our friend went to the counter, told the man he was being impolite and unkind, stated that she was a pastor, and then told him to stop this behavior. The man immediately stopped his tirade. The shoppers and clerks responded with relief and appreciation for her use of formal power.

Formal power is also limited by a much less explicit form of power, what we have called relational power. Years after his time at Trinity Church, Brian served as senior pastor in a larger congregation. The church board agreed with Brian to hire someone to initiate a new, vital ministry program in the church. Brian felt he knew just the right person for the job. But his choice was overruled in a vote by the board members. Instead, they chose to hire a person who lacked the needed skills, but who had a longstanding relationship with them as a member of the church. The power this member had with the board due to their relationship history was greater than the pastor's formal power to influence the hiring decision. Formal power was limited by relational power.

Questions to Ponder

1. List a number of formal positions you have held, and describe the power that came with each position. What boundaries did you experience to your power in each position? For each position, consider to what degree the roles, responsibilities, privileges, and limitations of your formal power were clearly described in a formal document. If they were not formally described, what were the challenges, risks, or benefits of having a less-explicit description of your formal power?

2. Reflect on a story you know about a person who used the formal power of their position inappropriately. How did this impact their organization?

Relational Power

Relational power, as noted in chapter two, is the capacity to act and to influence others based on interpersonal associations between people apart from organizational roles and titles. People gain relational power when they build long-term, strong relationships. This implicit and relationally based power can be even stronger than formal power. Through the development of trust and respect in relationships, people earn the right to be heard and thus gain relational power to lead. Often, the amount of power people have is based on the history, strength, and health of their relationships in the social systems where they live, work, worship, and play.

> Relational power is the capacity to act and to influence others based on interpersonal associations between people apart from organizational roles and titles. This implicit and relationally based power can be even stronger than formal power.

Mrs. Jones illustrates this well (see chap. two). She was the venerable third-grade Sunday school teacher many sought out for counsel due to her decades of faithful and caring relationships in the church. In this way she wielded much power to influence others in her church beyond her teaching role. In fact, Mrs. Jones had so much relational power that the church leaders would rarely make major ministry changes without consulting with her first. In a similar manner, Mia and Caroline had this implicit power to initiate a new ministry based on their long-term friendship with the pastor.

In our other case stories, Brian and Sue were both relatively new to their respective congregations. Therefore, they did not have common histories or strong relationships with the members and other leaders. However, the decision makers and actors in both of their cases did have strong relationships with each other. The relationship ties between Brian's board members and between the people that removed Sue's publicity were strong from many years of working together. The strength of these relationship ties is such that people may have supported the interests of others even though they may have actually disagreed with those interests.

Both Brian and Sue faced significant limitations in relational power. This reduced what they were able to accomplish even though both had formal power. Sue had such little knowledge of the pastors she worked with that she had no idea her initiative would provoke resistance. Furthermore, she was never told directly why her publicity was removed. This left her feeling powerless and without the trust and respect she needed from others to do her job. Her formal power was not enough.

In Brian's later reflections on what happened at Trinity Church, he confided that he seriously considered staging a protest against Pastor Joe's resignation when it came up for confirmation at the regional denomination meeting. However, he thought better of it, realizing that his capacity to function at the church would be greatly hampered by doing so. His protest would have added a major conflict and break of trust in his relationships with the church board members. This would have resulted in a significant decrease in his new and growing relational power. It was a tough decision for Brian to make: follow orders and continue to serve the congregation under the leadership of the board or pursue a more honest and loving process for Pastor Joe.

A ministry friend named Kayla served as a director in a large city church for a couple of decades. Kayla's experience was a unique example of relational power. She was the only nonordained person out of seven serving as a department director in the church. Therefore, she was the only director who did not get an official vote at the board meetings, which was a definite lack of formal power compared to the other directors. However, she demonstrated an amazing capacity to accomplish work based on her implicit, relational power. She explained it this way:

> What I have is power of influence. In my book, everything is done by relationships, absolutely everything. And they [the ordained staff] know that I am loyal and trustworthy to the end and will make that commitment to them. So, I use indirect power. And because of my longevity in the church, the senior pastor may not even know it, but we'll be in staff meetings and he'll look in my direction and say, "Isn't that right, Kayla? Isn't that right? You told us about this."

Although the senior pastor responded with deference to Kayla's relational power, he did not seem to have been conscious of it, nor of her relatively low amount of formal power compared to the ordained staff.

One of the other pastors did notice the power difference and asked Kayla about her lack of formal power with the church board vote. She responded with an insightful description of the strength of relational power:

> In the Christian world you've got to change hearts. That's where the gift of influence is the most important thing you can have. Ultimately influencing people's hearts and desires is more effective than just setting the rules. That's your best work. There are usually a half dozen different ways to get things done. I don't vest a lot of things in the big vote. There's too much ministry to be done in a million ways to let one decision ruin your effectiveness.

Kayla was limited in her capacity to act and influence in some ways, due to her lesser formal power in the church organizational hierarchy. Yet

Kayla's experience over the years demonstrated the important work of relational ministry with the people. Kayla felt that her effectiveness as a ministry director was not actually limited by the board votes since there were always many other ways to move work forward when one built trusting relationships in the church.

In the broader US culture, people often gain relational power via their appearance, possessions, or skills. For example, we tend to ascribe more than physical power to a tall, muscular man by assuming he would lead us well. Sporting a professional haircut and wearing a dark blue suit to the office might help a person gain a respectful hearing at a meeting. We also tend to defer to people who have more wealth, an expensive car, or a big house. Celebrities are regularly interviewed in popular media to speak with authority on topics on which they have no expertise. Their significant power due to personal resources lends to an increase in relational power in social settings.

In addition, dominant behavior increases implied power simply because the person *appears* to be more powerful. The person at the meeting with clever verbal skills, strong voice, and seeming expertise will often win the debate. Relational power from these social perceptions may add up significantly in a limited context, but relational power built up through actual relationships will outweigh all these other types.

In summary, over time relationships usually delineate what people are and are not able to do. Therefore, ministry leaders must be sensitive to and proactive about the relationships they have with other staff, officers, participants, and people in the community. Those who are effective in ministry tend to be aware of the strength and health of relationships within their organization and the effect those relationships have on their overall ministry. They are constantly working on developing trust and respect with the people they work with. As Brian shared, after years of ministry, "Leadership is not a title. The right to lead is earned. And it takes a while."

Questions to Ponder

1. Describe a time when people with formal power in an organization failed to get things done their way because of their lack of relational power.

2. It takes time and effort to develop significant relationships of trust and respect. What kinds of situations and activities help you develop the trust of relational capital in your organization? With your family?

3. Conversely, what kinds of situations and activities undermine or diminish your relationship capital in your organization? With your family?

Unequal Power in Ministry

Now we have come to a difficult but important issue. Most people entering ministry are idealistic about their own and others' capacities to act and to influence others. Our wishful thinking compels us to expect all the adults involved in our ministries to act with the same power for the same mission with the same compassion. That is, we hope to be playing on a level field and in a loving manner. Unfortunately, this often is not the case. Power is rarely equal between people, and power is easily used for selfishness and evil.

As Brian said, "I was really naive. I thought church life was pleasant, that people more or less loved each other, after a fashion anyway." In addition to this idealism, those of us who were born and raised in the majority white, male American culture may assume that equality and justice exists among all believers regardless of age, gender, ethnicity, class, financial status, relationships, or time in the organization. We may believe that every participant—or at least everyone in a leadership role—ought to have an equal voice. After all, the apostle Paul wrote, "There is neither Jew nor Greek, there is neither slave nor free, there is neither male nor female, for you are all one in Christ Jesus" (Galatians 3:28).

There is no question that from a biblical perspective we are all of equal value before God, created in God's image and adopted into God's family. Jesus even stressed that leaders are to be servants, not people who "lord it over" others like the Gentile rulers (Mark 10:42-45). Notice, however, that only some of the disciples were called to be apostles and "leaders" for God's people. And among the disciples who were leaders for the early church, there was a wide spectrum of power in their capacities to act and influence.

Modern ministry is no different. People are diverse. We are unequal in gifts, talents, roles, resources, and callings. These forms of inequality do not necessarily stem from injustice or the result of human rebellion against God. Many of these "inequalities" are God's design for diversity of skills and gifts in the body of Christ in order to build the church and participate in his redemption of the world (Romans 12:3-8; 1 Corinthians 12). Therefore, when we come together in organizations, we have diverse amounts of power. As Crouch helpfully summarized, institutions "almost never distribute power equally, in either quantity or quality."[6]

In this broken world, unequal power easily leads to injustice and repression of those with less power. "And yet," reasons Crouch, "not all unequal power prevents flourishing. In fact, sometimes unequal distribution is *essential* to flourishing."[7] Scripture demonstrates God's plan for our good through differing power in roles of leadership and responsibility. For example, after the exodus from Egypt, God said that only Aaron and his sons should serve the people as priests. Later, God called many others in the tribes of Israel to serve the people as kings and prophets. In the New Testament, the apostles direct the church to appoint elders for leadership roles. Other passages command children to obey and honor their parents, and call all of us to use our various spiritual gifts for the "common good" and the building up of "the body of Christ" (e.g., Exodus 28:1; 1 Samuel 16:1; Acts 14:23; Ephesians 6:1-2; 1 Corinthians 12).

In our case stories, both Brian and Sue, as new hires, assumed they were working on a level playing field with the other ministry leaders in their respective churches. They expected fair play, with equality and justice. They assumed they would have equal opportunities to exercise power in proportion to their formal titles and roles. They pursued work as if their power to accomplish tasks would be equivalent to and structured by their formal positions. And they thought this would be true for others as well. "Surely," they assumed, "mature Christian leaders would have the same trust and respect for each other." However, Brian's critique of himself was true for Sue as well. To assume power is equal, fair, and predictable in any context is naive and disingenuous.

The board members at Trinity Church wielded more power than both Joe and Brian. They secretly forced Joe to resign, and Brian would not have been able to stop them. Mia and Caroline also had unequal power but were able to compensate for that with the strength of their relationship with their pastor and many church women. Sue's lack of equal power and unhealthy communication patterns at Grace Church left her in the dark with broken trust in many directions.

"Ah," you might say, "this is what I hate about the idea of politics in the first place! Underhanded gamesmanship. Can't we at least expect that in the church we can escape manipulation, coercion, injustice, and conflict?"

Please read this clearly: As followers of Jesus Christ, we believe that practicing leadership requires people to shun unethical and unbiblical gamesmanship. At the same time, we believe that disagreements and conflicts over differing interests and agendas are inevitable and can even be profitable for learning. They certainly were in the ministries of the prophets, Jesus, and the apostles! All of us in ministry need to grow in biblical wisdom and realistic awareness of human uses of power.

Every theological tradition with biblical fidelity acknowledges that we live in a broken world. The Bible records that our first parents took steps of direct rebellion against our Creator God. Humanity has been suffering the consequences of our sinfulness ever since. Unjust and unloving power dynamics exist in every social system due to human sinfulness. Once we face this reality, we can begin to do something about it. Later we will discuss the steps necessary to bring more just and loving equality into relational and organizational environments. However, if we refuse to face the facts of unequal power use (both healthy and harmful) in ourselves and our organizations, we will not be able to function responsibly or redemptively. And the painful outcomes will continue to prevent our labors from thriving.

> All of us in ministry need to grow in biblical wisdom and realistic awareness of human uses of power. Unjust and unloving power dynamics exist in every social system due to human sinfulness. If we refuse to face the facts of unequal power use in ourselves and our organizations, we will not be able to function responsibly or redemptively.

Questions to Ponder

1. What actions could Sue have taken to prevent the removal of her publicity for the program on depression? What are ways Sue could have responded that might have furthered the healthier use of power in her church?

2. In what possible ways could Brian have responded to his board that might have furthered the healthier use of power in his church?

3. Name a relationship you are in where power is unequally distributed. Is the power formal or relational? In what ways do the power

dynamics in this relationship restrain your capacity to act or to influence others? In what ways do the power dynamics enhance your capacity to act or to influence others?

4. What criteria could you use to assess whether unequal power is legitimate or illegitimate in your organization? In your family?

Learning to See Power Dynamics

The power discussions of this chapter lead to four practical conclusions for working with people in ministry. First, because there are always differences in both formal and relational power within any group of people, we need to observe how power is exercised in each group or context we work in so we can more wisely manage our own capacities to act and influence.

Second, healthy leaders steward their power to help others use their own power, all for the group's common goals. This will help the team accomplish much while also accounting for the participation of each individual. Stewarding power must be done with justice and compassion, understanding that power which grows out of healthy relationships will nearly always be the strongest and most enduring.

Third, as leaders we need to be keenly aware that everyone is subject to the actions and the influences of others, both those with more power as well as those with less. As Americans, we are not nearly as independent and free to act and choose as we think we are. Humans are highly interdependent on each other. No matter how much or how little power we have, we are all called to respect others and to serve humbly, recognizing that our ultimate accountability for our use of power is to God.

> Because those with more power tend to be less aware of their power, healthy leadership at any level requires us to be students of people's interests and of the power dynamics in our organizations. Those with less power tend to be most aware of the power dynamics in any given context. Therefore, we should seek them out to learn from their perspectives.

And fourth, because those with more power tend to be less aware of their power, healthy leadership at any level requires us to be students of people's interests and of the power dynamics in our organizations.

Unfortunately, people often enter ministry without contemplating power. As a result, they can make painfully flawed assumptions about their own and others' abilities to get things done. Ministry leaders can be so unaware of how their use of power affects others that their actions and influence unintentionally result in abuse. The practical need to manage uneven power dynamics, regardless of context, is a reality of life. Each of us has been negotiating with power since we were born, even if we've been unaware of it. Managing uneven power between people requires focused reflection on where the uneven power exists and how power is being exercised in each context.

Fruitful ministry can and does happen in harmony, even when there are differences in formal and relational power. True, our selfishness and limited awareness may cause the use of power to result in unhealthy and unloving actions. However, unequal power does not require that people compete in conflict, either among themselves or with others. That is an unfortunate myth of current American culture. Unhealthy leaders usurp power with this myth by turning people against each other for the sake of selfish goals.

People cannot work autonomously in ministry; ministry is people work. We might be tempted to think we can minister fruitfully without others and thus not have to deal with politics. But whatever the context, we are accountable to others who have the power to limit or to enhance our capacities to work. This means that we do not have the final right or the ultimate responsibility for all decisions. However, there will be times when formal power must be challenged. In those times, our attitude should be one of respect and humility under our Lord Jesus Christ. We are always responsible to God and are ultimately under his power.

When power dynamics between people are unequal, it is important to consider carefully whether these asymmetries are legitimate or illegitimate, just or unjust, healthy or abusive. As leadership authors Mike Bonem and Roger Patterson explain, the implicit approach that many ministries employ is a variation of the "one genius" model. These ministries assume that the senior leader "imparts all the ideas and is responsible for giving direction, and the members and other staff are expected to accept and implement."[8] As image bearers of God, with stewardship and dominion over God's creation, we all need to consider more carefully how we use our power. Does our power lead to privilege and status, or does it result in fruitfulness, godliness, and creativity for ourselves, others, and the rest of creation? As Crouch summarizes, "When power is used well, people and the whole cosmos come more alive to what they were meant to be. . . . Flourishing [for all creation] is the test of power."[9]

Does our power lead to privilege and status, or does it result in fruitfulness, godliness, and creativity for ourselves, others, and the rest of creation?

Unhealthy leaders usually do not recognize how much power they have compared to others. It is far too easy to assume that others have the same capacity to act and to influence as we do. Those with more power can easily dictate who is involved in planning, decision making, and change, as well as what people accomplish once they are invited to participate.[10] Those with less power tend to be most aware of the power dynamics in any given context. Therefore, we should seek them out to learn from their perspectives.

Becoming a student of power dynamics requires intentional time for observation and reflection. This is what authors Ron Heifetz and Marty Linsky describe as "leaving the dance floor to get on the balcony." They write,

> Let's say you are dancing in a big ballroom with a balcony above. A band plays and people swirl all around you to the music, filling up your view. Most of your attention focuses on your dance partner, and you reserve whatever is left to make sure you don't collide with dancers close by. . . . But if you had gone up to the balcony and looked down on the dance floor, you might have seen a very different picture. You would have noticed all sorts of patterns. For example, you might have observed some people never danced at all. And others only engaged when the tempo increased.[11]

The only way we gain a clearer view of reality is by taking ourselves out of the dance of interaction and planning, even if only for a moment. "Otherwise," these authors explain, "you are likely to misperceive the situation and make the wrong diagnosis, leading you to misguided decisions."[12] They emphasize that "the process must be iterative, not static. The challenge is to move back and forth between the dance floor and the balcony, making interventions, observing their influence in real time, and then returning to the action."[13]

The following questions are designed to help us get on the balcony to observe what is going on with power in our organizations.

Questions to Ponder

1. Where are you in the organizational structure of your ministry? What formal power does that position provide?

2. What relationship groups are in your organization?

   How long have people known each other or worked together?

   What challenges have they faced together?

   What draws them together? Shared interests? Similar backgrounds?

3. How do your personal and work values correspond with the observable values of this organization? How do your values compare to the values of those in leadership above you? How do they compare to those under your formal leadership?

4. What is your relationship capital in this organization? To what extent do people perceive you as trustworthy? What can you do to develop healthier, stronger relationships?

5. How do you perceive the trustworthiness of others on your team and in your organization? With whom could you safely discuss your insights and perspectives about power?

6. Reflect on a recent work disappointment when you failed to reach a goal. Before the failure, what were your assumptions about your ability to get things done? In what ways have your assumptions changed as a result of the failure?

7. What words do you use to explain the uneven power dynamics in your contexts? What stories do you tell yourself about your own amount of power?

8. As you apply to join an organization, in what ways could you assess the formal and relational power structures?

Chapter **4**

The Branches and Roots of Interests

As described in chapter two, politics can be understood according to four key concepts: power, interests, negotiation, and ethical implications. Our leadership skills develop as we use these four concepts to reflect on and to analyze organizational dilemmas and relationship tensions. To explore the role of interests, let's start by looking at the experience of our friend Dave.

When Dave accepted a new job as associate pastor in a large suburban church, he brought a unique skill set to the position. Along with being trained for the pastorate, he was an experienced musician and worship leader. Together with his pastoral duties, the senior pastor asked Dave to lead the congregation toward worshiping with new contemporary styles of music.

Fully aware of the worship wars that such changes could create, Dave wisely asked pointed questions about how modifications to the church's existing style might affect the congregation and ministry staff. The senior pastor replied that the church board was unanimously behind these plans. In addition, the leadership had spoken with the music director about the changes. "She is excited about these new developments," the senior pastor reported to Dave.

Three weeks later, Dave led an evening service and oversaw the worship team. He thought everything went well. The senior pastor was enthusiastic; it was a good start. However, at the board meeting the following night, a supportive board member whispered to Dave a warning, "Expect some tension about what happened last night. Some people were unhappy about it." Dave was surprised and could not imagine what the problem could be.

At the staff meeting the next morning, the music director was clearly upset and unloaded a series of complaints. She felt that Dave had sabotaged her ministry by giving the impression that the music change was the start of something brand new. She had worked on gradually changing the music style for a couple years. Several of the musicians came to her after the service saying, "People aren't happy about this music change." One church member phoned the music director after the service to see how she was coping. The member suspected she would be quite upset at what Dave did.

How would you respond to the music director if you were Dave or the senior pastor? To his credit, the senior pastor apologized to both Dave and the director, taking full responsibility. The senior pastor explained that he had asked Dave to do exactly what Dave had done, and that he himself was wrong to assume the plan had been well communicated to others. Dave, in turn, apologized for any impression he had given that might have undermined the previous work of the music director. After the meeting, the senior pastor spoke with the musicians and key members of the congregation, again taking full responsibility for the matter. Over the following weeks the senior pastor more carefully shared all plans for Dave's continued involvement with everyone concerned.

The conflict in this story is not unusual. As leaders, we often think we've done a great job communicating to everyone involved in a change or new program. Only later do we discover that we've unconsciously stepped on toes, hurt feelings, and broken trust with team members. We often put a new idea into motion, assuming there is consensus on the plan. Later we discover that others are grumbling behind the scenes and subversively disrupting the plan.

Why are complaints and conflicts such a common problem when leading change? What is it about planning and implementing even the smallest of changes that energizes people toward disagreement and raises emotions so quickly? One key answer is *interests*, which everyone has.

Learning to See Interests

Interests are priority preferences. In other words, interests are the concerns that fuel people's emotions, motivations, and actions. People will work hard—often very hard—to make sure their interests are reflected in what they are doing and in how others' actions change the situation around them. Interests are often tied to our very identities. We rarely know and articulate our own interests well, let alone perceive those of others. Yet the ability to understand people's interests, starting with our own, is an essential skill for ministry. Without intentional reflection, we will unconsciously act to promote or protect our interests. And we can easily harm others in the process.

> Interests are the concerns that fuel people's emotions, motivations, and actions. People will work hard—often very hard—to make sure their interests are reflected in what they are doing and how other's actions change the situation around them.

People develop interests out of both individual and corporate goals, values, beliefs, personalities, expectations, predispositions, and experiences. And their interests may change quickly, depending on the context and relationships involved. In other words, interests surface as the strongest inclinations of the human will at a given moment. To gain understanding of interests, we need to grow in our capacity to perceive them, to name them, to empathize with them, and to manage them, both for ourselves and for others.

To perceive interests, we need to stop and reflect. This might sound simple, but it is not easy to do in our fast-paced world. To identify interests, we must slow down and ask, *Why am I doing or feeling what I am at this moment?* It takes practice to see and explicitly name interests motivating our daily activities. Once some interests are named, we can assess them and better control how they are driving us.

The next step of understanding is to learn to empathize with others who hold interests quite different from our own. We can respectfully acknowledge that they have deep concerns, even if we disagree with their reasoning and their resulting actions.

Interests can be merely momentary preferences, ones we compromise easily. Strong interests determine the hills we will die on, overriding other concerns and driving us to pursue change at personal risk. Some interests stem from deep values that connect to our life purposes, self-worth, and faith. Interests underlie the most heroic and the most evil actions. Consider God's interests of ultimate love in Romans 5:8: "God shows his love for us in that while we were still sinners, Christ died for us."

When reviewing the stories we've looked at so far, we discover that in each instance the key players were motivated by deep-seated interests. Interests moved each person to act for change and to seek to influence others toward approving or adopting those same interests. We will now explore four basic ways in which interests function.

1. People have different interests.

2. Those interests reflect the way people think life should be.

3. People gather together around similar interests.

4. People promote and defend their interests.

People Have Different Interests

Most of the people in our stories have had different interests. This seems obvious. But in daily life it is not so obvious. It is surprising how long it can take us to consciously realize that our actions are motivated out of interests and that others might disagree with those interests.

In every situation stakeholders have different interests. The term *stakeholders* is shorthand for the individuals or groups with something to gain or to lose as a result of the situation. For example, Dave wanted to make a good impression in his new pastoral position and to use his musical gifts to enrich the church. His interests also included pleasing the staff and the congregants with the worship music style changes. Since he was assured of full support from the leadership and congregation, he had no idea that the music director wanted to continue to change the music style gradually. She also had an interest in being appreciated for the years of work she had invested in this change. Dave unknowingly crossed her interests by flipping the music style in a single service and by not acknowledging her work.

In an earlier story, newly hired Associate Pastor Brian had strong interests in being mentored by the experienced Senior Pastor Joe. He was not interested in being a senior pastor at that time. Brian did not know the church board hired him due to their interest in having a pastor in place before they terminated Pastor Joe.

As the director of Christian education, Sue had strong interests to be successful in her role by helping congregants learn and grow through new programs. Sue assumed she understood the need for depression support groups at her church. Many agreed with her interests and approved her plan, including her supervising pastor, the Christian education committee, and the counseling pastor. However, the senior pastor apparently shut down the publicity. He had contrary interests. He thought that public acknowledgment of depression in the church was more hurtful than helpful, and he did not want the church fragmented into more weekly small group meetings. Furthermore, Pastor Mike and the bulletin volunteer had interests that led them to act in support of the senior pastor's interests and against Sue's.

The story of Mia and Caroline is deceptively simple. However, there are layers of interests at work in it. The women were only slightly interested in painting lessons or in parties. Their deeper interest was to strengthen what they perceived was a growing weakness in the church: the level of authentic relationships among the women. Having an evening event for women to learn to paint together was simply a vehicle to attain their deeper interest. Key to their success was that the pastor shared this deeper interest. In addition, they had other interests keyed to the success of the party. One that was hidden from the pastor was that they hoped to leverage its success to promote future relationship-building activities for the church.

As discussed in chapter three, we see many conflicting interests in Mark 3. The Pharisees and Herodians had interests in maintaining their power as religious leaders. Jesus' popularity with the crowds was threatening their capacity to influence people. Therefore, they watched carefully to see if Jesus would break their Sabbath laws. Jesus' interests in going to the synagogue were to preach and to demonstrate that the kingdom of God was near. Jesus fulfilled his goals, perhaps putting aside a lesser interest of not angering the religious leaders. Jesus responsibly managed his interests and the accompanying feelings of anger, grief, and deadly threat. What about the interests of the disciples, the disabled man, or those who simply came to worship that day? The text does not tell us, but we can imagine how their interests also played a role in their behaviors.

People's Interests Reflect the Way They Think Life Should Be

A second way interests usually function is that they are fueled by people's hidden assumptions about how the world should work. Interests may seem as limited as a momentary desire or passing concern. However, interests that affect how people work together more often stem from people's core values and worldviews. Strong interests are rooted in these personal convictions that reflect one's identity, concerns, values, and desires—which all point to deep desires for the future. As a result, people use the power available to them to pursue changes that exhibit their interests.

Let's take a moment to note the hidden assumptions or beliefs empowering the interests in the characters of our stories. Dave agreed to take on the role of assistant minister with the assurance that everyone, including the music director, understood his role in implementing a more contemporary music style. He assumed the music change should happen quickly under his leadership. He took full control of the evening service, assuming that all agreed with the way he led. It did not occur to any in the planning meetings to discuss *how* Dave should lead the change or how the current director had already been leading this change. Looking back, it is easy to observe that the music director was upset by Dave's leadership and believed the change in music style should be made slowly over time.

When Brian agreed to be the associate pastor, he had the strong but hidden assumption that "church life was pleasant, that people more or less loved each other, after a fashion anyway." When the board forced Pastor Joe to resign, why was Brian so disturbed? Stories of church conflict are countless. But for Brian, his deep-seated hopes that his first church experience would be one of peaceful learning and growing, as well as his assumption of how church life should be, were crushed.

Sue believed wholeheartedly in the depression support groups she was implementing. This was not just another ministry event to her. She assumed that depression was a real and significant issue for many in the congregation. Members of her family suffered from clinical depression, so she already had strong views on how churches *should* help. She assumed that any church would welcome such a ministry. She could not imagine that others on staff would not agree with her convictions about it.

In Mark 3, Jesus had strong theological interests beyond the action of healing the man's hand. He wanted others to accurately interpret and experience the Sabbath, contrary to the way the Jewish leaders enforced Sabbath rules. Foremost, he was interested in presenting the kingdom of God—its influence on what people believed and how they lived.

People Gather Around Similar Interests

A third, distinctive feature of interests is that, like the proverbial birds of a feather, people with similar interests flock together. We even gather around common interests unconsciously. Why do we do this? To build power and emotional support for our interests. Joined together, we have more capacity to shape our world and stronger influence to move others toward approving our agenda or joining our cause. We may even pretend to have the same interests as rivals, as long as it appears the rivals will promote some of our more important interests in return. Look at the coalitions that formed in each of our stories. The collective power of the group furthers the chances of success with the shared interests.

When Dave abruptly changed the music style for a worship service, people immediately gathered to oppose him. The music director and others in the music ministry, as well as some in the congregation, did not like the sudden change. Did it signal bigger changes to come? Perhaps it threatened their future plans. The disgruntled people quickly found each other after the service to discuss their concerns and fears.

The board members of Trinity Church united through their common interest in getting rid of Pastor Joe and in hiring Brian to help the church transition to a new senior pastor. After Pastor Joe resigned, Brian and his wife immediately united in a mutual, private fear for their job security at Trinity, and they began to look for a new church position.

Sue had aligned with several church staff and lay leaders who affirmed the need for depression support groups. The Christian education committee confirmed their interests and approved Sue's plan to organize the groups. Sue began the process by gathering group leaders who were excited with her about the new ministry. Alternatively, the senior pastor gathered Pastor Mike and the bulletin volunteer to align with his interests and to remove Sue's publicity.

The story of Mia and Caroline organizing a painting party is a great example of how people gather together to accomplish a common interest. These women found each other and then pursued their pastor in hopes of his agreement with their interests. The three together had the power to enact their common interests successfully.

Usually the Pharisees and Herodians held opposite interests. The Pharisees were theological conservatives who resented Roman rule. The Herodians were Jews aligned with the Roman government. But both groups were upset with Jesus. They felt he threatened their power and causes. While the Pharisees took great offense at Jesus' violations of their laws, the Herodians were alarmed by his seeming threat to Roman authority.

Both were intimidated by Jesus' ability to draw and influence crowds and perform miracles. Their mutual interests motivated them to come together and discuss how they might destroy Jesus.

"Emotional triangulation" is the name researchers give to this tendency for individuals with similar interests to join together in order to increase their power for a common cause. The act of forming these personal relationship triangles may be ethically neutral. It is the behavior of the group after it forms that requires moral reflection. Researchers note that

> a two-person relationship is notoriously unstable. As long as the relationship is calm, things remain steady. But all it takes is for one person to begin to feel uncomfortable with something about the other, and the relationship moves toward instability. To manage the increased anxiety, one of the two can bring a third person into the triangle. . . . The more intense the issue, the more people there are who will ultimately be engaged in the process.[1]

We see in each story that people join with others who affirm their interests. Those in relationship triangles will usually take action on their concerns. Together they have more power and will use it to shape their world and to influence others toward approving their agenda and joining their cause.

People Promote and Defend Their Interests

Because interests reflect what we think is best, we will use the power and resources we have to promote, advance, and defend our interests, often passionately. We are stakeholders. As individuals or in groups, our interests show that we have something to gain or to lose in the situation. Therefore, we will defend the cause when opposed or when feeling threatened.

For example, Dave felt strongly that the contemporary music style was best for the worship service. And his interest was affirmed by the senior pastor. As a result, his interests in leading the style change were heightened beyond mere job performance. Perhaps this is one reason why he was confident about changing the style all at once, thus strongly promoting his interests. His motivations for action were also tied to his identity as a skilled musician and worship leader. And these skills were explicitly highlighted as a reason for hiring him. When others complained after Dave led worship that first time, they were crossing his interests. Dave probably felt they were critiquing his talent, personality, and sense of vocational calling. It took concerted self-control not to lash out in defense of his actions and interests at the staff meeting.

After Dave led worship that first time, unhappy musicians and congregants immediately defended their interests by complaining to the music director. Because the director agreed with their complaints, she boldly expressed these emotions at the staff meeting. She thus strengthened the defense of her own interests for leading a gradual change in music style.

In Brian's story, the board members used many resources to promote their shared interests. They invested their resources of time, planning, and formal power to terminate Pastor Joe. In doing so, they placed their relationship power with other congregants at risk. In addition, they stretched the church budget to hire a new pastor to sustain the necessary functions of the church upon Joe's expected resignation.

In Sue's story, the senior pastor apparently defended his interests by exercising his formal power to have others quickly remove Sue's publicity. He promoted his interests through the actions of Pastor Mike and the bulletin volunteer. Pastor Mike and the bulletin volunteer apparently did not have stakes in the new support group ministry.

Once Mia and Caroline discovered they had the same concern to build relationships in their church, they took action to promote their shared interest with their pastor.

After Jesus healed the man with a withered hand on the Sabbath, it took a few years and much planning for the Pharisees and Herodians to get Jesus convicted and killed. And they had to triangulate with the Roman governor to succeed! Core beliefs and values were at stake, so the Jewish leaders went to great lengths to influence others to join their cause and to decrease the power of those deemed a threat, especially Jesus.

In each of our case stories, the interests of those involved motivated them to use power, to act, and to influence others. People naturally align with others who hold similar interests and conflict with those who differ. And if the stakes are high enough, people will employ whatever formal and relational power they have to further their interests. Therefore, to lead and minister more responsibly and wisely, we must learn the skill of perceiving and identifying our own interests and the probable interests of those in our contexts. This work, in turn, helps us to understand more clearly the broader interests of organizations and communities.

Questions to Ponder

1. Name several interests that represent the way you think situations should be in your organization.

2. Reflect on a time when you experienced a conflict with someone in your organization over one of those interests. In that conflict, did you seek to find others who would listen to your concerns, agree with you, or come to your defense? If so, how did they respond?

3. What other tactics, besides gathering others, did you use to defend or further your interests during the conflict?

Identifying Interests

How do we perceive and understand our own unique interests, let alone the interests of others? Where do our varying interests come from? And how can we identify the interests that stem from our organizations or communities? The reflective work of analyzing interests is a challenging but important leadership skill.

Many factors complicate the analysis of individual and group interests. To start with, people never have only one interest at a time. And a set of interests held at one time may even contain contradicting values and tangled logic. For any one situation, a person could have many interests due to varied investments and concerns about the outcome. Some interests are above ground. They are explicit, with obvious differences in strength and connections. These easily observed interests lead to predictable actions and emotions. For example, everyone knew Dave was a musician and eager to lead worship. They expected him to be enthusiastic about leading worship that Sunday night.

Many interests, however, are below ground, like the extensive, deep root system of an oak tree. Hidden interests may easily trip us up, creating conflict and disrupting progress. People are often unaware of their convictions and the depth with which they hold them, until these hidden interests are challenged directly or new experiences expose them. When Brian accepted his first pastoral position, he was not aware of his deep conviction that church leaders should agree and not have conflicts. Only years after he experienced the church board's ousting of Pastor Joe did he recognize that his thinking was naive. Since then, he has come to understand that conflict is normal, that differences need to be discussed, and that people grow in trust and understanding from this healthy conflict process.

Many root interests are hidden intentionally for self-protection. We bury these interests from others because they are so important, to reveal them would be too great a risk. For example, in Mark 3 the Pharisees had the explicit interest of watching Jesus. The crowds could see that they too wanted to be near him. But their deeper interests, which they did not admit to Jesus or to the crowds, were to discredit and eradicate Jesus. They would not risk the crowds turning on them in anger.

The more important the interest, the more directly it connects to our core (or tree trunk). These interests involve our identity, self-worth, and worldview. Unfortunately, these huge interests often drive fear-based actions.

> Human interests are like the branches and roots of a big oak tree continually growing from the trunk. Some are above ground like the branches and leaves. Other interests are below ground, like the extensive, deep root system. Diagnosing interests means figuring out some of the branch-and-root motivational convictions of ourselves first and then of others.

Therefore, when trying to discern important hidden interests, we need to ask, What do I fear? and What might others be afraid of in this situation? The music director at Dave's church was not merely irritated because her previous work was overridden. She was afraid of losing her credibility and perhaps her job. This fear spurred her to courageously speak up in the meeting. Sue was also fearful of losing her job if she continued to pursue the new small group ministry and happened to cross interests with the senior pastor. This fear paralyzed her from seeking out any more information about who removed her publicity.

Interests can span an almost limitless range of subjects and perspectives. Depending on the issue, interests can be unbiased or prejudiced, narrow-minded or open-minded, just or unjust, gospel-centered or self-centered. The branches and roots of people's interests intertwine and affect each other consciously and unconsciously. It is both unwise and ineffective to ignore the many values, goals, and complex motivations people have. The big oak trees of our interests are always present and influence any given situation.² To help us see the oak trunk, branches, and roots more clearly, we need diagnostic methods and tools.

Diagnosing Interests

Diagnosing interests involves figuring out some of the branch-and-root concerns and the core motivational convictions of ourselves first and then of others. It requires setting aside time specifically for this work. Because the enormous variety of interests can be hidden and intertwined, they can be difficult to identify. We all bring our own biases and cultural assumptions into the diagnostic process. Therefore, our interest identifications will be inexact. We must hold initial conclusions with humility and continue to gain further confirmation. The diagnostic challenge of accurately identifying interests can be daunting.

Naming and negotiating interests is a core political activity in ministry. If we do not properly identify and understand the interests of those involved in a given situation, we will not be able to engage in the healthy negotiations of those concerns. An understanding of interests provides us with awareness, perspective, and empathy of how we and others think, feel, and act regarding the issues at hand.

To understand our own interests or to identify the interests of others, we can start by gathering multiple perspectives and sources of information. Four different skills for this gathering work require intentional effort.

1. Asking penetrating and respectful questions of the stakeholders in the situation.

2. Listening carefully to others while withholding judgment.

3. Gathering information over a period of time.

4. Understanding others' interpretations, concerns, and fears.

It is a common mistake for us to assume others' motivations and concerns and then draw conclusions based on our own perceptions and interests. Instead, we need to learn to value understanding above the desire to confirm our own explanations. It takes practice and patience to have these conversations. But we have much to gain by talking about interests directly with those who have something to gain or lose as a result of the situation. Then, in further discussion, we should help them to gain a fuller awareness of how other individuals and groups have something at stake as well. Again, it takes practice to learn how to participate calmly in these conversations.

To start this diagnostic process, we need to reflect on our own interests and the strength of our desires to protect and promote those interests. Only then will we clearly see some hidden-root interests and submit them to God, whose interests are perfectly good and loving. This prepares us to seek understanding of others' interests with humility and wisdom. If we do not begin with ourselves, we will likely feel threatened when we encounter any conflicting interests from others. To the degree that we are unaware of our own interests and our power in promoting them, we can do much harm to others.

> Reflection-*in*-action is like the improvisation of a good jazz player. It requires us to apply prior knowledge and experience to the immediate circumstances and dilemmas at hand, all while managing emotions.

Reflection is a critical ability to develop in diagnosing interests. To increase reflective skills, consider two ways reflection happens in practice.[3] Situations in life are often puzzling, ambiguous, and troubling. Yet we must make judgments and decisions while in the thick of those situations, using "reflection-*in*-action." Think of this type of reflection as the improvisation of a good jazz player. It requires us to apply prior knowledge and experience to the immediate circumstances and dilemmas at hand, all while managing emotions. That's the challenge of improv!

After the situation, we can gain new insights by reviewing and reconsidering the consequences of our decisions, feelings, and conduct. This "reflection-*on*-action" requires discipline in our hurried culture. It requires a commitment to stop and the patience to be still and focus for a time on observations of what happened. Contemplation is hard work. We gain new understandings into our own interests, as well as the interests of others, by practicing reflective observing through both improvisation during and contemplation after the presenting situation.

Let's return to Brian's story. Walking into church on that Tuesday morning after his ordination, Brian might have felt a level of peace, excitement, and satisfaction after the celebratory weekend. This would be the time for his normal, weekly meeting with Senior Pastor Joe. Instead, a board member quickly ushered him into an office and informed him that Joe had "resigned." Brian was now responsible for the day-to-day operations of the entire church.

> Reflection-*on*-action is the discipline of reviewing and reconsidering the consequences of our decisions, feelings, and conduct. It requires a commitment to stop and the patience to be still and focus for a time on observations of what happened.

If you were Brian, what would your capacity for reflection-in-action have been during that short, unexpected meeting with the board member? What would you think and feel about Joe's resignation? About your role in the church? About the board members? About Joe? Or about your career plans? What might you say—or not say—to that board member in front of you?

What would your capacity be for reflection-on-action later in the day? What new insights might you develop about the interests of the board members? Your own interests? Or the interests of those in the congregation? How might this intentional reflection affect your emotions and actions? Simple tools and methods can enhance our capacity to do this type of reflection-in-action and reflection-on-action.

Basic Tools for Reflection and Naming Interests

As mentioned in chapter two, four simple yet provocative questions with ethical implications begin the critical thinking process about the negotiation of power and interests.

1. Who are the stakeholders in this situation?

2. What are the probable interests of each stakeholder?

3. How will those interests be represented during the negotiation process?

4. To what degree are we serving the welfare of God's church and the redemption of his world over our selfish interests?

It is crucial to work on these questions before any major planning or decision-making meeting. Writing out the answers to these questions will enhance the reflective process. By listing ideas on paper or a whiteboard, we are able to assess and to evaluate them more deliberately.

Once you are comfortable grappling with these questions personally, teach others this process. By pausing to answer these questions, meetings with conflict or the potential for conflict can become energized, optimistic, and collaborative.

During the meeting, draw a chart on a board or easel and encourage all to build their own lists (see table 4.1). Start with a column listing all the stakeholders that the group can name. Then add a column for interests and one for possible resolutions. Hopefully, people in the group will experience any tensions they feel decreasing and trust increasing as the list grows. People often feel heard when their interests are written on the board. They may also feel safe to name their own previously hidden or emotional interests because the group goal is to fill the board with possibilities.

Table 4.1. Identifying stakeholders and interests

Stakeholders List the individuals or groups that have something to gain or to lose in the situation.	Interests List what each has to gain or to lose in the situation.	Representing Interests List how the interests are accounted for in negotiating.

The next step in this reflection process is to consider observable ways interests are currently moving people to seek change and to influence others. Use the following questions to surface less obvious stakeholders and interests in order to deepen the discussion.

1. What issues are people having conflicts about?

2. How do people think these situations ought to be resolved?

3. Which persons are gathering over common interests? What common interests are they gathering around?

4. Who is promoting particular interests? What interests are they promoting?

5. Who is defending something or acting defensively? What are they defending? What possible fears might be driving their actions?

Diagnostic work for understanding interests requires the examination of multiple perspectives and sources of information. It also involves intentional reflection during and after action.

Questions to Ponder

1. What are some hidden, below-ground interests for your organization that you may have but would not share with any colleagues? What are some actions you have taken that reflected these hidden interests?

2. Consider a recent decision you were involved in making in your organization. To what degree were you accounting for the impact the decision might have on others? How much did that awareness (or lack of awareness) come to bear on the decision-making process?

3. What are some helpful ways you have learned about the interests of others?

In this chapter we have introduced the idea and importance of interests. In chapters five through seven we will provide more detailed diagnostic tools for making interests explicit, particularly when they develop out of our personal uniqueness, our organizational culture, and our societal-cultural background.

Chapter 5

Personal Interests

Everyone has interests. They are the highly complex motivations that lead people to act in one way or another. A central aspect in the politics of working with people is negotiating interests. Therefore, it is important to develop our capacity to recognize, name, and empathize with our own interests and the interests of others.

Three Sources of Human Interests

There are three broad sources of human interests: personal uniqueness, organizational culture, and societal culture.[1] The three sources overlap, as in the circles pictured in figure 5.1. In this chapter, as well as chapters six and seven, we provide multiple filters through which each source of our human interests can be analyzed. Each filter helps us see unique interests from that one perspective. In this way, understood interests can be clarified and unrecognized interests can be made explicit. This information can greatly enhance our capacity to negotiate interests with understanding and wisdom.

Personal uniqueness is a source of individual interests that stem largely from the person's background and personality. These personal interests include convictions and commitments about how life should work, which are more individual than broadly cultural. Personal interests can be as common as the source of disagreement between two friends over music styles. Or they can be as profound as differences in ministry philosophy that split up a missions team.

Organizational culture is like a road map that tells a specific group of people—be it family, business, school, congregation, parachurch ministry, or denomination—how and why to get things done. It provides the common source of interests expressed by people involved in a particular group. Organizational culture encompasses the formal, published structures of the organization as well as the relational, unwritten rules of behavior. *Formal* organizational culture includes the documented history, physical resources, mission and core value statements, policy and rule handbooks, job descriptions, and organizational charts. *Relational* organizational culture develops over time as people work together. The relational culture of an organization includes the stories people tell about their organization's history, their shared but unwritten values, the resources of relationship capital, the group expectations and communication patterns, and jargon. If formal organizational culture is like the streets marked on a city map, the relational organizational culture is the popular shortcuts for navigating the city.

Figure 5.1. Three sources of human interests

Societal culture is like an extensive road map that tells a larger group of people how to live together. Societal culture encompasses the unique history, orientations, resources, goals, language, rules, and values of a community or geographical region. The phrase *societal interest*s makes the distinction between interests grounded in the limited organizational culture of a workplace or ministry, and interests grounded in the more general culture of the area where people live.

We will look more in-depth at personal interests in this chapter and consider the others in chapters six and seven.

Questions to Ponder

1. Name some personal interests you have that are different from others in your family.

2. What are some adjustments you have made to adapt to the place where you work or worship? To what degree were these adjustments due to your personal interests conflicting with the organizational culture-based interests?

Diagnosing Personal Interests

Personal interests include deep-seated assumptions about how life should work. Our personal interests motivate us to act directly from our beliefs about what is moral, how we are to live, how others should treat us, and how we can influence any given situation.

> Personal interests include convictions and commitments about how life should work, which are more individual than broadly cultural. They motivate us to act directly from our beliefs about what is moral, how we are to live, how others should treat us, and how we can influence any given situation.

Let's consider personal interests in Dave's story. Remember that he started a new job as associate pastor, with directions to lead change in the Sunday worship music style. He probably had similar interests that most of us would have when beginning a new job. We probably desired to fit in, to succeed, to be trusted, to be valued, and to be supported by the supervisor. Dave assumed the senior pastor had effectively prepared the way for him to direct and change the worship music.

Now consider the personal interests the music director might have had about this new pastor. Did she feel uneasy or threatened by Dave's presence, expertise, and ideas? Had she given tacit approval to the senior pastor about Dave's participation without truly meaning to? The following four filters are useful for explicitly naming these types of personal interests.

1. Five facets of the whole person: physical, emotional, intellectual, social, and moral

2. Family of origin

3. Research-based personality profiles

4. Results or relationships tendency

Each filter describes specific, observable aspects of our personalities that can lead us to have predictable interests and resulting behaviors.

Personal Filter 1: Five Facets of the Whole Person

We humans are complicated creatures. Every aspect of our personhood interacts with every other part. However, to grow in self-awareness of personal interests, it is helpful to observe each aspect of personhood separately: the physical, emotional, intellectual, social, and moral (see 1 Corinthians 2:11; Galatians 5:16-26; Ephesians 4:15; John 15:1-11; 1 Peter 2:4-5). The goal is *not* to dissect ourselves by pitting one aspect against another. Instead, we seek to better understand the interests we promote out of these five categories.

Physical. Abraham Maslow is considered one of the fathers of modern psychology. One of his primary concerns was to understand what motivates people. He posited that "people are motivated to achieve certain needs and that some take precedence over others."[2] According to Maslow, the most basic level of human needs is physical, including food, water, warmth, rest, and safety. These physical needs influence our conscious and unconscious interests.

Consider the basic need for rest. If we attend an important meeting after a sick child kept us up half the night, our lack of sleep will probably make us irritable. As a result we have less patience for a colleague who doesn't understand the issues under discussion. Our physical state will heighten our interest to resolve the issue quickly and to move on to what we consider more important.

More serious physical needs involve the need for shelter and safety. Recall the feelings experienced by Brian after learning that Senior Pastor Joe had abruptly "resigned." Trinity Church no longer felt like a safe place to serve, physically or emotionally. Brian might not trust the board members to provide his job and paycheck consistently for the years he had planned to serve there.

Emotional. People often think that work on emotions is a soft skill that is trivial to the task of getting work done.[3] However, many leadership experts recognize that emotions influence every aspect of our personhood and even the success of corporations and communities. Management psychologists David Caruso and Peter Salovey write, "We believe that to ignore their role, to deny the wisdom of your own emotions and those of others, is to invite failure as a person, as a manager, and as a leader."[4]

The value and role of human emotions has been debated among Christians for a long time.[5] More recently, Christian theologians and counselors have acknowledged that emotions are a critical, God-given aspect of our personhood.[6] Pete Scazzero summarizes their conclusions, bluntly saying, "Emotional health and spiritual maturity are inseparable."[7]

Emotions can drive our interests. And yet it is hard to accurately identify our feelings or the emotions of others. One way to work on identifying emotions is to reflect on recent encounters with others. Emotions "are primarily signals about people, social situations, and interactions. The events that call forth emotions are typically interpersonal actions."[8] Sue was mildly concerned when her posters went missing. However, after the volunteer told her that her bulletin announcement had been cancelled, her fight-or-flight response took over. She felt her whole ministry had been undermined and took immediate steps to find out who had crossed her and why they had done it.

We can grow in our capacity to perceive when our emotions are at work *during* personal interactions with others by using the reflection-in-action skill discussed in chapter four. After the event, we can practice reflection-on-action by observing and reflecting on our thinking and acting in response to our emotions. Sue would have been wise to consider her own emotions, interests, and the possible interests of others regarding her publicity before taking any further action.

A friend of the authors is the chief operations officer of a faith-based organization. After reflecting on the emotions in his workplace, he recognized that the interpersonal methods of his boss were alienating others on the management team. For the health of the organization, he decided to address his concerns with his boss. He barely slept the night before this meeting and was highly anxious as he entered the room. By intentionally reflecting-in-action, he reminded himself that it was his responsibility to manage his emotions so that he could respectfully and calmly present his concerns. Throughout the conversation he monitored his tone of voice and nonverbal expressions. He didn't want his anxiety to diminish or to intensify his message.

The emotions checklist in appendix one is a tool to help us recognize the emotions we or others experience. Before and after times of interacting with others, try using this list to identify emotions in play during the situation. Then, consider listing the likely ways those emotions influenced or changed the interests of everyone involved.

Intellectual. People might assume that most interests are developed through our conscious, logical thought processes. Some are. However, most interests stem from opinions that are formed by more than rational thought or well-researched information. Intellectual interests develop from many sources and are acquired over years through growth in knowledge and in relevant experiences. These interests are influenced by family, schooling, geographic region, and culture. In addition, the level of conviction people have about any given issue will vary based on their unique personality and perspective on the subject.

How do you diagnose intellectual interests when they are so complicated? One method is to note the information sources that persons trust to provide accurate perspectives on reality. For instance, two colleagues had significant disagreements about how to set the church calendar dates. They both listed many reasons why their way would serve the community best. There seemed to be no room for collaboration until they discovered their background sources. One had aligned holiday dates with the nearby public school's calendar; the other had done the same with a private school's calendar.

In our information-overload culture, we are influenced by much more data than we are aware of. Advertisers count on this fact. We also have so many sources of global news that objective media reporting seems to be a thing of the past. Readers and viewers flock to blogs and websites that agree with their own biases. Therefore, we can gain self-awareness of our intellectual interests by simply listing our opinions and the resources that informed them. We can grow in our understanding of others' intellectual interests by noting what they read and watch. Just make sure you do not pigeonhole yourself or others. Leave room for people to grow and change through new information and experiences.

> In our information-overload culture, we are influenced by much more data than we are aware of. We can gain self-awareness of our intellectual interests by listing our opinions and the resources that informed them, and we can grow in our understanding of others' intellectual interests by noting what they read and watch.

Social. Recognizing patterns in how we relate to others provides insight about our social interests. Humans are social creatures who need loving relationships to thrive. The Bible teaches that fellowship is an integral part of a healthy Christian life (1 Thessalonians 5:11).[9] Our relational needs, identity needs, desire for acceptance from others, and fear of rejection can greatly shape our interests. Consider the time and effort required to establish and to sustain a trusted friendship. That exertion reflects deep social interests. Similarly, the reasons we avoid certain contexts and people also reveal social interests.

At a recent conference, Julie was sitting with a small group of people she had never met. The group had just heard a presentation on the importance of the protection of children in ministry. People in the group were responding by sharing their perspectives on the subject. Having grown up in an abusive home, Julie had many deep feelings about children's safety. But she also struggled to feel socially accepted. After quietly listening, she finally stirred up the courage to express an opinion. For the rest in the group, this might not have been a big deal, but after sharing her insights, Julie suddenly felt fearful and awkward, wondering if the others would reject her. Her prevailing interests at that moment were much more social and emotional than intellectual.

Moral. The moral aspect of life accounts for what we consider to be right and wrong, and how we choose to act. In Romans 12:2, the apostle Paul exhorts his friends to "not be conformed to this world." Rather, they are to be continually renewed, having their minds transformed in a way that takes "captive every thought to make it obedient to Christ" (2 Corinthians 10:5).[10] However, it is not unusual for us to assume our interests are appropriate without considering whether they reflect God's point of view. The apostle Paul even faced this challenge. At one point he shared with his friends at Philippi that many "seek their own interests, not those of Jesus Christ" (Philippians 2:21).

It is important for all of our interests, and especially our moral interests, to be under the review and critique of Scripture. Moral interests deal with matters that Scripture explicitly states are right or wrong (selfishness, immorality, gossip, hatred, lying, etc. [Galatians 5:19-21]), as well as with matters where Scripture is not so direct (styles of clothing and entertainment, what you eat and drink [Romans 14]). For gray issues requiring discernment, the

Scripture is full of insights and provides us with guiding principles. Regardless of the consequences or our own preferences, followers of Christ are responsible to learn to obey God's revealed truth, to ask God for wisdom in discernment, and to live in step with God's Spirit.

It is fitting for followers of Christ to cultivate the disciplines of Bible study and prayer to help review and critique their moral interests. Ezra, the Old Testament scribe, modeled this behavior: "Ezra had set his heart to study the Law of the LORD, and to do it and to teach [God's] statutes" (Ezra 7:10).

Questions for Personal Filter 1

Physical

1. Reflect on your current diet. What are you eating and why? What effect does your diet have on your interests? What impact does it have on how you promote your interests?

2. To what extent do you exercise regularly and adequately? What differences might that make in your daily concerns and capacities?

3. When was your last physical exam? How might the results influence your interests?

4. What are your sleep patterns? How do they affect your family or friends? Your work relationships? Your productivity? Your motivations?

Emotional

1. What is your capacity to reflect on your emotions during and after an interpersonal event? What motivates you to develop this self-awareness skill further?

2. In what ways have you been blindsided by your emotions recently? What was the effect of these emotions on your interests? On your capacity to think? On your communication with others?

3. Who can you safely talk to about your emotions? Who can help you identify your emotional interests more thoroughly?

Intellectual

1. What sources of media do you regularly consume? While watching or listening, try listing the media's interests based on what is mentioned or dramatized. To what degree do they align with your own interests? Note what topics or opinions are not mentioned.

2. What do you read regularly? What do you hope to gain from your reading? What draws you to read one source versus another?

3. What types of media do you quote or summarize to others? What interests of yours does this sharing reflect? What media sources do others refer to you?

4. Consciously observe some media ads. What assumptions are they promoting? What interests do they reflect?

5. What could you gain by reading some of the same books or resources that your work colleagues and others in your family highly value? Consider swapping a valued, marked-up book or periodical with a colleague in order to better understand each other's perspectives.

Social

1. When and how do you compare yourself to others? What do you do in response to your comparisons? What interests do these responses reflect?

2. How would you describe your various friendships? What influences do they have on your opinions, perspectives, and values?

3. Who in your life have you been able to talk to without concern for negative repercussions? What common interests helped create your deep trust in these people?

Moral

1. Consider some recent painful experiences you have had with others. How have these experiences shaped your social interests and actions?

2. What steps are you taking to have your mind renewed to the will of God? In what ways can you grow to see conflict situations more from God's point of view?

3. In what ways do you see your moral interests being influenced by media and other external sources? How do these interests compare to biblical principles or commandments?

4. To what extent has prayer shaped your personal perspectives on life's dilemmas?

Personal Filter 2: Family of Origin

In the field of counseling, the phrase *family of origin* refers to our nuclear family or those significant caretakers and persons we lived with for our first eighteen years of life. It may also include extended biological family of current and past generations. Our experiences in childhood and adolescence profoundly shape our personal interests. As well-known pastor Pete Scazzero explains,

> While we are affected by powerful external events and circumstances through our earthly lives, our families are the most powerful group to which we will ever belong. Even those who left home as young adults, determined to "break" from their family histories, soon find that their family's way of "doing" life follows them wherever they go.[11]

In order to identify the interests from our family of origin that molded us, one beneficial exercise is to draw and then explore a family diagram or genogram. Appendix two provides a description of how to do this. This appendix also provides many questions one can use to investigate the genogram and learn about particular interests based on patterns from family background.

Questions for Personal Filter 2

1. Even before working on a genogram, what are some strengths and struggles you identify in yourself from growing up in your family?

2. What aspects of your childhood neighborhood do you appreciate? What about your childhood town? How have these defined your expectations of how things ought to be?

3. What were your key experiences with church from birth to adulthood? How would you describe the religious culture of your upbringing? What aspects of it do you affirm? What do you challenge?

4. In what ways (positive and negative) have your childhood experiences impacted your current vision of ministry? Your perspectives on leadership? Your sense of how ministry ought to happen?

Personal Filter 3: Research-based Personality Profiles

The exploration of personality profiles can provide significant insight into personal interests. Numerous well-researched profiles are available, only some of which will be briefly explained here. They are self-administered or accessible through counselors, career centers, or life coaches. These profiles demonstrate personality differences in many categories. All the personality types in a profile are affirmed, with the specific categories described as neutral, neither inherently good nor bad. The results can provide a helpful general analysis of your personality and the values of your type. However, profiles can be expensive, and the results are quite limited compared to the uniqueness of each individual person. People should not use results to limit themselves or to label and limit others. Instead, profiles can provide a broader perspective and appreciation for the differences and values in the people around us. Thus, learning from personality profiles can greatly increase our understanding, respect, and empathy for those with differing interests from our own.

> Learning from personality profiles can greatly increase our understanding and empathy for those with differing interests from our own.

Some of the more popular profiles include the DISC behavior assessment, the Myers-Briggs Personality Inventory (MBTI), and the RightPath leadership assessments. These tools are designed to help people identify their unique talents, strengths, and struggles. They are intended to name typical default behaviors and are not constructed to detect emotional or psychiatric problems.

Other instruments are usually administered by mental health professionals and require interpretation and evaluation by these clinicians. Two of the more popular are the 16PF Personality Factor test and the Minnesota Multiphasic Personality Inventory (MMPI). While the 16PF is often used as a measure of normal healthy personality, it can also be employed as a clinical instrument to help diagnose psychiatric disorders. Similarly, the MMPI is a highly sophisticated test that identifies both healthy personality characteristics and psychopathology.

One pastor we know shared how helpful the Myers-Briggs was in identifying his natural interest in helping others. Before taking the profile, he was often self-critical, deriding himself as a "people-pleasing approval leech." After taking the MBTI he learned that this was a common strength and corresponding struggle for his personality type. Now he appreciates this characteristic in himself and does not expect others to be similarly wired. And he is much more mindful not to overfunction in his desire to please others.

An example of a newer personality profile helpful for exploring personal interests is the RightPath 4/6. This profile has a companion instrument called the RightPath Leadership 360 (L360).[12] The L360 requires twelve or more friends and work associates to rate the person in key areas of attitudes, behaviors, and skills. The L360 provides a significant way to receive honest, straightforward, and helpful comments from others. Most leaders who take it learn they are much harder evaluating themselves than others are. The use of these tools gives them new insights into their unique interests and how they relate to the interests of others.

Personality profile assessments provide many categories and spectrums of personal differences. To list a few, these profiles name the degree to which people drain our energy, whether we notice physical or emotional data first, our willingness to take risks, how dominantly or compliantly we act, whether we process information better verbally or internally, how concisely and bluntly we communicate, and how compassionate we are.

If you have not taken a personality profile or 360 inventory lately, consider doing so to learn more about your strengths, struggles, and how others experience your leadership. Invite those that work with you to join in this work of self-discovery and team building.

Questions for Personal Filter 3

1. What stories do you tell yourself about your strengths and struggles? What do these tell you about your identity interests concerning yourself and your sense of well-being, giftedness, and worthiness? Who can you ask for helpful, honest discussions about your strengths and struggles?

2. How do your strengths inform some of your deepest values and interests? How might your struggles be affecting some of your deepest values and interests?

Personal Filter 4: Tendency to Focus on Results or Relationships

Recognizing whether an individual is more focused on results or relationships is a personality difference that consistently shows up in research inventories. But it is also easily observed from daily interactions. All of us are responsible to get things done. At the same time, each of us must live and work with others in a loving manner. Both the ability to accomplish tasks and the skill of building relationships are important for success in most endeavors. But because of natural personalities and family of origin patterns, people tend to be hardwired to have a greater capacity and interest in pursuing either results or relationships. For example, when working at an office building or church, some of us go to the kitchen for coffee and return to our desks promptly. Others head to the kitchen, have multiple conversations with people along the way and forget the coffee.

> Both the ability to accomplish tasks and the skill of building relationships are important for success in most endeavors. But because of natural personalities and family of origin patterns, people tend to be hardwired to have a greater capacity and interest in pursuing either results or relationships.

When a ministry leader focuses mostly on tasks and results, others on their team may feel that their worth is based solely on what they get accomplished or how they perform. They may question their value as a fellow believer. As a result, their trust in the leader and their job satisfaction can diminish. And in time, their job performance may drop as well.

A young professional was a member of the worship ensemble at her church. While she admittedly was not very good on the guitar, she enjoyed playing with the group and even jamming together on free nights. The organization of the ensemble was pretty loose. So, she did not think about it much when she missed a few weeks of rehearsals, with the result that she was excluded from playing on the following Sundays. However, after a month of missing rehearsals, she finally asked the worship director, "Why haven't I been told about the practice sessions?"

"Oh," he responded, "a number of us felt you were holding us back musically, so we decided not to tell you about the rehearsals." Needless to say, the focus of this director, and perhaps others in the ensemble, was on musical performance to the neglect of their relationship with the young woman, who was deeply hurt by their rejection and deception. It also held the church back from accomplishing its goal of being a caring fellowship. The failure to do relationships well may mean we run a great program with no lasting kingdom impact.

On the other side, our leadership capacity to love people well decreases when we focus primarily on relationships to the neglect of results. Because he was a church planter, one young pastor's denomination required him to identify and work toward quarterly attendance and financial goals. This task was difficult for him. Because of his natural bent toward relationships, he felt these goals were superficial and inauthentic. So, he spent most of his time networking relationally throughout the community.

> The pursuits of *both* relationships and results are necessary goals for any leader. Only with healthy, growing relationships will results build toward significant successes with lasting effect.

When it came time for denominational review, the review board reprimanded the young pastor for not working on his goals. Then his fledgling congregation complained—first to the pastor and then to the denomination—that the worship services were sloppy and that the pastor failed to follow through on his responsibilities. The pastor responded by spending even more time with people in the community. Eventually the denomination leaders replaced him with someone who could hold the tension between pursuing relationships and results.

Questions for Personal Filter 4

1. Interests can be below ground, functioning unconsciously and yet strongly influencing behavior. How aware are you of the ways your preference for results or relationships affect your daily routine? Consider asking several people you trust about their perceptions of your focus in this area and how it affects others.

2. How has your preference for either results or relationships influenced your personal decisions, leadership, and friendships? Consider the effects of your preference in the following areas:

   - working with others
   - working under deadlines
   - your capacity to listen
   - your capacity to follow through on tasks
   - your criteria for measuring success

- your willingness to set and enforce standards
- your ability to feel and show empathy

3. Compare and contrast experiences with good friends and with daily work associates. For each person, do you tend to emphasize people or productivity? Do you emphasize getting work accomplished or the others' feelings? Look for a pattern over time to help you diagnose these personal interests.

Concluding Thoughts

Personal interests are individually held convictions and commitments about how life should work or what should be possible. These deep-set motivations develop as people grow from childhood into adult life. An individual's life experiences and perceptions of those experiences create a unique profile of convictions, beliefs, and identity. The four filters can help us gain self-awareness both of our unique interests stemming from our personalities and of how these interests influence what we do. In chapter six we explore interests that develop from organizational culture.

Chapter 6

Organizational Interests

Personal uniqueness, organizational culture, and societal culture are three main sources of human interests. In chapters four and five, we introduced the concept of human interests and looked at filters to diagnose personal interests. In this chapter we will explore filters for recognizing and evaluating people's interests formed in organizational cultures.

An organizational culture develops uniquely in each context, be it family, business, school, local church, parachurch ministry, or denomination. Here we will focus on ministry organizations, though the filters discussed can help identify interests in any type of organizational setting.

A challenging aspect of organizational culture is that it is a mix of formal and relational structures within the organization. The formal structures include the documented history, physical resources, mission and core values statements, budgets, policy and rule handbooks, job descriptions, and organizational charts.[1] The relational structures develop over time as people work together. These structures include the stories people tell about their organization's history, their shared but unwritten values, the resources of relationship capital, the group expectations and communication patterns, and jargon. Because of these many formal and relational aspects of organizational culture,

> The relational structures of organizational culture develop over time as people work together and include the stories people tell about their organization's history, their shared but unwritten values, the resources of relationship capital, the group expectations and communication patterns, and jargon.

the majority of the culture is hidden, like the roots of the big oak tree discussed earlier.

The relational side of an organizational culture might conflict with the formal and publicly expressed mission and interests of the ministry. In addition, different levels of leadership may or may not be in sync with the relational culture of those they manage. Or different teams in an organization may have their own ways of working. For example, in Sue's story the senior pastor was out of sync; he was not working with the same values and relationship expectations of the committees and staff Sue worked with. The senior pastor's personal interests conflicted with the relational culture of open communication and collaboration under his leadership. Furthermore, Sue and those working with her felt that the senior pastor's values conflicted with the formal mission of the church.

Most ministries are nonprofit organizations made up of partnerships between volunteers, professionals, and other participants. Therefore, the relational aspects of the organizational culture are often much more substantial than in business organizations and can lead to deeply felt but hidden interests. Ministry teams share mutual experiences, commitments, visions, and values that frame the group interests.[2] They also share resources, expectations for behavior, and unspoken rules, which include sacred cows or customs that members refuse to question or discuss. When Jesus drove the money changers out of the temple, he was breaking the rules of the organizational culture and confronting the organizational interests of the Jewish leadership. Jesus condemned them for valuing financial profit and sacrificial rules (formal organization culture) over the worship of God (relational organization culture [John 2:13-17]). The regular members of the Jewish community did not openly question Jesus' criticism during most of his public ministry.

As people become involved in an organization, they learn the organization's culture, as well as the microcultures formed by groups within the organization. Over time, new members' actions and attitudes mirror the group's rituals and practices. Usually, they either adapt to the organization's values and expectations or decide to leave it.

A friend recently moved from a church where everyone wore blue jeans with untucked shirts on Sunday to a church where congregants typically wore business attire. This clothing difference reflects the organizational culture our friend will need to adjust to. And with time, our friend will probably adopt other interests that come from the new church culture.

Diagnosing Organizational Culture-based Interests

Organizational culture can be described as "the way we do things around here," which leads to member interests being "the reasons I do things this way around here."[3] A common culture provides people with shared experiences, by which they develop similar expressed and hidden interests. The members' interests are reflected in the office furniture, the way people dress, the stories people tell about their organization, unique traditions, who their heroes are, and what people celebrate as success.[4]

Organizational culture types are similar to personality profiles, with unique characteristics, strengths, and struggles. Researchers of organizational development have formed keen insights into the ways that

> Organizational culture can be described as "the way we do things around here," so member interests would be "the reasons I do things this way around here" and are reflected in the office furniture, the way people dress, the stories people tell about their organization, unique traditions, who their heroes are, and what people celebrate as success.

systems, including ministry organizations, function.[5] For example, our colleague Philip Douglass has developed a detailed study of church personality based on the Myers-Briggs Personality Profile.[6] Tools like this help name organizational culture similar to how chapter five describes personal interests.

Below are four filters for identifying organizational culture and the resulting member interests. While not revealing all the driving interests of an organization's members, these filters provide helpful snapshots of the various characteristics that the group likely shares.

Organizational Culture Filter 1: Company Values

The work of management professors Kim Cameron and Robert Quinn is particularly helpful in diagnosing organizational interests in light of their values orientation.[7] While originally developed to evaluate corporate contexts, we have found their work helpful in understanding nonprofits as well.

Cameron and Quinn describe organizational culture as "the taken-for-granted values, underlying assumptions, expectations, collective memories, and definitions present in organizations and their members."[8] Some of the questions they use to gather data about an organization's culture appear under "Questions for Organizational Culture Filter 1." They use this data to identify four value orientations that describe the dominant interests of the members. We have renamed these four orientations as collaborative, control, creative, and competitive culture types.

A *collaborative* culture is one that seeks to create a family atmosphere of collaboration, unity, relational commitment, and employee development. There is an emphasis on trust, people liking each other, and loyalty. Teamwork, mutual participation, and consensus are prominent. Leaders are expected to be warm and supportive, serving more as facilitators and coaches than as directors.

> **Four value orientations which describe the dominant interests of an organization's members are collaborative, control, creative, and competitive culture types.**

A *control* culture focuses on stability. People highly value clear rules, procedures, consistency, efficiency, and predictable work. There are clear, hierarchical lines of decision making and accountability. Leaders are monitors who measure outcomes and enforce the rules.

A *creative* culture is change-oriented.[9] People are expected to be adaptable, innovative, and risk oriented. These cultures want to be on the cutting edge of new knowledge and programs. Leaders are innovators who sell their vision, encourage flexibility and growth through failure, and are willing and happy to break the rules.

A *competitive* culture is oriented toward being the biggest and the best. It leverages resources, including its people, to aggressively gain market share (or the ministry equivalent). Leaders are hard-driving producers who are tough and demanding. People highly value comparisons to similar organizations and a regular review of numerical data.

Every organization has a blend of these four values. However, Cameron and Quinn assert that "almost always, one or more of the culture types dominate an organization."[10] Furthermore, they note that the concept of organizational culture "is distinct from the concept of organization *climate*. Climate consists of temporary attitudes, feelings, and perceptions of individual members. Culture is an enduring, slow-to-change, core characteristic of organizations."[11]

In order to use Cameron and Quinn's framework to diagnose the organizational culture you are reviewing, begin by answering the following questions. Each set of questions will identify important, though often unexpressed, company interests. Consider how the answers reflect one or more of the four cultural values (collaborative, control, creative, or competitive). Then, imagine how the interests of organizational members reflect these cultural values. Finally, take your initial findings and review them with others who know the organization and use their feedback to critique and improve your analysis and the health of the organizational culture.

Questions for Organizational Culture Filter 1

1. What are the dominant characteristics of the organization? Is it more collaborative, controlling, creative, or highly driven and competitive?

2. How do the leaders lead? To what degree do they mentor others? To what degree are they risk oriented? Focused on efficiency? Fixed on production? Concerned about people feeling valued and successful?

3. How are employees managed? To what degree is the environment team focused or individually competitive? Which is encouraged more, conformity or creativity?

4. What provides the organizational glue? How prevalent is a shared trust? To what degree is the vision and mission important for daily functioning?

5. What are the organization's strategic emphases? New challenges? Status quo? Stretch targets?

6. How does the organization gauge success? What is most celebrated as progress?

Organizational Culture Filter 2: Ministry Programs

Ministry programs reveal the convictions and culture of a ministry: theological convictions, budget convictions, and convictions of time and other resource priorities. Therefore, another way to identify the more hidden culture of a ministry is to review the plans, programs, schedules, and commitments of the staff and active members. This type of reflection highlights probable interests stemming from the organizational culture.

Often activities happen in ministry where only the planners know the true interests behind the events. In the story of Mia and Caroline, they did not simply want to have an art program. They proposed this activity based on their deep concern for the development of relationships among women in the church. If outsiders heard about this activity, they might think, *What a fun thing for the church women to do.* If they pondered why church leaders would use time and resources for the event, they could venture a guess. To gain a more precise answer, they could ask Mia or Caroline about the story behind the

> One way to identify the more hidden culture of a ministry is to review the plans, programs, schedules, and commitments of the staff and active members.

program and thus gain a clearer understanding of the real interests motivating the activity.

Similarly, Sue did not plan the depression support groups at Grace Church simply because she thought it was a nice idea. She heard the need expressed from a number of groups in the church. Quite a few single-again adults shared their anxiety about facing another holiday season. And the counseling staff asked for her help supporting those who struggled with depression since holidays can highlight loneliness and life disappointments for both groups.

But Sue did not realize that individuals were asking her to start a new program that was counter to some hidden rules in the church. The pastors and administrator who removed her publicity also had stakes in Sue's program. Perhaps they believed that strong faith and the current ministries of the church should be enough to address the needs of the people. Sue's program did not represent their perspectives or interests, so they did not want resources going to it.

> By looking closely at ministry plans and programs that are or are not happening, one can often identify the most influential interests in the organization.

By looking closely at ministry plans and programs that are or are not happening, one can often identify the most influential interests in the organization. The reasons may be based on budgetary concerns or even on long-standing traditions. But the ministry's culture will strongly influence the member interests that underlie the priority activities.

Questions for Organizational Culture Filter 2

1. What are the central programs in the ministry? What are the most traditional programs? What are the official rationales behind each activity? Who proposed each one?

2. What are the stories members tell about the importance of these activities? What reasons do people give for being involved? What goals do members hope each activity will accomplish?

3. What are some possible programs that are not supported by your ministry organization? What is the official rationale behind these choices? What are the stories members tell about why these programs are not pursued?

Organizational Culture Filter 3: Results or Relationships Focus

Just as individuals tend to focus on building either results or relationships, so do organizational cultures. And the people within the organization will respond to that cultural default by prioritizing one over the other. Organizational behaviorists Robert Goffee and Gareth Jones developed a model to evaluate these interests in any organization, be it church, parachurch ministry, or business. They suggest there are two general categories of interests that frame how people interact with one another in the organization. We have reframed their categories by using the terms used previously as a filter for personal interests: *results* or *relationships*.[12]

A *relationships*-oriented work context refers to an organizational culture where care and concern for others is a higher value and priority than getting work done. Therefore, when under pressure, people are expected to take time to build relationships and trust. Coworkers see one another as friends and companions. People show respect for shared ideas, attitudes, and values. Employees are encouraged to associate on equal terms as peers.

> Just as individuals tend to focus on building either results or relationships, so do organizational cultures. And the people within the organization will respond to that cultural default by prioritizing one over the other.

A *results*-focused organization is focused on accomplishing tangible goals. Therefore, the culture moves people to get work accomplished. In this environment people relate to one another primarily on the basis of their work responsibilities. They may not necessarily know each other, like one another, or hold similar interests beyond their shared official tasks.

By making a matrix of relationship-and-results priorities, Goffee and Jones developed a typology of organizational cultures that can be applied to ministry systems as well. Consider where you have experienced ministry cultures that were more similar to one description over the others in table 6.1.

Table 6.1. Ministry organizational culture based on relationship or results

	High Relationship Priority	Low Relationship Priority
High Results Priority	**Communal Organization** Most ministries desire to have this culture. People are interpersonally attracted to and care for one another. And missional goals are set, accomplished, and celebrated. This culture is inherently unstable and thus rare. When friendship networks solidify, the culture becomes networked. When programs dominate over relational priorities, it becomes mercenary.	**Mercenary Organization** Here people cooperate together to attain individual objectives and tasks. The prevailing attitude is, "If you help me achieve my tasks and goals, I am attracted to you." Large churches and parachurch ministries often reflect this culture. Participants come to express their giftedness and to have their needs met, while the staff directs people and resources to accomplish the organization's agenda.
Low Results Priority	**Networked Organization** This culture benefits from strong loyalties and sincere friendships. Its club-like atmosphere comes from strong rituals, which reinforce the community. However, these relationships accomplish little from a missional perspective. The people are focused on meeting their internal needs.	**Fragmented Organization** In this environment people derive benefit from the autonomy and freedom granted to individual members. There is a lack of coordinated effort as people pursue their own agendas. Not many ministries could remain viable in this context since personal interests are bound to conflict, thus preventing accomplishments and success on the organizational level.

Questions for Organizational Culture Filter 3

1. Based on this four-part model of table 6.1, how would you classify your current church or ministry culture?

2. What interests does this model identify as characteristic of your organization's members and leaders?

3. How long have you been involved in your current organization? What personal interests have you modified to reflect the organization's culture? What personal interests has the organization's culture strengthened?

4. How has your involvement in this ministry changed your pursuit of relationships at work? How has it changed your sense of mission and success?

Organizational Culture Filter 4: Stubborn Cultural Qualities

In their book *The Practice of Adaptive Leadership*, Ronald Heifetz, Alexander Grashow, and Marty Linsky provide three categories useful in discerning organizational interests: structure, ethos, and defaults.[13] They explain how these stubborn cultural qualities take root and grow over time in organizations.

> From the first day in the life of an organization, the elements begin taking shape. People make decisions about how to interact with each other, which ideas will be shared and which will not, what jokes are appropriate and funny, who gets the floor during debates and meetings, and what kinds of performance will be rewarded. . . . An organizational system takes on a life of its own, selecting, rewarding, and absorbing members into it who then perpetuate the system. . . . Over time [the culture and resulting interests of the members] become deeply ingrained, self-reinforcing, and very difficult to reshape.[14]

This reinforcing quality of organizational culture helps to explain a common experience in ministry. Staff members come and go, yet the ministry does not seem to change in significant ways. If leaders knew the more hidden qualities of their organizational cultures, they would have

> The reinforcing quality of organizational culture helps to explain a common experience in ministry. Staff members come and go, yet the ministry does not seem to change in significant ways. If leaders knew the more hidden qualities of their organizational cultures, they would have a much better chance of leading change.

a much better chance of leading change. The next several pages contain summaries and filters for these three stubborn cultural qualities.

Structure. Organizational structure includes rules and patterns for such things as compensation, hierarchical reporting, and hiring procedures. These practices can be used to explore basic managerial commitments of an organization. Collect this data by using both personal observations and interactions with employees and ministry participants. You can also examine written and online documents of the organization. After compiling answers to the following filter questions, share them with some of the people you previously interviewed. See if they agree with your conclusions. And remember, if others disagree with your perspective, that does not necessarily mean you are inaccurate. We all have different viewpoints, but the discussion itself could help everyone see the organizational structure and interests more clearly.

Questions for Organizational Culture Filter 4: Structure

1. How is compensation determined? Who decides? What are the criteria?

2. Who receives formal recognition in the organization? Who receives informal recognition? For what reasons? How is recognition delivered?

3. Draw the formal organizational chart of departments or teams. How strict are the reporting relationships? How strict are the communication lines? Draw them in.

4. What are the hiring procedures? Who is involved? Who makes the decisions in the process?

5. Consider how employees are reviewed. To what degree are standardized forms and written expectations used for the reviews? Who performs the reviews? What are the criteria?

6. How is the board of directors formed? What influence does the board have on the way the organization functions? To what degree are they involved in day-to-day operations?

7. What are the formal, public organizational plans (including statements of mission, vision, values, and goals)? How available is this

information to the broader community? To what extent is the broader community invited to respond to the plans?

Ethos. The *ethos* of an institution describes its unique character, including underlying dispositions and guiding moral beliefs. Researchers Heifetz, Grashow, and Linsky point to four elements that make up an organization's ethos: its folklore, rituals, group norms, and meeting protocols.[15] These four elements are usually not written down or formally documented. But they have a powerful influence on what is considered acceptable and unacceptable behavior in the organizational culture. Thus, they affect member interests.

Folklore is collection of stories, customs, jokes, and legends that circulate within an organization, usually by word of mouth. These stories are told over and over again, at the coffee maker, over meals, during orientation or new member classes, and at goodbye parties for departing staff. Heifetz, Grashow, and Linsky would advise us "to unpack each story and read between the lines, looking for clues about what is allowed as well as what is off-limits."[16] See "Questions for Organizational Culture Filter 4: Ethos" for questions we have developed to use in a cultural diagnosis.

> Folklore, rituals, group norms, and meeting protocols make up an organization's ethos and have a powerful influence on what is considered acceptable and unacceptable behavior.

Our friend's experience provides an example of folklore. When she joined the staff of a mission organization, she quickly became aware of numerous unwritten procedures that reflected a controlling organizational culture. Then she heard a story about the long-departed founder of the mission. "I was told how he would tell all new employees they must keep their window blinds at a forty-five-degree angle to present a uniform appearance to outsiders looking at our building. And he would actually monitor this, checking offices to see if the blinds were properly adjusted. If not, he would personally go into the office and correct the angle." After hearing this story, our friend had a better understanding of the history behind the mission's traditionally accepted restrictions.

Rituals are the second aspect of organizational ethos. Rituals are practices repeated time and again under similar circumstances. They can range from the way the organization celebrates birthdays (or not), the way scheduled meetings are run, which liturgies are used, and when programs are held during holidays. Every ministry has rituals that continue year after year, usually without being questioned. By understanding which rituals an organization has established and which it does not have, we can discover interesting aspects about the ministry's organizational culture.[17] Observations about rituals may also unearth deeply hidden interests of the leaders.

The Sunday following the tragedy of 9/11, one senior pastor had his congregation stand and repeat the Pledge of Allegiance. Eight years later, when this pastor left the church, a candidate for the senior pastor position was surprised to discover the pledge was still a weekly occurrence in the worship service. He later learned how involved the church leadership was in national government issues, a fact found nowhere in official and public documents about the church.

> Consider whether your ministry's probable group norms reinforce the status quo or indicate openness to change, learning, and growth.

We know of one rather new, very large church that people consider highly innovative. Yet even they have developed numerous rituals, including one that would surprise many Christians. Because they pour significant time and effort into their Christmas Eve services, they always cancel worship on the Sunday after Christmas, no matter what day of the week Christmas falls on each year. They encourage members and regular attenders to worship in other churches on that Sunday. Staff and members obviously have numerous interests keeping this ritual in place.

Group norms are the third element of organizational ethos. Group norms identify the assumed, informal rules about appropriate behavior for individuals. They govern how people relate to one another in an organization.[18] A friend and seasoned pastor once served in a congregation that had three different worship services. For the first service, he would come to church dressed in a suit and tie. For the next he would remove the suitcoat and tie for a more comfortable look. That evening he would lead worship in jeans. Participants in each service had group norms he adapted to.

Refer to "Questions for Organizational Culture Filter 4: Group Norms" for questions developed to gather facts and clues on group norms. Consider whether your ministry's probable group norms reinforce the status quo or indicate openness to change, learning, and growth.

Meeting protocols are the final element of organizational ethos. They reflect the formal and hidden rules of how meetings are supposed to go. One can learn much about an organization's health and culture by observing the meetings. "Protocols include what kinds of meetings are held regularly, who gets invited to them, and how the agenda is established. They speak to how power is distributed in the organization and what information is exchanged."[19]

> One can learn much about an organization's health and culture by observing the meetings.

After over fifteen years of service in a parachurch youth ministry, an experienced minister accepted an invitation to join the adult ministry staff team of a large church. In his youth ministry organization, all local staff participated in the weekly meeting covering strategy and planning. He just assumed that the church staff would operate in the same way. Imagine how surprised he was to discover that he was not invited to attend the church board meetings unless he was asked to come for a specific purpose.

Questions for Organizational Culture Filter 4: Ethos

Folklore

1. What tends to happen when someone disagrees openly with the boss, senior pastor, or officer?

2. Why have people been fired? Why did some people resign from the organization?

3. How did the person with the longest tenure in the organization achieve such longevity?

4. Why did the founders create this ministry? Why have the founders left or stayed?

5. Consider a recent, significant disagreement in the organization. What happened? Who was involved? How did leadership handle the situation? What stories do colleagues tell about the process?

6. How has the organization handled misfits or people who did not obey the organizational culture well?

7. Who wields the real power (capacity to act and influence) on the board? How do they steward their power?

8. In what ways has the organization celebrated success? Managed failure?

9. What are the ministry's stories, customs, jokes, and legends you have repeatedly heard?

Rituals

1. What events and regularly scheduled activities do everyone assume will happen in your ministry?

2. Consider your ministry's annual calendar, monthly events, and weekly routines. What established rituals are in your ministry? How were they started? What did they accomplish when they began? Why do you think they have continued? To what degree are they still useful toward advancing the stated mission? What unique organizational interests might be displayed by these rituals?

Group Norms

1. Who gets to call whom by their first name? When are formal titles used?

2. What dress is appropriate and in what context?

3. Whose office doors remain open or closed during the day? When do doors close?

4. What jokes are okay to tell?

5. How, when, and where do people socialize? How are email and cell phones used?

6. How is conflict managed? Who tends to play repeated roles in managing conflict?

Meeting Protocols

1. What kinds of meetings are held regularly? Who gets invited to them? Who plans the meeting and to what extent? How is the agenda established? Who facilitates the meetings?

2. To what degree are meetings designed for decision making or information sharing?

3. To what degree is there room for dialogue, questions, creative thoughts, evaluations, constructive conflict, and learning from mistakes? What percentage of a meeting involves receiving directions from an authority?

4. To what degree are stakeholders' interests discussed at meetings? How do people negotiate for their interests? How are decisions made?

5. To what extent are attendees allowed to speak on subjects beyond their areas of responsibility?

6. In what ways and to what extent is conflict accepted, orchestrated, or marginalized?[20]

Defaults. Defaults are habitual and assumed beliefs and actions that people in organizations rely on for stability and predictability. "Defaults are the ways of looking at situations that lead people to behave in ways that are comfortable and that have generated desirable results in the past."[21] Defaults have worked well over time. Therefore, members will find them easy to fall back into when the ministry is faced with a dilemma or crisis. And every organization faces these problems. Unfortunately, default responses are rarely suitable to a new challenge. It would not be a challenge or crisis if default modes actually resolved it.

Consider ministries facing financial challenges. For some organizations, these financial issues fit a cyclical pattern. As a default response, the senior leadership addresses the financial challenge by making a percentage budget cut across every department. The assumption is that this is a fair way to handle the problem. As a result, the ministry staff begin to assume that around the same time every year their budget will shrink. Therefore, the staff inflate their budget projections, thus becoming a default response to the senior leadership's response. As a result, the financial problems and anxiety were cyclical, but not solved. The cultural defaults had a direct effect on the interests of the department heads in budgeting. What kept the default mode in place? People's interests were to avoid changes in financial procedures.

Heifetz, Grashow, and Linsky make this important comment about the difficulty in changing defaults: "Overriding your organization's defaults often requires [that you take on] behaviors that feel uncomfortable and risky. . . . Indeed, it is a default's very familiarity that causes organizations to cling to it long after it has stopped being so widely useful."[22]

Seasoned ministry leaders are rarely able to diagnose their own defaults. This is why it is important to gain objective perspective on your organization. One way to do this is to hire outside consultants to observe your organization. Another way is to provide opportunities for new hires to speak, in safe confidence, of what they observe within their first six months. A third way is to create places for middle management to speak into their experience of the organizational culture. Often leadership 360-evaluation instruments can provide a confidential way to share such information and to name and question default modes of behaviors.

Questions for Organizational Culture Filter 4: Defaults

1. What are some organizational defaults that you once questioned but now have become accustomed to in your ministry?

2. Ask a couple of friends who are not members of your organization to attend an activity or worship service. Have your friends make lists of insider activities or language they notice but do not understand.

Concluding Thoughts

In summary, the four filters just discussed help us distinguish some important aspects of organizational culture. Every ministry has a distinct personality, with above- and below-ground characteristics that reflect "the way we do things around here." It often takes months, sometimes years, to uncover these cultural pressures and the resulting interests of the members. Culture affects everyone involved in the ministry, from the top leadership to the youngest participant. And the interests of everyone are molded by the organization's culture. The more we recognize the unique characteristics of our ministries, the better opportunity we will have to navigate the culture responsibly, to understand the various interests of its members, and to lead change toward a healthier, more fruitful organization.

Chapter 7

Societal Interests

This is the third chapter in the exploration of the political concept of interests. Human interests are specific, high-priority preferences at a given time that lead people to act and to influence others. Our interests stem from many possible sources. Chapters five and six examined various filters to identify both personal and organizational interests. This chapter considers the influence of the broader culture on people's interests. These societal interests can be even more hidden from our awareness than ones shaped by personal uniqueness or organizational culture.

Broad cultural settings are described by many categories, including geographic regions, linguistic areas, religious ranges, ethnic communities, socioeconomic groups, and even generational units. Of course, it is simplistic to assume that all the people from any group, even a small group of friends or family, have been affected the same way by cultural influences. However, that is how culture works; people habitually function as if most around them agree on how the world should be and how we should act in it.

This chapter presents five filters for identifying societal cultures and the interests people develop from living in them. These are just a few of the many categories we could use to discern cultural differences. These filters provide a starting place to increase capacity for identifying hidden cultural interests more readily. They use five standard sociological categories for distinguishing cultural differences and values: generations, geography and demographics, communication styles, time orientation, and power distance.

The societal interests of people usually originate from the place and culture where they grew up. For a simple example, as a young adult, Tasha, one of the authors of this book, naively assumed that she could move from one geographic region of the United States to another without it affecting her daily ways of life. However, this assumption was shattered once she transitioned from the mountains of northern New Mexico to the city center of Houston. There she experienced conflicting expectations of appearance, language, and behavior. She quickly adapted by wearing lipstick, saying "y'all" instead of "you guys," and storing most of her food in the refrigerator instead of on the counter.

Jesus spoke to societal culture issues, as well as personal interests, in his dialogue with the Samaritan woman at the well (John 4). By merely addressing her directly for conversation, Jesus challenged her societal assumptions. She asked, "How is it that you, a Jew, ask for a drink from me, a woman of Samaria?" (v. 9). Jewish men at that time would not have acknowledged the presence of a Samaritan woman, let alone received something she had touched. In the course of their conversation, Jesus also addressed societal matters such as marriage, gender, and religious norms.

Societal Culture Filter 1: Generations

Sociologists describe the various generational groupings reflected in the Western world. They have used category names like *traditionalists* (born before 1946), *baby boomers* (born after World War II and before the mid-1960s), *Gen Xers* (born 1965–1980), *millennials* (born 1981–2000), and *Gen Y* (born after 2000).[1] The researched theory is that a person's generational time frame affects the rituals, relationships, perspectives, and interests of that group of people in a common manner.

> A person's generational time frame affects the rituals, relationships, perspectives, and interests of that group of people.

A significant influence on traditionalists was the experience of growing up during the Great Depression and facing the rigors of World War II. However, for millennials the 9/11 terrorist attack, social media, and social justice protests have had a very different impact.

One set of researchers developed a fascinating chart that highlights cultural differences between the generations.[2] Their criteria for generational differences includes who the generation views as influencers; what their core values are; what their key attributes are; how they view family, education, work and leadership; and what their opinions on retirement are.

We recently spoke with a seasoned boomer pastor who was sensitive to the concerns of his millennial staff. He explained, "I used to hang out with previous staff like their contemporary. Now my staff views me as a parent or even a grandparent. Whether or not I like it, I've had to adjust to their perceptions." Apart from age differences, the interests of his younger staff are likely influenced by their generation's sense of fear and instability in the world, high rate of divorce, absent fathers, and the rarity of meaningful relationships with grandparents.

Questions for Societal Culture Filter 1: Generations

1. Reflect on the various generations represented in your community or in your ministry. How do you see the varied interests of these groups reflected in these contexts?

2. How did your perspectives differ from those of your parents? What topics caused conflict? Where did you find agreement?

3. Consider going out for coffee with a few friends from different generations. As a group, try to identify significant influences that have shaped differing perspectives.

Societal Culture Filter 2: Geography and Demographics

Geographic regions of the country often maintain different cultural norms and interests. Take the experience of author and professor of missions James Plueddemann, for example. Although he navigated many different cultural contexts for decades in his missionary life, he shared that one of the most challenging took place in a geographical domain in the United States. He served for three years on a school board in the Deep South. When the board asked him not to serve a second term, he painfully learned that there was much about Southern culture and leadership that he did not understand. He reflected, "I learned that some of the trickiest cross-cultural challenges can occur within what we think is our own culture, but in reality is a unique subculture."[3]

Socioeconomic differences make up another demographic that leads to cultural differences and varying interests between people. The main concerns of socioeconomics focus on financial resources, employment, education, and ethnic diversity. The key socioeconomic factors that shape us are our educational level, income level, the income level of our parents, lifestyle preferences and opportunities, and our profession or occupation.

The recent marriage of friends illustrates these differences. He grew up in a lower-middle class home. While never lacking the basic necessities, his existence was certainly "no frills" compared to his bride. She grew up in an upper-class family, where country-club memberships, designer clothes, and European vacations were the norm. One can easily imagine some of the conflicts they had to navigate while serving together on the staff of a collegiate ministry.

Ethnic and social groupings are also key demographics to consider when identifying cultural differences and the resulting interests. Many subcultures exist within a single community. Diagnosing probable interests involves identifying these subcultures and respecting the interests they represent. It is unfortunate that many Christians from majority social-ethnic groups maintain an attitude that their interests are what is truly important or the "proper way" of looking at things. The lack of eagerness to learn from Christians of other groups hampers the growth and unity of the church.

> It is unfortunate that many Christians from majority social-ethnic groups maintain an attitude that their interests are what is truly important or the "proper way" of looking at things. The lack of eagerness to learn from Christians of other groups hampers the growth and unity of the church.

The experience of Luis illustrates this challenge. As a Hispanic pastor ministering in the United States, Luis chose to be credentialed in a denomination of traditional Western European origin. After he passed his ordination exams, a respected denominational leader approached him and said, "Your worship style isn't biblical. But I'm sure after being with us for a few years, you will come to understand how true worship should take place." Months after this incident, Luis was still upset, alternately having feelings of anger and depression. His experience is similar to that of many minorities trying to collaborate with white Americans. All groups involved have much to learn about the varied perspectives and interests of those from other cultures.

**Questions for Societal Culture Filter 2:
Geography and Demographics**

1. How would you gather information in order to accurately identify the interests of the general population in your geographic region?

2. How do these interests compare with the geographic interests of your childhood?

3. What are the demographics of your area: the educational levels, occupations, employment rates, and lifestyles? How do these influence the interests of people in your community?

4. What are the ethnicities represented in your community? What are their cultural distinguishing characteristics? How could you welcome and celebrate some of these cultural differences?

5. What differing interests are you already aware of in ethnic groups of your ministry or community? How can you learn more about the different perspectives and interests of these people?

Societal Culture Filter 3: Communication Styles

Filter 3 differentiates people on a spectrum between those who use explicit words for communication (low-context culture) and those who use more implicit, nonverbal signals and body language for communication (high-context culture). High-context cultures perceive positional roles, cultural norms, and their surroundings as part of the communication process. Low-context cultures largely ignore this information in their communications.

In general, the United States and Canada are low-context cultures. This means people tend to send and receive messages in a direct manner using many words for clarity. They base their understanding more on the literal meaning of what is said than on subtexts coming from facial expression, tone of voice, physical environment, cultural expectations, or other non-verbal cues. When people in low-context cultures communicate their interests, they focus on using literal words without subtlety. To a person from a high-context culture, this form of communication can seem very rude and presumptuous.

One theological seminary the authors know well is an example of a very low-context subculture. The classrooms are very plain and have bare, beige walls. The faculty dress simply and comfortably, rarely using their titles. Instead, they focus on using words (many words) to make their ideas and interests explicit. Their facial expressions and tone of voice are usually pleasant and steady, which may not help their communication if it seems monotone. Students warn each other about the professor who sounds angry when he is actually just excited about discussing an idea. This lack of implicit and subtle communication can seem quite rude for students from high-context environments, like those from East Asia.

> When people in low-context cultures communicate their interests, they focus on using literal words without subtlety. To a person from a high-context culture, this form of communication can seem very rude and presumptuous.

A counselor friend grew up in an emotionally abusive home in which adult family members interpreted most facial expressions or gestures negatively. The communication was a high-context style. Therefore, she was trained to be hyperaware of the way people were feeling based on their nonverbal expressions. When first married, her husband, who came from a rather low-context family culture, was baffled when she kept asking, "What do you mean by that look?" She now has a highly effective ministry with women who have suffered from abuse. Her women clients have a difficult time expressing their pain and grief. But she has a vast capacity to understand the burdens and concerns of the women she works with even when they cannot explain it with words.

Questions for Societal Culture Filter 3: Communication Styles

1. Did you grow up in a low- or high-context communication culture? What about your home? On a spectrum of low (1) to high (5) context communication, where do you prefer to communicate?

2. How would you describe the communication style of your ministry? How does this communication style affect the expectations and interests of those involved?

3. Consider a recent conflict within your ministry team. To what degree did the differing communication styles of individual team members add to the misunderstandings?

Societal Culture Filter 4: Time Orientation

In most Western and highly industrialized cultures, the notion of time is directly linked to the clock. Time is considered a limited resource to count and to manage. People who grew up with this clock-time orientation tend to be highly aware of their daily schedules, as well as the commitments of others. Their interests in managing time can be observed in their plans, schedules, and efficiency. And they usually draw a sharp line between work time and personal time.

Conversely, agricultural and rural cultures tend to view time seasonally and do not focus on counting minutes. Time is the opportunity for one event after another, where the length of the event is not usually predetermined. People from this event-time orientation are more patient and spontaneous with their schedules. Their interests focus on the event at the moment and the requirements for them in that event. Thus, they appear much more casual about starting and ending times than those from a clock-time orientation. An unexpected friend popping in will usually get priority over a planned appointment.

A pastor friend grew up in a small country town, so he generally operates with an event-time orientation. Because of his laid-back, relational style, the elders of his urban church decided to hire an administrative pastor to help with the church management. The pastor established a regular meeting at the beginning of each week with the administrator. The first few times they met, the pastor was late. When he came in the office, the administrator had a scowl on his face. In the administrator's view, the pastor was in the wrong. But from the pastor's perspective, it was more important to finish the conversations he was having before going to his next meeting. Their differences in societal culture backgrounds made for conflicting interests.

Questions for Societal Culture Filter 4: Time Orientation

1. What is your ministry's general attitude toward the stewardship of time? To what degree is your organization prioritizing the clock over the events?

2. How has the ministry handled staff or participants who function from a different orientation on time? What is considered "on time"? When do people consider it important to be on time?

3. Regarding your own ministry style, how do you hold the tension between apparent interruptions and viewing interruptions as ministry opportunities?

4. How do people manage interruptions in your ministry organization?

Societal Culture Filter 5: Power Distance

Power distance refers to how far apart leaders and followers feel from each other. Low-power contexts occur when leaders and followers socialize together and address each other as peers. In these collaborative environments, followers expect to have input through a democratic decision-making process. A high-power-distance environment, however, is much different. Followers address their leaders formally and do not expect to socialize with them. The followers assume that leaders should have more authority, respect, and status symbols. Decisions are made unilaterally by leaders who assume they will be obeyed without question. Here is how Andy Crouch describes this cultural difference:

> In high power distance cultures, power is made visible and tangible, and dramatic differences in power are seen as a natural, indeed crucial, part of a healthy society. In low power distance cultures, on the other hand, visible hierarchy and signs of power are discouraged. Those with power are expected to treat others as equals, not as subordinates. . . . America, today, is about as low power distance as it has ever been—and so is the American church.[4]

One significant exception to this is African American churches. Again, author Andy Crouch helps us understand this. His longer explanation below is well worth reflecting on.

> I have had the great gift, at several seasons of my life, of worshiping and working in African American churches. It took me many years, as a young white man, to understand why leaders in the black church so often carry themselves with what initially seemed to me like excessive amounts of visible authority. A pastor wearing an expensive suit, driving a late-model car, and protected by layers of administrative staff and formality, presents very little apparent vulnerability to the world. . . . I gradually came to understand that black church leaders in fact bear a tremendous amount of vulnerability, even if it is not readily apparent. Their vulnerability can be personal: vanishingly few white Americans who drive late-model,

high-end cars have ever been stopped by police simply on suspicion that the vehicle is not theirs—whereas many, many black pastors have experienced this insult to their dignity and accomplishments. But more importantly, as representatives of a historically subjugated community, black pastors live every day bearing the nearly unbearable burdens of a *community* that has been shaped by oppression and violence, prejudice and ignorance. And the appropriate response to this hidden vulnerability is in fact public dignity—representing the community not just in its vulnerability but in its God-given, image-bearing authority. It may be appropriate for a pastor in a privileged and powerful community to emphasize his vulnerability by saying, "Just call me Dan." But it is entirely appropriate for a pastor in a community of vulnerability to model authority and expect to be addressed, especially in public, with his full title and family name.[5]

> The low-power-distance culture in the United States provides us with another challenge to our interests in ministry. We can value the appearance of equal power in our ministries so much that we fail to notice and value the interests of those with less power.

Many low-power-distance Americans react very strongly against the idea of high-power distance in relation to their leaders. Rarely do they understand that people expect and rely on these symbols in a high-power-distance culture. "Scripture seems to leave room for some flexibility regarding power distance in leadership style but not in leadership attitudes," suggests Plueddemann. "The heart of every leader must be humble, seeking the good of others and suspicious of one's own motives."[6]

The low-power-distance culture in the United States provides us with another challenge to our interests in ministry. We can value the appearance of equal power in our ministries so much that we fail to notice and value the interests of those with less power. As Crouch says, "But in a low power distance culture, it is especially easy for the powerful to forget their power. It can deceive us into thinking that power is not an issue that requires our attention, let alone a matter for

> The stewardship of our power, in the interests of Christ, requires us to observe power dynamics much more explicitly so we can use it for the flourishing of all.

discipleship. And the ones most likely to be deceived are the ones with the most power."[7]

Perhaps this is the strongest reason for us to grow in our awareness of cultural power distance. The stewardship of our power, in the interests of Christ, requires us to observe power dynamics much more explicitly than we usually do—so that we can use power for the flourishing of all.

Questions for Societal Culture Filter 5: Power Distance

1. Identify the power-distance practice in your ministry. How does your own personal power-distance preferences compare to the culture of your organization?

2. In what ways does your organization's power-distance culture affect the interests of the members? What can you affirm about these priorities from a biblical perspective? What can you challenge?

3. How would you evaluate your willingness to serve in relationships both where you possess more power and where you possess less?

Conclusion

Chapters four through seven described many concepts about interests and filters for diagnosing them. Understanding interests is an important skill to develop in order to work responsibly with people. Identifying key interests helps us better address the true issues that concern both ourselves and others. Of course, we will not be able to identify all of the interests at play in any given situation. But what people do in any circumstance depends in large part on how thoroughly they perceive what's going on.[8]

The more interests we are aware of, the more comprehensively we will understand why people are using their power the way they do.

At any point in time there are multiple types of interests involved in human interactions. These interests are formed by our personalities, organizational cultures, and societal cultures. People hold their interests for many reasons, some of which we have explored through the use of these various filters. Some interests are clearly evident, but most are not influencing us consciously. They are unconscious motivations and values, hidden like roots of a big oak tree. In addition, interests can be held with varied levels of intensity.

Much of life takes place in the crossfire of conflicting interests.[9] The interests people most value reflect the way they believe life should be. In organizations and broader societies, the cultures describe "the way things are done around here." Participants in the cultures align their interests with these cultural values and perspectives. Similarly, people join with others who hold similar interests to act and influence others in their social systems. And people do this with the power they have available. The process of promoting one's interests in relational contexts through the use of power is called negotiation. This is the theme of chapters eight and nine.

Chapter **8**

Negotiation, Power, and Interests

A happily married couple recently told Bob about their regular "pizza fight." Most Friday nights the family has pizza together. The husband, a hospital chaplain, comes home after a long week of comforting staff and patients. He wants a break from caring for others for a while. His wife is homeschooling three children. When he walks in the door, she is relieved to have another adult who can help with household responsibilities. So, who will order the pizza? The negotiation becomes a battle.

We all are negotiating all the time, whether we are aware of it or not. It is what people do; we promote our interests with the power available to us. A conventional definition of *negotiation* is the "process whereby two or more parties with both common and conflicting interests come together to talk with a view to reaching an agreement."[1] Regardless of the specifics of a situation, politics—the negotiation of interests in relational contexts of power—is a constant activity in life and ministry.[2]

The previous chapters laid building blocks for understanding how the politics of ministry work. To review, there are four main activities involved in this political work. First, we must perceive the dynamics of *power* among people, including the relationship capital that already exists or must be built with those involved. Second, we need to understand the different *interests* people hold. Third, we explicitly engage in *negotiation* between

> Negotiation takes place when two or more persons with common or conflicting interests work toward reaching an agreement for future action. In negotiation people use their power— the capacity to act and to influence others—to further their interests.

the people involved. And finally, we must consider the *ethical implications* of actions, decisions, and resulting consequences. In this chapter, we are focusing on the third activity of negotiation.

Negotiation takes place when two or more persons with common or conflicting interests work toward reaching an agreement for future action. In negotiation people use their power—the capacity to act and to influence others—to further their interests. The negotiation process can take minutes or years. It rarely takes place in a single conversation, and it is certainly not a linear process.[3]

Ministry leadership involves leading change and growth. This means making decisions—lots of decisions—every day. Decision-making takes place by gathering information, developing strategic plans, evaluating progress, and communicating directions, all in various contexts. These activities can be helpfully summed up with one term: *planning*. And planning always involves politics.

Our ministry plans may be as simple as making a shopping list for a small dinner gathering or as complicated as preparing a family camp for several hundred people. But regardless of the number of people or activities, planning involves working with others in a process over time. And that is when *negotiation* happens, when people bring their available *power*, and their relevant *interests* into the planning and change process.

The Planning Table

People rarely make ministry plans or engage the process to change something on their own. We may think we are acting alone at points in the process, but others almost always become involved, whether we invite them or not. Therefore, ministry leadership requires that we interact with others. All of these interactions are brought to what authors Cervero and Wilson call "the planning table."[4] The *planning table* represents the metaphorical place where people communicate with and influence each other during negotiation for decisions and change. The planning

> The *planning table* represents the metaphorical place where people communicate with and influence each other during negotiation for decisions and change. The planning table may be actual tables, hallways, offices, emails, texts, shared documents, conference videos, and phones.

table may be actual tables, hallways, offices, emails, texts, shared documents, conference videos, and phones.

In each of the case stories we have looked at so far, the key participants were consciously or unconsciously negotiating at the planning table. In other words, they were using their available power to further their interests with others in the planning and change process. The formal and relational power people have defines what they are and are not able to do at the planning table.[5] Take a moment to remember when Dave led worship for the first time. People expressed their frustration and hurt regarding his worship leadership. They joined the metaphorical planning table by complaining to each other and the music director, thus pushing Dave and the senior pastor to engage in the negotiation process by considering their interests.

While developing depression support groups for Grace Church, Sue put much time and effort into negotiating her interests with everyone she assumed was at her planning table. But she did not count on the senior pastor and his close associate having different interests. They held much more formal and relational power in the church than she did. They cancelled her plans, and she did not even realize they were at her planning table.

At Trinity Church, the board members met several times at an actual table to plan what to do with Pastor Joe. The board intentionally hid their discussions from Brian, excluding him from the planning table. Then, the board met at the country club "table" with Pastor Joe to convince him to resign. Finally, they brought Brian into the process two days after his ordination when a board member simply informed him that Pastor Joe had resigned.

In response, Brian brought his own set of interests to the same metaphorical table of negotiation. He had limited formal power as a newly ordained associate pastor. Because he was new to the church, he had virtually no relational power. He quickly realized that it would be futile to resist the actions of the board members. However, he did have some capacity to act. Brian decided he would leave the church as soon as a new senior pastor arrived.

Questions to Ponder

Review a recent time when you were planning a ministry event.

1. How much of the planning or change process was intentional? How much happened spontaneously?

2. List all the individuals or groups ultimately involved in the negotiation process (those who influenced the planning with their available power and their relevant interests).

3. Note places and times when each person or group was at the planning table (communicating and influencing each other concerning the plans and decisions).

4. Consider how your formal and relational power compared to the power of the others at the table.

Four Key Aspects of Negotiation

Four actions take place during negotiation; chapter two described each one briefly. All four actions of negotiation occur during the planning and implementation of any ministry event.

First, people bring *their own specific, complex,* and often *hidden interests* to the planning table. That is, they do not engage in the negotiation work from an impartial position. Second, people promote their interests *between each other,* thus potentially utilizing their power resource of relationship capital. In other words, negotiation happens between real people that have varying amounts of trust and health in their relationships with each other. Third, they consciously or unconsciously *choose how to use the power* available to them—their capacities to act and to influence others—during the process. Fourth, people's actions during and after the negotiation process will either *strengthen or diminish the ongoing interests and power* of those involved. When people leave the planning table, their interests and power are changed. Note that the third and fourth aspects often go unrecognized in the negotiation process.

> Negotiation involves four unique actions:
> 1. People bring their own specific interests to the process.
> 2. People promote their interests between each other.
> 3. People use the power available to them to promote their interests.
> 4. People affect the ongoing interests and power of those involved by their actions during and after the negotiation.

To review these four negotiation actions, let's identify them in Dave's story. The music director was upset about the way Dave brought changes in music style to the worship service. She knew and trusted that the senior pastor allowed for open sharing of grievances at meetings. So, she *brought her specific interests to the process*. She also let others know how she was thinking and feeling; she *promoted her interests with others*. Her formal power at the church was not significant. She held a part-time position and was not on the church board. However, she had a great deal of relational power based on years of service in the congregation. She also had power based on a fair amount of relationship capital with the senior pastor due to her years of serving with him. And her concerns about what Dave did were confirmed by other musicians and members of the congregation who had grumbled to her. Emboldened by the power based on her knowledge of the pastor, her relationships, and the united interests she held with others, she presented a series of complaints at the next staff meeting. She *used the power available to her to promote her interests*.

Consider the response of Dave and the senior pastor to the music director's complaints during the staff meeting. Dave could have reacted defensively by saying that she was not in the dark about these decisions and that he (Dave) was only responding to the directives of the senior pastor and church board. The senior pastor could have exercised his formal power and "put the director in her place," telling her to stop festering a negative, divisive attitude and to submit to his leadership. However, they both chose a different method of negotiation. They used their power to promote their priority interests of upholding the unity of the church through healthy communication, care, and humility.

The senior pastor was consciously aware of the power dynamics in the room and that his actions *during and after this meeting would affect the ongoing interests and the power of those involved*. He began by apologizing to both Dave and the director, taking full responsibility for the complaints, saying he had asked Dave to do exactly what he had done. The senior pastor said he was wrong to assume that Dave's roles had been well communicated.

If Dave had assumed that his formal title and power overruled the music director's, he might have defended his actions with a "my way or the highway" attitude. This could have led to a huge congregational conflict over the music style. However, Dave was influenced by the senior pastor's actions. The meeting was affecting his *ongoing interests and power.* So Dave also apologized for any impression he had given that might have undermined the previous work of the director. Over the next few months Dave worked at building trust and a healthy relationship with the director. The senior pastor spoke with the musicians and key members of the congregation, again taking full responsibility for the matter. Furthermore, over the following weeks the senior pastor more carefully shared all plans for Dave's continued involvement with those concerned. *People's actions after the meeting were continuing to affect the ongoing interests and the power of those involved.*

The fourth aspect of negotiation informs those at the planning table that there is much more at stake than just the final decisions. Both the process and outcome of any negotiation will affect the future capacity of those involved to function in the ministry. When a negotiation is successful, the people involved generally grow in trust and respect for each other and their diverse interests. Thus, their ability to influence and to act in the future will increase. When planners experience a setback at the planning table, their power to promote their interests will likely diminish.[6] If Sue had been on staff at Grace Church for fifteen years with a long track record of successful ministry, her announcements for depression support groups would most likely *not* have been pulled without her knowledge. As it was, Sue definitely felt that her power to lead ministry at Grace Church had significantly diminished.

> Both the process and outcome of any negotiation will affect the future capacity of those involved to function in the ministry. When a negotiation is successful, the people involved generally grow in trust and respect for each other and their diverse interests. Thus, their ability to influence and to act in the future will increase.

The negotiation of interests occurs as an ongoing political process throughout any ministry. The "planning table" represents the places and processes where people express concrete concerns and make decisions together. When leading change in ministry planning, many variables are constantly at play at the table. These include the specific content of programs, time and calendar commitments, facility availability, relationship dynamics, and budget allocations, just to name a few. And these elements influence and change the formal and relational power dynamics of those involved. The next section explores how these factors come together as participants consciously and unconsciously choose *how* to negotiate at the table.

Questions to Ponder

Consider further the planning experience you reviewed previously.

1. How would you describe the relationship capital between the people at the planning table? (The amount of positive feelings, goodwill, grace, trust, and ready forgiveness shared between each other.)

2. Add to your lists the specific interests each person brought to the planning table.

3. What was the available power each person brought to the planning table?

4. How important was harmony in the planning process?

5. To what extent did you and others suppress your opinions and thoughts to keep the peace instead of expressing your disagreements honestly?

6. To what extent were you able to analyze the situation during the negotiation? What strategies did you use to express your interests? How well did each work?

7. How did the outcomes of the planning and program enhance or diminish each person's

   • future capacity to act and influence in the organization?

   • future involvement in similar ministry?

   • future relationships of trust with others involved?

Four Cells of Negotiation Strategies

Most ministries hold harmony and unity as high values. So, negotiations often happen in quiet consensus. However, in almost every planning context there are power and interest differences among the stakeholders. We should not suppress legitimate differences just so we can keep up a false appearance of harmony. Conflict can be the healthy and necessary work of honest negotiation.

At the planning table, people will need to confer, discuss, and argue while making judgments about what to create and implement in their ministries. These negotiations are neither neutral nor objective. And they may occur in relational contexts as difficult to read. Therefore, leaders must make best guesses in choosing a strategy for their negotiation actions that matches the situation. They must also be prepared for the renegotiation of important interests if the process needs reiteration to move in a healthier direction.[7]

> In almost every planning context there are power and interest differences among the stakeholders. We should not suppress legitimate differences just so we can keep up a false appearance of harmony. Conflict can be the healthy and necessary work of honest negotiation.

The following four-cell model represents different strategies people take when negotiating. The cells account for the amounts of power and the interests of the stakeholders involved.[8] The model illustrates the significant difference between power and interests. Based on power and interests comparisons, each person or group at the planning table will find themselves in one of four cells, with resulting strategies for action.

During ministry planning, those involved have interests that are either shared or conflicting. *Shared interests* are convictions and motivations in which people agree. Mia and Caroline held shared interests with their pastor concerning the need for the women of the church to build relationships. *Conflicting interests* are viewpoints and values in which people differ. Dave had conflicting interests with the music director over how to lead a change in musical style during the worship service. The stakeholders also have similar or different amounts of power (their capacities to act and influence in the given situation). When people have conflicting interests, those with more power will usually seek to achieve their goals by asserting that power.[9]

We will now examine the four-cell model of negotiation strategies (see table 8.1).

Cell one: Collaborate. When there are *shared interests* with *equal power relations*, a responsible negotiation strategy is to collaborate. People collaborate by coming together to address and solve issues. They cooperate willingly. In these kinds of negotiations people can treat each other as allies or friends. Their trust grows during the process, and everyone works together in a mutually supportive way.[10] When the people at the table are aware that they are collaborating in cell one, then the work will likely feel empowering, motivating, and highly productive.

As good friends, Mia and Caroline often shared their thoughts and convictions. And they usually agreed with each other. Their idea for the women's painting event came out of these conversations based on similar interests. They collaborated by forming plans.

Mark 3 describes a stunning example of collaboration, where the Pharisees and Herodians responded to Jesus healing the man with a withered hand. These two groups of Jewish leaders were normally at great odds with each other concerning who should govern the people. They shared fairly equal power relations in the community. In this situation, their shared interest in destroying Jesus caused them to join forces and collaborate.

Table 8.1. Four-cell model of negotiation strategies

	Equal Power	Unequal Power
Shared Interests	Cell 1 Collaborate	Cell 2 Network
Conflicting Interests	Cell 3 Bargain	Cell 4 Many possible actions depending on having more or less power

Cell two: Network. When there are *shared interests* with *unequal power relations*, a proper approach to negotiation is networking. People network when those with less power intentionally engage those with more power to help accomplish a shared interest. Those with less power in cell two have the challenge to form and maintain relationships with people of similar interests who hold more power at the planning table.[11]

After friends Mia and Caroline collaborated on the women's event, they networked by meeting with the pastor to propose their plan. Though all three were good friends with similar interests, the pastor held more formal and relational power in the church. By networking with him, Mia and Caroline were able to leverage their shared interests to promote the idea for the women's painting event.

When ministry planning takes place in the first two cells of shared interests, participants tend to work together in mutually supportive ways. The amount of power that people bring to the table is relatively unimportant because everyone has a similar set of interests. Participants are on the same page, so there is little or no worry that some may leverage their power to undermine others. Negotiations are generally friendly, noncoercive, and often free of conflict.[12] Unfortunately, people assume all ministry planning happens this way and are usually unprepared to function in the other two cells.

People new to ministry leadership need help understanding that while they enter with a level of formal power, they do not yet have relational power. Therefore, they will often be at the planning table in cell two or four, where power is unequal; and they will have less power than most others will have. Earning trust and respect over time by choosing to align interests with others in cell two is a vital negotiating strategy if they are going to promote any of their interests in the future effectively. A time-honored cliché speaks to this: "You've got to earn the right to be heard." Or as a pastor once shared, "You've got to find out who are the influencers, build a relationship with them if you can, and work through them."

> People new to ministry leadership need help understanding that while they enter with a level of formal power, they do not yet have relational power. Therefore, they will often be at the planning table in cell two or four, where power in unequal; and they will have less power than most others will have.

Cell three: Bargain. When there are *conflicting interests* among those with *equal power*, people negotiate by bargaining. In cell three, people come to the planning table anticipating the need to compromise on lesser interests and values. The only example of cell three bargaining in the previous case stories occurred when the Trinity Church board offered Senior Pastor Joe a "generous deal" in exchange for his quiet resignation.

Years ago a friend served a church where the previous pastor had a major conflict with a board member's daughter. She wanted the tune *Ave Maria* in her wedding ceremony. The pastor refused, basing his denial on theological convictions. The father appealed to the church board, which approved his daughter's song choice. In response, the pastor threw his resignation down on the table and threatened, "The *Ave Maria* goes or I go." The friend concluded this story with sound advice. "Well, the pastor went! When it comes to these conflicts, you've got to keep the overall picture in view. You have to be very careful and selective. And you're going to lose some battles. If you're going to die over an issue, it better be worth dying for."

In *bargaining*, final agreements will *not* satisfy everyone's interests. However, people negotiating in cell three (with conflicting interests among those with equal power) need each other to get things done and will seek out areas of common concern. Unlike the negotiation strategies in cells one (collaboration) and two (networking), the *way* people utilize power in cell three determines the outcomes due to the conflicting interests but equal power. In the end, one party may feel quite defeated compared to the others due to how people choose to exercise power.[13]

Bargaining strategies for using power are numerous. Depending on the context, positive and negative examples of such strategies include withholding or sharing information, keeping items off the agenda, keeping others away from the planning table, inviting new stakeholders to the table, educating others about relevant hidden interests, and remaining calm and pleasant at the table. A person needing to bargain in cell three faces the challenges of which persons to involve, which persons to trust and to what degree, and how much weight to give relevant interests. One also needs to be ready to give in when necessary to create a better context for ongoing negotiations. Thus, accepting short-term compromises often becomes a typical negotiating strategy.[14]

One Sunday, a church-planting pastor was leading the first worship service of a fledgling congregation. The pastor spotted a man he recognized as one who had created disruptions in other area churches. This man was wealthy and had used money to throw his weight around, always expecting people to do things his way.

After worship, this rich man asked the pastor if they could have lunch that week. At the meal, the man said, "I have a few questions to ask you about *our* church." Thus, the cell-three bargaining began. Knowing the church would probably lose the man's significant financial support, the pastor countered, "You are welcome to attend the church. But it will never be *your* church. You will not be a board member in this church, and I will do everything I can to keep you from being an influencer." The pastor negotiated this hard line to protect the church; he did not want a troublemaker at the planning table.

> A person needing to bargain in cell three faces the challenges of which persons to involve, which persons to trust and to what degree, and how much weight to give relevant interests. One also needs to be ready to give in when necessary to create a better context for ongoing negotiations.

Conclusions

This chapter investigates how people bring their interests to the ministry planning table to consider needs and goals, form plans, and make decisions. The negotiation process describes what takes place. It results in changing the power, interests, and relationships of all the stakeholders, whether or not they are included in the process.

Power and interests influence negotiation strategy and practice. People have either shared interests, where concerns are essentially the same, or conflicting interests, where perspectives differ. Power, the capacity for participants to act and influence, can be either equal or unequal compared to the others involved in the negotiation.

As a result, a four-cell model illustrates the different actions of negotiation based on the dynamics of power and interests. This chapter focused on the first three cells. In the first two cells, participants assume everyone is working together in a mutually supportive way because their interests align. Generally, people in these cells do not even recognize they are part of a negotiation process. They are simply working together to accomplish common goals.

However, in cell three people must bargain since interests are in conflict, though power is equal. People are attuned to these differences and will notice whether or not others recognize, respect, or address differing interests. In this cell, wise leaders will choose between varied options with great care, seeking to understand differing interests and to build relationship capital. In chapter nine we will look at cell four, the most challenging place for negotiating. This is because both power and interests are significantly different between the people at the planning table.

Questions to Ponder

1. Consider further the planning experience you reviewed earlier. Based on people's actions, in which cell was most of the negotiation process taking place?

2. Describe a recent time of planning in cell one (shared interests and equal power). What actions were involved in the collaboration? Describe how that work felt to you.

3. Describe a recent time of planning in cell two (shared interests but unequal power). In what ways did the people with less available power network with others to move the work forward?

4. Describe a time when you thought you'd be planning in cell one, only to learn that you were negotiating in cell three because the people at the planning table did not have the same interests.

   - At what point did you realize the interests were in conflict? Describe how that felt.

   - How did your actions change after you realized the interests were different?

   - What were the outcomes of that negotiation?

Chapter 9

Negotiation in Cell Four

Chapter eight introduced a four-cell model that illustrates the different actions of negotiation based on the dynamics of power and interests, and described those actions in the first three cells. Now we look carefully at cell four. Of the four possible situations we could find ourselves in during negotiation with others, the most challenging is when there are conflicting interests *and* unequal power between the people involved and affected by the change. This common yet highly challenging situation is called cell four in our model (see table 8.1).

When people engage their power and interests to influence each other during negotiation and change, they are at the planning table, metaphorically if not literally. In the other three cells, attitudes and actions at the planning table are more easily optimistic and calm. Not so in cell four. Emotions can run high, and anxiety is present due to people's interests being at risk. In cell four, those with the most power will usually assert it to achieve their interests. This in turn leads to real possibilities for manipulation, harm, or even abuse of others at the table.

People working in ministry often have to negotiate in cell four. Most of our case stories take place primarily in this cell, where interests and power are significantly different. As we look at the experiences of Brian, Sue, and Dave, we see they were not aware that they were in cell four until there was a crisis. Only when others directly challenged their interests did they come to the painful realization that they had less capacity to act than they assumed and that their interests conflicted with the interests of others involved.

It is naively optimistic to assume that everyone on a ministry team will hold common interests and that they all will negotiate planning in cell one or two. From a human perspective, Jesus ministered most of the time in cell four. His interests aligned with God's and, so, often conflicted with a broken world and sin. During his public ministry, Jesus generally had less power than his opponents did in the Jewish civic and religious leadership. He had almost no formal power, but his relational power with the disciples and the crowds gave Jesus the capacity to act for a time at the planning table.

Let's look again at the four-cell chart that represents the different strategies people take when negotiating.[1] As we have already noticed, when people have conflicting perspectives, those with the most power will usually assert it to achieve their interests.[2] Based on power and interests, each person or group will find themselves in one of the four cells, with resulting strategies for action.

Each planning context defines the options available for negotiating. In the context of cell four, where people have differing interests and unequal power, each participant will choose from a range of strategies illustrated on two spectrums (see figs. 9.1 and 9.2). The comparative amount of power that people hold determines which spectrum they are working from, one for those with more power or one for those with less. To negotiate more wisely, people should consciously choose between the various actions possible so their actions are in line with core values and biblical imperatives. In cell four, where anxiety is usually high, we can easily react to the situation such that our actions compromise our own goals and values. We may find ourselves in ethical knots in cell four, so we devote chapter ten to ethical considerations.

Cell Four for Those with Less Power

The two spectrums of focus in this chapter describe examples of cell-four negotiation strategies. The first spectrum shows the types of actions available to those with less power; the second shows actions for those with more power to act and influence in the situation. Both spectrums illustrate a continuum from the more aggressive actions on the right to the more passive actions on the left. Definitions and illustrations for each place labeled in the two spectrums will describe what it looks like to negotiate at the planning table in cell four.

This first spectrum describes the possible negotiation actions for those with less power compared to other stakeholders involved in the planning process (see fig. 9.1). Just because a person has less power does not mean they have no options for continued involvement in the process. When we find ourselves in a cell-four situation with less power, we still need to consider how our choice of action can further our goals and values.

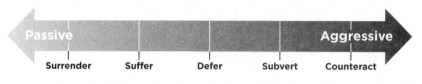

Passive ———————————————————— Aggressive

| Surrender | Suffer | Defer | Subvert | Counteract |

Figure 9.1. Spectrum of options for those with *less* power in cell four

Counteract. To counteract in cell four (the option on the far right) means to take concrete actions against the competing interests of others (not against people themselves). A predominant form of counteracting is confrontation, when one person or group figuratively or literally goes face-to-face with another person or group in order to examine, compare, or oppose their position on an issue.

> To counteract in cell four means to take concrete actions against the competing interests of others. It usually involves going face-to-face with another person or group in order to examine, compare, or oppose their position on an issue.

When the music director was upset over Dave's leadership of the Sunday evening service, she *counteracted* by listing many complaints at the next staff meeting. And when Sue discovered that her publicity had been removed, she *counteracted* by asking for an explanation from the volunteer who prepared the Sunday bulletin.

Another way to counteract involves presenting opposing information. A seminary student friend received financial aid from her home congregation while pursuing her degree. Rumors reached her ears that some leaders in her church were accusing her of misusing the stipend. She *counteracted* by sending reports to the church board, including copies of her grades and tuition bills.

> Fundamentally, both *counteracting* and *subversion* are strategies that move against the dominant interests of a people group by mobilizing people to negate the effects of those interests.

Subvert. In cell four, subversion does not mean the corruption of what is good. Instead, it means to engage a "process by which the values and principles of a system

> To subvert means to engage a "process by which the values and principles of a system in place are reversed," which can be a moral and responsible way to respond in the cell-four situation. We call this redemptive subversion.

in place are reversed."[3] Sometimes subversion is a moral and responsible way to respond. It's helpful to call this "redemptive subversion." For example, King Herod asked the wise men to return to him after finding the "King of the Jews" (Matthew 2:8). Herod was using *subversion* in a deceptive, evil way, acting like he also wanted to worship this child when he really planned to kill him. However, the wise men used *redemptive subversion*. After being warned in a dream not to return to Herod, they departed to their own country by another way (Matthew 2:12).

A Christian counselor friend was working with a woman distraught by the condition of her marriage. He encouraged her to have her husband come to the next session. But the husband adamantly refused, saying they did not need any help. So, our friend tried something else. He told the wife, "Go home and tell your husband that I said he doesn't have the guts to come in here." The husband was at the next session. The counselor used *redemptive subversion* by appealing to the husband's pride.

> Redemptive subversion can help move an individual, family, or organization from dysfunctional to healthy patterns.

Redemptive subversion can help move an individual, family, or organization from dysfunctional to healthy patterns. Look at Jesus' ministry. The religion of the Jews had degenerated into a legalistic system that actually went against the purposes of God as written in the Old Testament. In small and large ways (from eating grain to raising Lazarus from the dead), Jesus worked to reverse the values and principles of the broken world's system. Jesus' actions were the essence of *redemptive subversion*.

Fundamentally, both *counteracting* and *subversion* are strategies that move against the dominant interests of a group by mobilizing people to negate the effects of those interests.[4] Andy Crouch refers to this as "coercion," stating, "The legitimate role of coercion is to make room for flourishing, especially by restraining whatever fundamentally threatens the integrity of God's creative image bearers."[5]

Defer. In cell four, to *defer* means to yield to the contrary interests or judgments of another who has more power in the negotiation. When Brian heard that Senior Pastor Joe agreed to resign, he felt the actions of the board members were unjust. He even considered speaking against Joe's resignation at the regional meeting of their denomination. However, Brian realized his capacity to change the church board's decision was quite low. In addition, he believed such resistance would only aggravate the problem. So, he *deferred* to the board and accepted the pastor's resignation.

> To *defer* means to yield to the contrary interests or judgments of another who has more power in the negotiation.

In the Old Testament, the people of Israel asked the prophet Samuel to give them a king so they could be like the other nations. Samuel was deeply upset by their request. In response, the Lord said to him, "Obey the voice of the people in all they say to you, for they have not rejected you, but they have rejected me from being king over them" (1 Samuel 8:7). With grave words of warning, Samuel *deferred* to the wishes of the people and gave them a king.

The circumstances around Jesus' birth provide exemplary examples of deferring. When the angel Gabriel addressed Mary, she *deferred* to the will of God, even though it meant facing the humiliation of becoming pregnant out of wedlock. And when Joseph was told by the angel not to divorce Mary, he too yielded to the will of God.

Suffer. To *suffer* means to submit to or to be forced to tolerate injury or grief of some sort, including loss, distress, pain, or even death. Several persons in our case stories *suffered* to some extent as a result of being in cell four during change. When congregants criticized Dave for his leadership of the Sunday evening service music, he *suffered* humiliation. Sue *suffered* from embarrassment, anger, and distress when she had to cancel the depression support groups due to the senior pastor's opposition.

> To *suffer* means to submit to or to be forced to tolerate injury or grief of some sort, including loss, distress, pain, or even death.

In the Old Testament, Moses' mother knew Pharaoh had commanded that all Hebrew males be killed at birth. At first, she *subverted* this decree by keeping her baby hidden. When this was no longer possible, she *suffered* great stress, sorrow, and loss by putting her child adrift in a basket on the river. This was also an act of redemptive subversion.

Twice in 2 Corinthians the apostle Paul shared instances of *suffering* he experienced in the name of Christ (2 Corinthians 4:8-12; 11:23-29). And the author of Hebrews, in his famous chapter on faith, outlined the painful *suffering* experienced by saints in the Old Testament:

> Some were tortured, refusing to accept release, so that they might rise again to a better life. Others suffered mocking and flogging, and even chains and imprisonment. They were stoned, they were sawn in two, and they were killed with the sword. They went about in skins of sheep and goats, destitute, afflicted, mistreated . . . wandering about in deserts and mountains, and in dens and caves of the earth. (Hebrews 11:35-37)

Likewise, the apostle Peter presented an extended teaching on *suffering* (1 Peter 2:20).[6] While he told his readers that there was no credit in suffering for sin, he explained that when one does good and suffers for it, it is gracious in the eyes of God. Suffering is often one of the few options for those with less power in this world who seek to walk in obedience to God's ways.

Surrender. To *surrender* means giving up or yielding the power to act in line with one's own interests. By surrendering, those with less power choose not to resist but to allow those with more power to have their way.

Christians will face moral dilemmas when deciding whether or not to quit. Believers should not *surrender* on matters in which they believe the truth of God or the proper application of that truth to life is at stake.[7] For example, Bob attended a Bible study years ago where the topic of discussion was dishonesty. After the study, one participant commented to Bob, "I'm a Christian, and I know what the Bible says about lying. But I'm also in a business where lying is an expected part of our work. If I can't lie, I won't be able to feed my family. So, I lie." This man erred in *surrendering* his responsibility and power to obey God and *deferred* to the social pressure in his business.

Followers of Jesus are called by God to *surrender* their desires to the purposes of God as understood through the lens of Scripture. In Romans 12:2 Paul exhorts his readers, "Do not be conformed to this world, but be transformed by the renewal of your mind, that by testing you may discern what is the will of God, what is good and acceptable and perfect." Paul later models this for us in his view of his own imprisonment for the sake of the gospel throughout his letter to the Philippians.

For a final example, consider Polycarp, the second-century bishop of Smyrna who had been discipled by the apostle John. His story of martyrdom provides an extreme example of Christian faithfulness in a cell-four context. In Polycarp's time, the young church was harshly persecuted by the government of the Roman Empire, largely because the believers

> To *surrender* means giving up or yielding the power to act in line with one's own interests.

would not sacrifice to the gods or call Caesar Lord. So others considered them a great threat to society. Many Christians were tortured and executed for their faith and refusal to sacrifice to the gods.

At a very old age, after fleeing and hiding from those searching for him (*subversion*), Polycarp was betrayed by someone in his own household and seized by authorities. The proconsul and magistrate tried to persuade him to apostatize in order to go free. However, Polycarp replied, "For eighty-six years I have been his servant, and he has done me no wrong. How can I blaspheme my King who saved me?"[8] Polycarp *surrendered* to their threat of execution and *suffered* in burning at the stake.

Cell Four for Those with More Power

Ministry leaders will often find themselves in cell-four contexts where they have greater power to promote their interests above the competing interests of others. *How* we use our greater power in these situations is of critical importance in ministry and discipleship.

First, we do well to remind ourselves that in our sinfulness we will tend to use our greater power to achieve our interests *efficiently*. To counter this bent, we need to take time to reflect, pray, and test our interests against God's redemptive interests for all his creation to

> As ministry planners, we would be wise to use our power and the required time to gain a thorough understanding of the interests of those with less power at the planning table. In addition, we should learn about the interests of those who do not even have a seat at the table and yet will be directly affected by the decisions being made.

flourish. Multiple times in Scripture, God exhorts people to be extremely careful in the way they use their power, especially concerning those who are vulnerable.[9] Therefore, as ministry planners, we would be wise to use our power and the required time to gain a thorough understanding of the interests of those with less power at the planning table. In addition, we should learn about the interests of those who do not even have a seat at the table and yet will be directly affected by the decisions being made.

In this second spectrum for cell four (see fig. 9.2), notice how the actions change in degree of aggressiveness: from demanding one's interests on the far right to giving up one's interests on the far left. Unlike the first spectrum (of actions for those with *less* power in cell four), this spectrum (for those with *more* power) also illustrates a change in the degree of control one has in the planning and decision making: from full control on the far right to giving up all control on the far left.

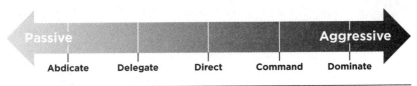

Passive				Aggressive
Abdicate	Delegate	Direct	Command	Dominate

Figure 9.2. Spectrum of options for those with *more* power in cell four

Dominate. Domination is the use of power to control others and to suppress their actions for self-determination. This cell-four choice should not be exercised by those in ministry leadership. It is not a godly use of power in cell-four contexts of planning and leading change. Such action breaks Jesus' command that his disciples not "lord it over" others but serve others in love (Matthew 20:20-28). To dominate others is to show disrespect to them as equals in worth and dignity as God's image bearers. This form of extreme manipulation leads to the emotional abuse and injury of others.

> **Domination is the use of power to control others and to suppress their contrary actions against one's own interests. It is not a godly use of power in cell-four contexts of planning and leading change.**

A church youth ministry intern was eager for the teenagers to critically evaluate popular media with biblical criteria. At one Friday night gathering, he chose a clean clip from an R-rated movie to show and discuss with the teens. The next morning, several parents complained to church board members about what they considered to be an inappropriate choice by the intern. One dad wanted the intern fired immediately. The church board called an emergency meeting with the intern the next day. After listening to the intern's story about what happened, the board moderator, who was good friends with the angry dad, told the intern that his job was on the line unless he ceased using popular media. The moderator continued to *dominate* the intern by adding that the intern had to apologize to the parents for his poor choice, without trying to explain why he showed the movie clip.

Command. To *command* is to use one's power to exercise an authoritative influence over the specific actions of others. This action in cell four can be an ethically responsible option for Christians. By God's grace, we are able to give instruction with the clear expectation of being obeyed, and yet do it in love. For example, in times of emergency (fire, injury, etc.), command-giving from one with authority for protecting people is likely the only wise option when there is no time to negotiate.

Some situations feel like emergencies, even though they are not life-threatening, because the time frame to act is so short. For example, during a retreat planning meeting, the campus ministry staff suddenly realized that no one reserved the conference facility they planned to use. With just a month before the set retreat date, the ministry director *commanded* one of the staff members to call the facility immediately, while he continued leading the meeting. The director figured that there was not a moment to lose. If the facility was already booked, much planning time and effort would be wasted, and the retreat would probably have to be cancelled. *Command* may be a wise action for the person with more power at the planning table.

Under normal circumstances, however, wise leadership requires allowing for plenty of time to discuss and work out the details of plans with those affected by the change. Therefore, *commanding* other adults is rarely the best option for negotiating interests. It is obvious that a parent's command to a child "Don't touch!" is a loving response when the child reaches toward a hot stove. It is far less obvious

> Wise leadership requires allowing for plenty of time to discuss and work out the details of plans with those affected by the change. Therefore, *commanding* other adults is rarely the best option for negotiating interests.

> To *command* is to use one's power to exercise an authoritative influence over the specific actions of others.

to envision a situation when those with more power *should* use a command in order to promote the well-being of other fully capable adults. *Commands* tend to stop communication, break trust and respect in the relationship, and limit the process for gaining understanding of interests.

In Sue's experience, the senior pastor seems to have had authoritative influence over the specific actions of his associate pastor and bulletin volunteer. He *commanded* his associate, who then *commanded* the volunteer, to delete Sue's bulletin announcement and to take down the other publicity for the new small group ministry. No one took the time to consult Sue. Each simply obeyed the wishes of those in positions over them. In response, Sue felt too embarrassed, dishonored, and threatened to speak to either of the pastors about it directly.

Recently, a friend who served as a church music director started a music ensemble made up of single adult church members. After working with this group for months, she asked the pastor if they could present a selection of their music in the worship service. With his agreement, they prepared a piece. At the Friday night rehearsal, the pastor listened from the back of the sanctuary. The next morning, he told the director, "That selection isn't going to work with my sermon." Having less power, the director *counteracted* by explaining how hard she had worked with the group and how excited they were to sing in the service. The pastor responded with a *command*. "That's not my problem. They aren't singing that song in the service." The director *deferred*. Nonetheless, the pastor lost the respect and trust of many people by issuing that command, and thus lost some power to act and to influence.

Direct. To *direct* means to give authoritative oversight by determining the general course of action or to provide planning decisions in advance of a change process. A great deal of ministry is initiated by a leader providing *directions* to others in the planning and execution of programming. The important distinction in cell-four actions between *commanding* and *directing* concerns the amount of control those with more power choose to maintain in the planning process. In *directing,* the leader at the planning table allows others to give input and to make decisions in more detailed matters. The leader is choosing to have less control over the specific manner that others carry out the course of action.

In one of our stories, Sue was *directing* many pieces of the new support group ministry: selecting and ordering workbooks, recruiting and training facilitators, developing publicity, and securing agreement from her supervisor and the Christian education committee. Many people gave input into the decisions and new ministry design. But they all agreed to work with her organizing *directions* in recognition of her title and formal power to lead the ministry.

Another example of directing involves a pastor who discovered that a church board member and spouse were using teaching materials in Sunday school that were not theologically appropriate for the church. Since the pastor did not have strong relationships with the couple and did not want them to feel singled out, he chose not to confront them directly. Instead, he used his formal power to *direct* a study team of the church board to look into the general matter of curriculum used in the church. The team decided that the couple should no longer be allowed to use the materials and graciously *commanded* them to cease.

> To *direct* means to give authoritative oversight by determining the general course of action or to provide planning decisions in advance of a change process. A great deal of ministry is initiated by a leader providing *directions* to others in the planning and execution of programming.

Delegate. *Delegating* involves appointing, entrusting, and authorizing a person or group to act in one's place. The one with more power turns over responsibility and empowers others to act and make decisions in line with the specified goal. In cell four, leaders negotiate using *delegation* by trusting those with less power to represent their interests well, even though the leader's interests conflict (knowingly or unknowingly) with the interests of their subordinates. In doing this, leaders are placing their interests at risk, as well as sharing their capacity to act by increasing the others' power to act. If the subordinates follow through by acting in line with the leader's interests, they may change their interests to be more in line with the leader's.

When the board members of Trinity Church called Brian to be an associate pastor, they did so in order to *delegate* the responsibilities of church operations to him once Pastor Joe resigned. However, one board member did not expect this

> *Delegating* involves appointing, entrusting, and authorizing a person or group to act in one's place.

delegation of power to Brian to backfire on one of his other interests. Soon after Pastor Joe left, this older board member became angry and manipulative at a board meeting, trying to force the group to agree to his idea. Brian responded with the use of his formal power of being moderator of the board by calling out the bad behavior. The board member apologized to Brian as moderator for the way he had acted.

Throughout his ministry, Jesus *delegated* responsibility for building his kingdom (Mark 6:7-13; Luke 10:1-12; Matthew 28:19-20; John 21:15-17; Acts 1:8). The disciples (as well as all of us who have come after them) had mixed interests with God's purposes. Yet Jesus graciously allows his church to participate as strategic partners in his plan for the redemption of all his creation. Of course, at his return Jesus will make all things new by his authoritative *command*. But even in the new heavens and earth, Jesus will *delegate* to his church a role in his eternal purposes.

Abdicate. When leaders fully *abdicate*, they relinquish their formal responsibilities and accompanying title, thus failing to accomplish their assigned duty. In the cell-four context of ministry negotiation, a limited form of *abdication* happens when the people with more power walk away from the planning table, literally and figuratively. They may not relinquish their titles or all their other responsibilities, but they do cease asserting their interests and stop using their power in the process, at least for a time. They deliberately allow the interests of others to succeed and attempt to drop all responsibility for the specific situation.

> In the cell-four context of ministry negotiation, a limited form of *abdication* happens when the people with more power walk away from the planning table, literally and figuratively. They may not relinquish their titles or all their other responsibilities, but they do cease asserting their interests and stop using their power in the process, at least for a time.

This limited form of leader *abdication* in the planning process would rarely be a godly action for Christians. To give up responsibility in the midst of the planning process would probably be a selfish, sinful action when one is leading ministry out of a God-given vocational calling and capacity to pursue kingdom interests. Ministry leaders cannot daily pick and choose which responsibilities they will fulfill and which they will drop. Others will still consider them to be accountable to all their responsibilities.

A director of Christian education (DCE) served a large congregation for a number of years. The senior pastor asked the DCE to make significant changes in the ministry, and the DCE did this. However, a month later, volunteers in the ministry complained directly to the senior pastor about the changes, thus *subverting* the DCE's authority. The senior pastor *abdicated* his responsibility for directing the changes. He acted as though he knew nothing about them. Instead, he placed all responsibility, and now blame, directly on the shoulders of the DCE under his authority.

In the New Testament, Acts 10 describes how God dramatically taught the apostle Peter not to make distinctions between Gentiles and Jews when sharing the gospel. Peter experienced the conversions of the Gentile Cornelius and his household. Later, however, Paul had to confront Peter on this issue. While in Antioch, Peter was eating with the Gentile Christians, but when some Jewish Christians arrived from Jerusalem, Peter separated himself from the Gentiles. In separating himself, Peter *abdicated* his responsibility to demonstrate that all believers had equal standing before God and in the church (Acts 10:9-33; Galatians 2:11-14).

Observations on the Four Cells

The unique contexts of power and interests in every negotiation indicate which cell the people are in during the planning table process. Within each cell there are a variety of options available for action. Choosing among the options is most important in cell four, as illustrated by the two spectrums examined earlier. More nuanced spectrums could be made for the other three cells as well.

Negotiations can move from one cell in the chart (see table 8.1) to another during the planning process, as people's power and interests change. In fact, wise leaders should seek to move cell-four negotiations in the direction of the other three cells. This is not a call for flat organizations or the denial of unequal power. It is a warning that little good can be accomplished if people perceive they have less power and are stuck in cell four at the planning table with conflicting interests. Those with more

> Negotiations can move from one cell in the chart to another during the planning process, as people's power and interests change. Wise leaders should seek to move cell-four negotiations in the direction of the other three cells.

power at the planning table can easily err in assuming that others at the table have equal power as themselves, simply because they are involved in the process. As a result, these leaders will attempt to bargain as if everyone was in cell three, with equal power but differing interests. This poor strategy will only further deteriorate the relationships since the others are actually in cell four. To address the more important and true problems, those with more power must become aware of the conflicting interests and sometimes even the suffering of those under their power in cell four.

The planning process will move out of cell four when healthy leaders use their capacities to consider the interests of those with less power and to empower them to engage the process well. These wise leaders value a trust-building, collaborative process more than the goal of merely gaining their own interests. Movement out of cell four requires those with more power to limit their power and modify their interests voluntarily, while advocating for others. This work takes patience, careful listening, and asking good questions so that all will better understand the competing interests. It also requires those with less power to exercise the courage to speak up respectfully and honestly.

> The planning process will move out of cell four when healthy leaders use their capacities to consider the interests of those with less power and to empower them to engage the process well, toward collaborative teamwork and a common goal.

The story of the angered music director who confronted both Dave and the senior pastor during a staff meeting illustrates good leadership moving the meeting process out of cell four. The senior pastor valued trust and teamwork over being right and in charge. He listened carefully to the worship leader's complaints, cared about her injury, and responded by acknowledging his own failure, accepting responsibility for the music style changes Dave had implemented. Dave gained an understanding of the competing interests, recognized how his leadership during the service offended the music director and others, and apologized for his failure to understand. The actions of these two pastors moved the ongoing planning out of cell four toward cell two, where the interests became shared and focused on the need for better communication.

Unlike the abbreviated case stories given here, most planning and change processes involve multiple agendas and complicated interests.[10]

As we saw in previous chapters describing sources of interests, most people will not be conscious of all the interests they themselves bring to the planning table, let alone the interests of others. While Jesus was sincerely concerned for the man with the withered hand, he was well aware that there were much bigger issues at stake in this healing. For example, questions from those present such as, What is the proper interpretation of the Law? Who is Jesus and where did he get such power? and Will the religious leaders tolerate this itinerant preacher? were at issue in that moment.

> True ministry leadership involves considering the people who are affected by the decisions, programs, and changes, and seeking to understand their interests.

A challenge for wise leadership is remembering that ministry is not simply identifying participants' needs and developing programs. Ministry leadership involves considering the people who are affected by decisions, programs, and changes, and seeking to understand their interests. This involves listening carefully to those who have something to gain or to lose as a result of the planning decisions. Leaders must learn what matters to these stakeholders and identify what cell they are negotiating in. The behaviors of those at the planning table usually make it obvious what cell they are in, if only we will take the time to understand. Ministry planners may find their work diminished, dismissed, or even terminated unless they take others' interests into account and invite people with relevant interests to the planning table.

Questions to Ponder

Describe a time when you thought you would be working in cells one or two, with shared interests, only to learn that you were functioning in cell four.

1. Did you have more or less power than others in cell four? Describe how that felt.

2. What actions did you take while working in that cell?

3. What actions did others take during that negotiation process?

4. What steps could have been taken (or were taken) to move out of cell four?

5. What was the outcome of that negotiation?

Conclusion

People usually enter ministry because they want to participate in God's redemptive work in the world. They want to see people come into a personal relationship with God and to grow in faith and love. Often ministry leaders and participants expect their experiences to be similar to that of Mia and Caroline, where ministry negotiation happens primarily in cells one and two, where interests are alike. However, far too often, like Brian, Dave, and Sue, people discover they are laboring in cell three (with differing interests but equal power) and four (with both differing interests and power). This work can be very discouraging and is not for the fainthearted. It involves patiently working with people through deep learning and change. Long after Brian's initial shock at Trinity Church and then after years of fruitful service in the pastorate, he quietly reflected, "You've got to learn to love the process more than just the outcome. If you don't love the process, you're not only going to be bald—like I am—but you're going to be frustrated to the point of giving up."

Chapter 10

Ethical Issues in the Politics of Ministry

This chapter explores some of the ethical challenges of the negotiating process. As described in the ethics section of chapter two, four simple yet provocative questions help to define the key ethical issues of ministry politics.

1. Who are the stakeholders in this situation?

2. What are the probable interests of each stakeholder?

3. How will those interests be represented during the negotiation process?

4. To what degree are we serving the welfare of God's church and the redemption of his world over our selfish interests?

The specific focus in this chapter concerns the choice of actions and use of power exercised in cell four, where people have differing interests and unequal power (see table 8.1). Ethicist David Jones states the big picture of the Christian life this way: "The controlling purpose of the Christian life is the glory of God; the impelling motive of the Christian life is love for God; and the directing principle of the Christian life is the will of God as revealed in Christ and the Holy Scriptures."[1] We glorify God by loving him and by responding to God's love and grace with our obedience to him.

However, even while seeking to do the will of God, people will still have different interests. And they usually join with others who hold similar interests to promote their agendas. We all advance our interests by using the

> Ministry politics is grounded in the way people apply their ethical commitments in daily practice. And nowhere is this seen more clearly than in the negotiation process of cell four, where interests conflict and power is unequal.

power available to us, working out our convictions and concerns in practical, day-to-day settings. In doing so, we reveal our true values in the way we exercise power to promote our interests.[2] Therefore, ministry politics is grounded in the way people apply their ethical commitments in daily practice. And nowhere is this seen more clearly than in the negotiation process of cell four, where interests conflict and power is unequal.

Cell Four Decisions and King David

The biblical stories of David struggling with King Saul provide helpful examples of someone navigating issues in cell four (see 1 Samuel 17–26). David's early experience with Saul was in cell two, where there was a clear formal power differential between the king and his subject. David shared the interests of Saul and served Saul well in defeating Goliath, working as armor bearer, and serving as a musician comforter. However, after David experienced great military successes against national enemies, King Saul grew jealous and sought to kill David. This dramatic change in Saul's interests moved their relationship into cell four. We can analyze their actions using the cell-four spectrums, which were explored in detail in chapter nine.

When King Saul first seeks to kill David, David is protected by Saul's son Jonathan. David *defers* to the king by continuing to serve him in leading the army. But eventually David makes a moral decision, choosing to save his life by *counteracting* the king and fleeing from Saul, thus also choosing to *suffer* exile. In this exile David made a series of other decisions to continue to *suffer* and to *defer, subvert,* and *counteract* the king's interests.

In 1 Samuel 19–26 we find David constantly on the run from the king. Saul viewed David as a direct threat to his authority. David, based on the clear interests of God's revealed will, tried to maintain a proper respect for God's authority represented by King Saul. David never initiated conflict with the king though he was taking steps to protect his own life and the lives of his followers. He used *subversion* when he cut off the edge of Saul's robe while hiding in a cave. Later, he repented, believing in hindsight that he broke God's moral law to respect governing authorities. He confessed, "The LORD forbid that I should do this thing to my lord, the LORD's anointed, to put out my hand against him, seeing he is the LORD's anointed" (1 Samuel 24:6).

Another time David decided to *subvert* Saul by sneaking into his camp and stealing Saul's spear and water jar. David's associate Abishai urged

David to kill the king. Abishai said God had given Saul into David's hand. David, however, refused to break what he understood to be God's moral law even though his own life was threatened, saying, "The LORD forbid that I should put out my hand against the LORD's anointed" (1 Samuel 26:11).

We see in David's example that decision making in cell four can be challenging. We would do well to imitate David in reviewing and learning from the actions we make in the pressure of cell-four conflicts. Cell four requires us to develop this capacity for reflection-in-action followed by reflection-on-action (as discussed in chap. four). These decisions are difficult. Sinful mistakes are easy to make here. In reflection-on-action, David concluded that he had broken God's moral law by cutting off the edge of Saul's robe. Perhaps his repentance for "putting out his hand" against Saul made him aware of his limits when he later snuck into Saul's camp and yet still refused to kill Saul.

Challenges of Cell Four

See figures 9.1 and 9.2 to review the basic types of actions available to people in cell four. Figure 9.1 represents the person or group that has *less* power. Figure 9.2 represents the person or group that has *more* power. Both spectrums illustrate a continuum from more aggressive actions on the right to more passive actions on the left.

The following are common concerns about the options on each spectrum:

- I don't know how to figure out what option is best in cell four.

- I'm unclear if one end of the spectrum is preferable to the other or if being in the middle is ideal.

- I attach negative meanings to several words on each spectrum, so those actions do not seem like possible choices for a Christian.

- My goal is to completely avoid doing politics in cell four.

These concerns make sense. Candidly, the more we have reflected, prayed, and taught about this, the more we are aware that there are no simple formulas for how to act in cell four. An analogy may help. Bob had the privilege of working for many years in the area of divorce recovery. One of the most important lessons he learned was that while there are normative statements in Scripture about marital disruption, the applications of these principles to distinct situations are far from uniform. Each case presents unique issues and different challenges and so requires creative application of biblical principles with humility and grace.

The humble, gracious application of biblical principles is also required in the negotiation process, particularly in cell four. The choice of action requires reflection, prayer, and discernment. Every situation and context is unique. Sometimes conflict reflects understandable disagreements in perspective. At other times, there is long-standing organizational dysfunction involved. In addition, there are situations where personal characteristics of the people involved resist change, even to the degree of character disturbances or psychiatric disorders. However, in all conflicts, issues of sin—some recognized and others not—are at work in each person. For we are still in the sanctification process of becoming more like Jesus.

Nevertheless, ministry leaders are regularly required to make personal and organizational decisions in cell four. Sometimes these decisions are wise and further the good work of all involved. More often, however, though made with the best intentions, decisions end up being a mixture of wisdom and error, with harmful unintended consequences. Sometimes people give up and walk away (*surrender* or *abdicate*) when they should have hung in there. Other times people stay to fight when they should drop the issue (chosen to *suffer* or to *delegate*). Cell-four work requires us to pursue biblical wisdom, to seek wise counsel from others, to repent of sin, to seek forgiveness, and to walk by faith in the power of the Spirit.

Since every situation is unique, we must choose from the spectrum of options summarized in the model according to the specific situation. While we should consider relevant biblical principles of behavior, no one can give a standardized answer of what to do in every cell-four negotiation. A person's moral interests deal with matters that Scripture explicitly states are right or wrong. But moral interests also concern gray issues where Scripture is not direct or is silent on the specifics. These gray issues require wisdom and insights provided by the guiding principles found in the Bible. The decisions (and outcomes) are still the responsibility of each individual. Regardless of the consequences or our own preferences, followers of Christ are responsible to learn to obey God's revealed truth, to ask God for wisdom in discernment, and to live in step with God's Spirit.

> **Cell-four work requires us to pursue biblical wisdom, to seek wise counsel from others, to repent of sin, to seek forgiveness, and to walk by faith in the power of the Spirit.**

At times, choices in cell four simply come down to matters of opinion. Sometimes we simply do not have clear teaching from the Bible on decisions we must make. In these situations the best we can do is to name this reality and have everyone clearly explain their personal preferences, calling them as such. Cell-four conflict can be over this very point. One person will think the issue is a matter of opinion, while another believes it is a matter of biblical obedience. In these circumstances, we do well to remind ourselves of Proverbs 18:2: "A fool takes no pleasure in understanding, but only in expressing his opinion." Scripture clearly calls us to protect the unity of the church and not to judge one another or quarrel over opinions (see Psalm 133; John 17:20-26; Romans 14:1-12; Ephesians 4:1-16).

Questions to Ponder

1. Recall a time when you were in a cell-four experience. Did you have less power or more power? What choice(s) did you make in response? Where would you place yourself on the spectrum of possible actions?

2. What scriptural principles came into play in the way you managed your cell-four experience?

3. When have you faced a disagreement with a fellow Christian in which one of you felt it was a matter of opinion and the other felt it a matter of biblical obedience? How was it resolved? If faced with the same challenge today, would you make the same decision you did then?

Ray's Story of Negotiation in All Four Cells

Ray served in pastoral ministry for over forty-five years. A formative experience in his life came when a number of his church board members turned on him. "This was probably one of the most hurtful times in my life," he confessed. "I had been very close to these people."

The story begins when Ray learned that the newly elected chair of the church's women's ministry suddenly replaced the women's Bible study teacher of many years. Ray requested that the teacher be reinstated. But by that time the teacher would not take the job back. She felt too hurt and did not want to work with the chair.

This replaced teacher had three friends who were upset by what had happened. Their husbands—board members in the church—took up their wives' offense by going after Ray. "They started picking on everything," he explained. "At budget time, they even fought against all the staff getting any kind of raise, because they didn't want me to have one." Finally, these men took Ray to breakfast and, to use Ray's words, "tore into him" about the church and everything they perceived was wrong with it.

A short while after that breakfast, a handful of other board members asked Ray for a meeting. "We sat down," he continued, "and they said, 'Ray, we know the criticism you've been under. You're going through a tough time right now. But we don't want you to be discouraged, and we certainly don't want you to think about leaving. Don't worry about this. We'll take care of it.'"

At the next board meeting, the three members who were critical of the pastor started complaining, saying, "We're not being fed." At that moment one of the other members spoke up.

> You know, I've had that problem too. There have been times in my life when I didn't feel like I was being fed. And as I reflect upon it now, the problem was not with the feeder, the problem was with me. There was sin in my life. And you know, that's your problem. So, how can we pray for you?

Clearly, while this board member sought to support the pastor, his blunt accusation against the three hit hard and lacked any grace that might have helped build healthier communication. The meeting ended in dead silence, and the three board members resigned their church memberships the next week.

Consider the actions of these church leaders through the negotiation strategy spectrum.

- Three women with less formal power than the women's ministry chair do not like a decision that the chair made. (They *suffer* and *subvert*—cell four.)
- The three women share their complaints with their board member husbands. (The women *network*—cell two.)
- The husbands draw together into a coalition based on the common interest of supporting their wives' grievances. (The husbands *collaborate*—cell one.)

- With several actions, from arguing over salary increases to tearing into the pastor, the board members (husbands) attack the representative of the system they deem culpable for their wives' unhappiness, Pastor Ray. (Their complaints cause much *bargaining* during board meetings—cell three.)

- Then, with their combined power of three against one, they start making demands on the pastor directly during the board meeting. (Their aggressive complaints are actually *commands* for change—cell four.)

- Other board members notice the conflict, not only with the pastor but with their own interests to support the pastor. First, they meet with the pastor assuring him of their support. (They *collaborate*—cell one.) In the board meeting, they change the topic by questioning the spiritual condition of the three men. (They attempt to *bargain* with the three to get them to stop attacking the pastor—cell three.)

- The bargain ends quickly, however, with the three men finding themselves with less power (cell four). They choose to *surrender* by leaving the church altogether.

It would have been difficult for Pastor Ray to have identified the interests of the negative three men on the board prior to the experience. However, as circumstances unfolded, he quickly became aware of them. These members were not simply interested in the change of a Bible study leader and the resulting unhappiness of their spouses. They had many other hidden interests in conflict with the church and with the pastor, which fueled their political actions. In hindsight we often discern deeper interests that are moving people to act in situations.

Cell-Four Decisions in Ray's Story

Ray's story is one that demonstrates both healthy and hurtful processes in cell four. The concerns of the three men on the board could have been addressed through open, honest cell-three *bargaining* in which all parties hold similar power but with conflicting interests. This is what Jesus commends in the Gospel of Matthew.

> If you are offering your gift at the altar and there remember that your brother has something against you, leave your gift there before the altar and go. First be reconciled to your brother, and then come and offer your gift. Come to terms quickly with your accuser while you are going with him

to court, lest your accuser hand you over to the judge, and the judge to the guard, and you be put in prison. (Matthew 5:23-25)

If your brother sins against you, go, and tell him his fault, between you and him alone. If he listens to you, you have gained your brother. But if he does not listen, take one or two others along with you, that every charge may be established by the evidence of two or three witnesses. (Matthew 18:15-16)

However, these three board members chose to negotiate their interests within cell four. People often go to cell four by the choice of their actions, when they could have stayed out of cell four. They perceived, or feared, that they had less power to pursue their interests. This perception is often incorrect. Believing they had less power, they chose to negotiate with actions on the less-power spectrum. They used various forms of *subversion* and *counteraction* to challenge Pastor Ray. Perhaps the other board member was unknowingly seeking to move the conflict into cell three by bluntly confronting the dissenters during the board meeting. Using *direction*, this single board member, knowing he had the support of others, accused the three of sinning in how they were acting. The response of the three was similar to the Pharisees' and Herodians' silence to Jesus' questions in Mark 3. Remaining in cell four, feeling defeated and with less power, these board members chose to *surrender*, cutting off all relationships by leaving the church.

Key Reasons Christians Conflict in Cell Four

Much of Jesus' ministry looks like it took place in cell four, where power is uneven and interests clash. Similarly, the book of Acts reveals that the apostles often ministered in cell-four circumstances. However, the majority of the conflicts presented in the Gospels and Acts were between Jesus or his disciples and nonbelievers. How should we think about cell-four conflicts between fellow Christians, like in Ray's story?

Jesus prayed for unity among believers and taught Christians to love one another. Similarly, in many of his letters to the churches the apostle Paul exhorted Christians to live and work in unity together (e.g., John 13:34-35; Ephesians 3:14-21). From this New Testament emphasis on unity, one could develop the idea that relationships, work, and even conflicts among followers of Christ should only happen in the first three cells. Yet the book of Acts and the Epistles reveal that conflict did happen between Christians in cell four, where interests and power were uneven between the parties involved. Paul had serious conflicts with Jewish Christians trying to force Gentile believers to be circumcised and follow the Jewish law (see Acts 15, Galatians, and 2 Corinthians). Paul also strongly corrected others who claimed to be Christians but lived in a manner inconsistent with the gospel (see Philippians 1:15-17; 2 Timothy 3:1-9; 4:14-15). In the book of Revelation, Jesus addressed with severity the problems in the seven churches (Revelation 2–3). Clearly, cell-four conflicts were not absent among New Testament believers.

Similarly, as we have seen from stories in this book, much present-day ministry happens between believers in cell four. Why is this so common? Why can't Christians either work through conflicting interests or agree to disagree with mutuality and respect, since they follow the same Lord and are all equal members of God's family?

The answers to these questions would fill many books! The following responses to these questions are suggestive rather than exhaustive. There are at least four basic reasons why so much ministry conflict happens in cell four: the pro-

> There are at least four basic reasons why so much ministry conflict happens in cell four: the progressive nature of sanctification, failures in discipleship, power dynamics in organizational culture, and character or personality disorders.

gressive nature of sanctification, gaps in discipleship, power dynamics in organizational culture, and character or personality disorders.

1. The progressive nature of sanctification. One reason so much ministry conflict happens in cell four is because all human beings are sinners who fall short of the glory of God (Romans 3:23).[3] Though we are made in God's image (Genesis 1:26-27; 1 Corinthians 11:7), all humankind is under the guilt and power of sin (Jeremiah 17:9; Romans 1:18–3:20). We are not sinners because we sin. Rather, we sin because we are sinners, born with a nature enslaved to sin.[4] Through the new birth of regeneration by grace through faith in Christ, God called us out of spiritual darkness and ended our slavery to sin. We have the sure hope of becoming like Christ by the power of the Spirit. Yet we are still called to fight against our sin in daily life. Thus, we have a lifelong "unending battle with sin."[5]

When it comes to the politics of working with people, the implications of our sinful condition are profound. Humankind's broken condition is behind much of the conflict seen in the stories we have studied. Whether it was the way Senior Pastor Joe was "encouraged" to resign, the disappearance of Sue's advertising, or board members attacking Pastor Ray, all of these conflicts involved human sin.

As Jesus taught, it is much easier to see the speck in someone else's eye than the log in our own (Matthew 7:3-5). Each one of us is in the process of sanctification, which involves "walking in the light," allowing God's Spirit to reveal our sin and convict us of how we have fallen short (1 John 1:5-10). We would do well to remember that when we face a challenging conversations, we are sinners redeemed only by God's mercy.

> Through the new birth of regeneration by grace through faith in Christ, we begin a lifelong process of being freed from sinful habits and of being formed in Christlike character.

Our sanctification process also requires the humility of letting others correct us with truth and considering their alternative perspectives. In Galatians 6, Paul told his readers, "If anyone is caught in any transgression, you who are spiritual should restore him in a spirit of gentleness. Keep watch on yourself, lest you too be tempted" (v. 1). We are reminded of the prophet Nathan directly addressing King David, exposing David's sins of adultery and murder (2 Samuel 12:1-14). This confrontation between Nathan and David began in cell four, where David had much more organizational power and was likely held in higher esteem by the people. David's humility in receiving Nathan's challenge (moving them out of cell four into cell two), together with his public repentance recorded in Psalm 51, reflects the continued work of God's Spirit in his life.

Compare David's response to that of King Saul when Saul's son Jonathan addressed his father's sin (1 Samuel 20:26-34). King Saul felt deeply threatened by David's military victories. Jonathan warned David of Saul's intentions and excused David from participating in a ceremonial meal, where Saul planned to kill David. When Saul learned of Jonathan's actions to thwart his plan, he exploded, cursing his son and throwing his spear at him! (Saul went off the far end of the cell-four spectrum, from *dominate* to destroy.) Saul sinfully chose the opposite of humility and repentance.

His reactions are symbolic of the responses some leaders have when questioned by subordinates.

Regardless of our age, organizational position, power, or interests, God calls us in love to work out our "salvation with fear and trembling" (Philippians 2:12). This includes confessing our sins to one another, speaking truth into each other's lives, evaluating our own convictions and the insights of others, and repenting of our sin (James 5:16; Luke 17:3; Galatians 6:1-2; 1 John 3:19-24; Galatians 6:3-5).

> As Jesus taught, it is much easier to see the speck in someone else's eye than the log in our own.

Questions to Ponder

1. Go back to the cell-four incident you reflected on earlier in the chapter. What steps might have been taken in that experience to move everyone into cell three?

2. What does it mean for Christians to "walk in the light" with one another? How does that reflect an "unending battle with sin"?

3. Describe a time when your broken human condition consciously or unconsciously produced a cell-four conflict. What choices along the spectrum of power did you make? Did God convict you about this in any way? If so, what did you do when you were convicted?

2. Gaps in discipleship. A second reason ministry conflict happens in cell four is what we call "gaps" in the discipleship of many believers. Some churches and ministries have clear plans to help believers grow and mature in Christ. Other believers move through a more spontaneous and unstructured spiritual pathway. Few of us reflect on our own spiritual growth, considering areas of strength and struggles and gaps in our experience or understanding. Christian discipleship programs have particular emphases as well as areas that are underdeveloped. No one curriculum can help us to grow in every way.

In some ministries discipleship connotes a concise, defined time frame. People say, "I was discipled by so and so," or "I've been discipled," as if they had attained a certain level of experience or understanding. But the Bible reflects the idea that discipleship is a lifelong, whole-person process. In Deuteronomy 6:5, Moses says we are to "Love the LORD your God with all your heart and with all your soul and with all your might." Jesus said that this command, together with "You shall love your neighbor as yourself," summarized all the Law and the Prophets (Matthew 22:37-40). The terms *heart, soul,* and *might* indicate that discipleship involves all aspects of our being. The command indicates that this is a lifelong endeavor.

Similarly, the apostle Paul presents growth in Christ as a lifelong process. In writing to the Colossians he states, "As you received Christ Jesus the Lord, so walk in him, rooted and built up in him and established in the faith, just as you were taught, abounding in thanksgiving" (Colossians 2:6-7). Discipleship is an ongoing process. Paul did not consider himself complete in Christ or having arrived at maturity without sin (see Philippians 3:12-16). Furthermore, Paul presents many who were involved in the Colossians' discipleship (Colossians 4:4-17). Discipleship happens in community.

> **The Bible reflects the idea that discipleship is an ongoing, lifelong, whole-person process. Discipleship is an ongoing process that happens in community.**

Much discipleship curriculum in the United States focuses on biblical and theological knowledge. Though it is important to know the Scriptures and sound doctrine, grasping this material does not necessarily equate to maturity in Christ. For example, early in his ministry a pastor chose two persons to become deacons because they "seemed to know their Bible and had a proper theology." He continued to tell the story:

> We didn't think about how these folks lived and how they related to other people. It turned out these new deacons were authoritarian in their leadership. They beat people over the head with their theology. I learned the hard way that Bible knowledge and proper theology do not necessarily make someone a mature disciple. We have to look for the fruit of the Spirit in their lives.

When Paul outlined to Timothy the qualifications necessary for church leadership, he certainly referenced knowledge of Bible and doctrine (1 Timothy 3:9; Titus 1:9). But he also outlined numerous characteristics of personal, social, and lifestyle maturity that would demonstrate the fruit of godliness.[6] Many ministry leaders today would not measure up to the criteria for leadership that Paul describes. This lack of maturity shows up as harmful reactivity in cell-four conflicts.

Many of the characteristics and behaviors that Paul lists as signs of spiritual maturity reflect what is popularly referred to as emotional intelligence (EQ). Pastor and author Peter Scazzero describes this as a critical aspect of discipleship.

> There was a time in my life when . . . the agonizing pain of a major crisis had me writhing in anger and shame—*me*, the guy who had tried so hard to be a committed and loving Christian, who was so sincere about serving God and his kingdom. . . . That is when I discovered the radical truth that changed my life: that emotional health and spiritual maturity are inseparable.[7]

He later adds, "Because people are having real, and helpful spiritual experiences in certain areas of their lives—such as worship, prayer, Bible studies, and fellowship—they mistakenly believe they are doing fine, even if their relational life and interior world is not in order."[8]

How does this relate to ministry in cell four? When writing to his younger protégé Timothy, the apostle Paul sternly warned, "Do not be hasty in the laying on of hands" to set aside people for leadership in the church (1 Timothy 5:22). When spiritually or emotionally immature people are formally empowered to lead God's people, differences in interests that arise will usually lead to unhealthy conflict management. This is seen in many of our case stories and found throughout the history of the church. As one person vividly put it when reflecting on years of experience with church leadership selection:

> The culture of the church flows out of the maturity of the leadership. You have to guard the church from people wanting to move up through the ranks for the wrong reasons. These are not side issues. They are the very things that destroy churches. The wrong people getting the wrong positions at the wrong time exerting the wrong influence and pretty soon the church is torn apart.

It is easier to address these discipleship issues before a person is vested with formal leadership power. The church has the challenging responsibility of the ongoing shepherding and discipleship of all believers, wherever they are in their spiritual journey.

Questions to Ponder

1. In the context where you became a Christian, what did it mean to be discipled?

2. How do you believe being a Christian should influence a person's character? What do you think when you hear about a Christian leader who demonstrates a lack of emotional maturity?

3. How should discipleship influence the mental, physical, social, and moral aspects of life?

3. Organizational power dynamics. A third reason why ministry conflict often ends up in cell four has to do with the power dynamics found in organizational cultures. As we shared in chapter six, organizations have personalities. As people become involved, they are socialized into the ways of the organization's system. Participants' actions and attitudes begin to mirror subtle rituals and practices reflecting expectations for proper conduct. Organizational culture is seen in the office furniture, what people wear, what stories the organization tells itself, who the heroes are, and what topics people speak about to brag about the organization.[9]

Organizational culture can be defined as "the way we do things around here."[10] Leadership author Richard Daft explains the power of organizational culture well:

> Walk into the headquarters of Patagonia, and you will likely see people wearing flip flops and shorts. . . . The feeling inside headquarters is relaxed, yet vibrant; people work hard, but they also have fun. Compare that to the headquarters at Exxon Mobil, where most employees are in conventional business attire and the atmosphere is tinged with competitiveness and a rigorous, analytical approach to taking care of business. . . .
>
> Culture is the unwritten, feeling part of the organization. . . . Everyone participates in culture, but culture generally goes unnoticed. It is only when managers try to implement new strategies, structures, or systems that go against basic cultural norms and values that they come face to face with the power of culture.[11]

Daft also cautions, "Negative cultural norms can damage a company just as powerfully as positive ones can strengthen it."[12] He explains that "when relationships both within the organization and with customers, suppliers, and partners are based on honesty, trust, and respect, a spirit of goodwill exists and people willingly cooperate to achieve mutual benefits." However, "relationships based on cutthroat competition, self-interest, and subterfuge can be devastating to a company."[13]

Sadly, churches and ministries may exhibit the negative characteristics and cultures Daft describes. Dysfunctional environments quickly create cell-four working contexts where trust is diminished. People will protect themselves and their interests by using whatever power they have available. When this happens, the toxicity creates distrust and anxiety, which undermines the whole purpose of the ministry. For example, consider how Brian felt after Pastor Joe was forced to resign. He shared, "I was scared to death. For the first time, I saw how precarious the pastor's position can be. It was a wake-up call to be more aware. And probably a lot less trusting." A culture of distrust, anxiety, and competition moves people into cell four, and their behaviors will reflect one of the two spectrums.

A hierarchical structure is used in most organizations, including ministries and churches. There is nothing inherently wrong with this. However, in this broken world hierarchical structure is formed using a chain of command where communication typically flows from the top down. Amy Edmondson, a professor at Harvard Business School, argues, "Hierarchy, by its very nature, dramatically reduces speaking up by those lower in the pecking order."[14] It is only by concerted effort of bosses to seek out feedback and humbly receive it that this tendency can be minimized and real learning and productivity can take place.[15]

Chapter seven explained how a hierarchical structure often creates what is called a high-power distance culture.[16] This is when leaders do not view themselves as peers to subordinates.[17] The more rigid the system, the less democratic the decision-making process. This in turn creates an environment where decisions are made unilaterally by leaders, who assume subordinates will obey without question.

Is it appropriate in Christian organizations for a high-power distance culture to develop between Christians? Yes, it is possible for Christian leaders to have godly attitudes of humility and service while expressing broader cultural norms of high-power distance. However, ministry leaders do well to assess continually the gospel health of their ministry's organizational culture. Andy Crouch states the assessment criteria clearly, writing, "The best test of any institution, and especially of any institution's roles and rules for using power [organizational culture], is *whether everyone flourishes* when everyone indwells their roles and plays by the rules, or whether only a few of the participants experience abundance and growth."[18]

One extreme characteristic of unhealthy organizations is manipulation. This is a common complaint in ministry cultures described as "too political." A friend expressed this in connection with the four negotiation cells. She said, "A word that kept coming to my mind after our conversation was *manipulation*. How can one function in cell four without being manipulative?"

We found the following comment by leadership author Preston Ni helpful at this point.

> It is important to distinguish healthy social influence from manipulation. Healthy social influence occurs between most people, and is part of the give and take of constructive relationships. In manipulation, one person is used for the benefit of another. The manipulator deliberately creates an imbalance of power, and exploits the victim to serve his or her agenda.[19]

Every form of negotiation involves social influence. It is what normally takes place when a person's emotions, opinions, or behaviors are influenced by others.[20] Manipulation, on the other hand, means taking advantage of people dishonestly—often using fear, obligation, guilt, and sometimes direct or indirect threat to punish if an individual does not comply with what the manipulator desires. Exploitive people manipulate others in seeking to control, intimidate, exaggerate, or distort the truth to get what they want.[21]

The two cell-four spectrums illustrate distinct sets of actions available for either those with more power or for those with less power (see figs. 9.1 and 9.2). However, *either* party can use their power to manipulate the other. We desperately need wisdom and the power of the Spirit to avoid choosing to manipulate others. It is never appropriate for those who claim to follow Christ to employ psychologically oppressive means to get what they want. If manipulation is being used as part of an organization's culture, one may need to employ legal means to stop such organizationally approved behavior. If this is not possible or does not work, one should consider leaving such an unhealthy organization.

Questions to Ponder

1. An organizational culture of distrust, anxiety, and competition moves people into cell four, such that their behaviors will reflect the two spectrums. To what degree have you experienced this in an organization? If you have experienced such a culture, consider the behaviors

of the people there that you observed and compare them to those on the two spectrums for cell four.

2. Preston Ni presented the difference between healthy social influence and manipulation. Describe a time when you believe you exercised healthy social influence. As you reflect back on the experience, how did you handle it? Describe a time when others exercised healthy social influence on you. How did it feel?

3. When have you felt manipulated by another? How did you respond? How do you feel about that situation today? Conversely, consider a time when you manipulated someone else. How would you evaluate your actions?

4. At what point would you think the time had come to leave an unhealthy organization?

4. Character and personality issues. A fourth, and very weighty reason why ministry negotiation processes often happen in cell four, concerns the character or personality of the people who rise to leadership positions. In his article "Why Bad Guys Win at Work," Tomas Chamorro-Premuzic explores how people with personality issues often ascend to leadership roles. He explains that personality issues, like narcissism, are more common in the population than we think. Persons can score high on a narcissism profile and yet other people will not be aware of the depth of their disorder, either at work or at home.[22] Let us explore this more specifically in regard to research on leadership.

Personality issues in leaders. Studies have shown that narcissistic types of personality characteristics positively correlate to gaining leadership positions in organizations. Chamorro-Premuzic explains this sad reality of our brokenness and the impact on our organizations.

> An impressive 15-year longitudinal study found that individuals with psychopathic and narcissistic characteristics gravitated toward the top of the organizational hierarchy.... [This] explains why bad guys often win—their success comes at a price, and that price is paid by the organization.... And the more polluted or contaminated the environment—in a political sense—the more these parasitic personalities will thrive.[23]

Another way of looking at these issues is through the lens of what psychologist George Simon calls "character disturbance." Simon suggests that personality disorders and character disturbances lie at different ends of a continuum. On the one hand, a personality disorder is "of such intensity, inflexibility, and intractability that it impairs adaptive functioning."[24] On the other hand, a character disturbance describes persons whose characteristics are linked to their dysfunctional attitudes and thinking patterns. He asserts that their shallow, self-centered relationships, their moral immaturity, and their social irresponsibility "all stem from an underdeveloped conscience and reflect significant deficiencies or disturbances of character."[25]

People with character or personality issues can function and succeed in society without being diagnosed with clinical pathologies. Or, as organizational psychologist Manfred F. R. Kets de Vries says, "The state of mental health of senior executives is much more subtle. They can't be too crazy or they wouldn't have made it to a senior position—but they are nonetheless extremely driven people."[26] This is important for ministry leaders and organizations to understand, for Christians are not exempt from these sobering research findings.

When combined with the broken, sinful condition of humanity, perhaps it is merely a matter of degree to which character disturbances or disorders can be found in everyone—including ourselves. Cultural apologist Francis Schaeffer stated that God's sanctification work in us can lead to substantial healing, but full healing does not come until Jesus returns or calls us home.[27] All of us have pathologies that we will struggle with until we are made faultless in glory. But on this side of eternity, these characteristics can propel people to higher positions in their organizations.[28]

Personality issues in leaders affect the organization. The characteristics that help leaders with personality issues succeed can severely impact the immediate and long-term health of an organization. Kets de Vries explains, "The behavior of a company's chief executive will have a profound effect on an entire organization."[29] And Richard Daft states, "Though ideas that become part of the culture can come from anywhere within the organization, an organization's culture generally begins with a founder or early leader who articulates and implements particular ideas and values as a vision, philosophy, or business strategy."[30] The emotional health and maturity of the leader usually determines the health of the organization. If the leadership tends to operate in cell four, then the culture of the organization will look like cell four.

Psychologist Diane Langberg explores how persons who display character or personality issues in leadership can have a profoundly negative impact. She delineates several kinds of power, including physical power, verbal power, emotional power, knowledge power, skill power, and position power. She continues,

> When these kinds of power reside in one person, it is a phenomenal combination. Think about it. Take a strong physical presence, an articulate voice, emotional sway, and psychological and theological knowledge and put them all together in a room with someone in crisis, whose struggles and pain have rendered them somewhat inarticulate, who is theologically uncertain and whose history carries instances of victimization—you have a potential for the *abuse of power*. Words, knowledge, skill, and position can all be used in concert to move or convince another human being who is vulnerable. Sheep are used to feed egos, give a sense of adequacy, build reputations, and feed sexual appetites.[31]

Responding to personality issues in leaders. Considering the options in cell four, how can leaders with *more power* manage those who work with them and exhibit character or personality disorders? The leader's options range from encouraging the other to take developmental steps toward healing to requiring the person to take a reduced role in ministry or to firing the person from the ministry position. Ministry leaders have the responsibility to shepherd those who work with them toward maturity in Christ, which includes wholeness and psychological health. Open and honest conversation, together with discipleship, coaching, mentoring, or therapy can potentially lead to growth and change in character and personality issues.

When people with character and personality issues resist addressing their problems, or when professionals diagnose that there is little potential for them to change, significant steps may be necessary. Leaders will need to reassign or diminish such people's responsibilities or terminate their employment. However, even in the most difficult of circumstances, these steps must be taken in a spirit of grace, always treating others as we ourselves would want to be treated (Matthew 7:12).[32]

How should believers manage organizational and relational difficulties in cell four when they are in positions of *less power*?[33] We have already looked at Jesus' directives in Matthew 18:15-17 as an important option in cell three, where power is equal but interests conflict.

> If your brother sins against you, go and tell him his fault, between you and him alone. If he listens to you, you have gained your brother. But if he does not listen, take one or two others along with you, that every charge may be established by the evidence of two or three witnesses. If he refuses to listen to them, tell it to the church. And if he refuses to listen even to the church, let him be to you as a Gentile and a tax collector.

Matthew 18 provides principles that govern conflictual relations between Christians. In his commentary on the Gospel of Matthew, R. T. France clarifies the power dynamics involved in this passage, saying that the context is of "two brothers/sisters" who "stand on an equal footing."[34] This comment suggests that the passage does not apply to dealing with someone who exercises greater power in a toxic or abusive manner, especially when employment is involved, since the power to hire and fire is threatening to those employed.

Mary Alice Chrnalogar is an expert in helping people heal from participation in extremist religious groups. She agrees that Matthew 18 does not apply to those with unequal power in the same way as to those with equal power. She makes an important distinction between the first step of individual confrontation found in Matthew 18 and confrontation of leaders as instructed in 1 Timothy 5:19-20. There Paul writes, "Do not admit a charge against an elder [formal church leader] except on the evidence of two or three witnesses. As for those who persist in sin, rebuke them in the presence of all, so that the rest may stand in fear." She argues the first step of confrontation toward those with greater power is at the second level of Matthew 18, which includes two or three witnesses.[35]

Perhaps this is what occurred in Pastor Ray's story. The three board members had been verbally attacking Ray for weeks after their spouses were upset with the choice of a new teacher for the women's Bible study. Because they brought no evidence or witnesses to charge Ray, they were not following Paul's instruction concerning the confrontation of church leaders. In the final board meeting, in front of the whole board another member accused the three of harboring unrepentant sin. In doing this, he could have been following Paul if he had already brought charges and witnesses concerning the three men. Since these men did "persist in sin," the next step toward the health of the church would have been to rebuke them in the presence of the board.

In his research on managing toxic leaders, Kelly Dehnert suggests a variety of responses to unhealthy leaders with more power. These responses are similar to the spectrum of responses we offer to those with less power in cell four. They include confronting, seeking justice from those in higher authority, or leaving the organization.[36] However, he asserts that extreme care must be taken when someone chooses to confront a toxic leader. There is a great amount of literature on how to help people resolve differences. Yet this literature usually assumes "that people are playing fair and that there is not significant dysfunction in one of the individuals or organizations involved."[37] Kets de Vries stresses the challenge of seeking resolution from a person with more power. He says there is "a fine line between a battle worth fighting and a battleground worth fleeing."[38]

It is helpful to remember Daniel's experience with Babylonian king Nebuchadnezzar and his son Belshazzar. Daniel 1–3 clearly shows that Nebuchadnezzar was an authoritarian leader who exhibited extreme character issues. However, God supernaturally confronted Nebuchadnezzar, who was humiliated by living and acting like a brute beast for "seven periods of time" (Daniel 4:25). At the end of this ordeal, Nebuchadnezzar humbled himself before God, and God restored him to his senses and to the leadership of the kingdom. It is possible for people with character disturbances to learn, change, and grow.

Belshazzar, son of Nebuchadnezzar, did not learn from his father's experience. He seems to have resumed an authoritarian and godless leadership style similar to the way his father acted before God's intervention. Though Belshazzar was confronted by God, there is no indication he repented. The result of Belshazzar's refusal to change was his downfall and the destruction of the Babylonian empire (Daniel 5).

Kets de Vries, together with Danny Miller, describes the difficulty of changing a toxic organizational culture. "Some problems are so deep-seated or severe that they would not even be amenable to change. . . . They represent long-standing, deeply ingrained ways of perceiving, interpreting, and behaving on the part of coalitions of very powerful members of the organizations. These patterns are very hard to alter, even when their dysfunctional consequences are obvious."[39] However true this is, by the grace of God and the power of the gospel, such change may be possible when there is repentance and learning.

Questions to Ponder

1. On a piece of paper, list five characteristics of the best boss you've ever had. After doing this, list five characteristics of the worst boss you've ever had. How did issues of character influence these characteristics?

2. Research shows that unhealthy character issues may be positively linked with gaining leadership positions, even in Christian organizations. What steps would you suggest to protect an organization from vesting formal power in such persons? How would you counsel an organization to proceed if such an unhealthy person was already in a leadership role?

3. How do you think the guidelines for relational reconciliation in Matthew 18 apply to conditions in cell four? How would you seek to handle a disagreement with an unhealthy leader who has more power?

Gospel Work in Cell Four

One of the most difficult settings where ethical questions are worked out in cell four is when someone needs to be fired. We close this chapter by sharing the story of how one employee was terminated in a gospel manner that reflects careful consideration of the stakeholders and their interests. It is a story of conflicting interests and unequal power where those with more power exercised it with grace.

Walt is chairman of the board of a family business whose motto is "Perfect Products, Perfect Service, Treat People Right." As Walt explains, "The policy our organization sustains with employees is one of communication, respect, and treating them as I would want to be treated. Our most important resource is our employees. So, we develop committed relationships with accountability."

Walt goes on to share the details of this particularly challenging situation of leading in cell four.

Our greatest challenge has been with substance abuse. We had to terminate one employee who got involved with heroin. We went more than nine yards with him. We gave him job changes and rehabilitation opportunities. He was tested and tested and failed over and over. And the union supported us in finally exercising the "third strike" rule. The union leaders and those of us in management came to the conclusion together to tell the employee, "You don't want to work here, and we don't want you here, so you need to move on to another career. But you still need to go to a rehabilitation program and admit yourself. And you need job training." So, we paid for all that. And he's gotten himself clean. That was tough, but the conclusion was righteous.

Walt was in a position of having more organizational and relational power than his employee. Yet he went out of his way to demonstrate respect and care for this employee and for the union that represented him. It required lots of time and many conversations of bargaining and networking to keep moving the conflict out of cell four. Together, Walt and the union officials extended grace by providing multiple opportunities through rehabilitation and job changes. Finally, when the decision was made to terminate, all invested parties collaborated (cell one!). And even then, grace was extended by paying once more for rehabilitation, as well as providing job training so that the terminated employee might find a new career. People used power to help others flourish. Is it any wonder that most who work for this business are loyal employees?

The way people work out the themes of politics will always reflect their ethical convictions. As Steve Garber recently put it, "When we choose against grace, we choose for an eye-for-an-eye, committing ourselves to the survival of the fittest. The jungle works that way, but that is a world and worldview away from how most of us want to live—how most of us need to live."[40]

Chapter (11)

Tom Moves into a Political Struggle

A Final Case Study

This chapter takes an extended look at how the main concepts of this book can be seen in a single ministry case study. This story is from an early experience of our friend Tom, who has been in ministry now for decades. While it may be impossible to find a single experience that includes every point we've discussed, this one provides plenty of true-life material to work with the foundational ideas of negotiating ministry.

Before we dive into this story, it is important to note that Tom was the only person interviewed about the story. This means we only have his perspective on what happened. So the story reflects his biases. Therefore, in analyzing Tom's experience we will speculate about the circumstances and perspectives of those involved. Speculation happens in the analysis of any situation. However, when we are doing a diagnosis of our own life circumstances, we must name our biases and test our conclusions. We do that by using the insights of others to check our assumptions and analyze our perspective.

Note also that this extensive analysis work of a single story helps us practice the leadership art of "getting off the dance floor and onto the balcony." We do this in order to gain more objectivity and to see new possibilities in the midst of complicated, political circumstances. This dance metaphor from chapter three explains how we gain a clearer view of reality by intentionally stopping to reflect on our context, even if only for a moment. If we do *not* do this, Harvard professors Ronald Heifetz and Marty Linsky warn, we are much more likely "to misperceive the situation and make the wrong diagnosis, leading [us] to misguided decisions."[1] In this chapter we practice the art of gaining a better understanding of negotiating ministry from the balcony.

Tom's Story

After graduating from seminary and serving as an assistant pastor for two years, Tom agreed to explore a church-planting opportunity in Tennessee. While visiting the area, Tom and his wife spent time with a twelve-person plant team who desired to start the new church. He also met with members of the church planting committee of his denomination's regional board. This committee would oversee both the finances provided by the regional board and the planting process until the church became self-sustaining.

During this visit, Tom was repeatedly told of the great need for a church of this type in the region. Committee members told him that another similar denomination had attempted a church plant in the area, but that plant, Valley Church, had folded over a year ago. Members assured him there was no other church in the area of the theological style or nature envisioned for this plant. Tom and his wife agreed to move to Tennessee and lead the new church plant.

As Tom moved into his Tennessee apartment, he spied a blue sign advertising Valley Church, the very church that he was told had folded. He later learned that the initial members of his plant team had come out of an angry split from Valley over a year earlier. His regional board's committee had not searched out the facts. Furthermore, while vetting people for the plant's leadership team, Tom learned that some in his plant team were still embittered toward the people at Valley.

Over the next year, Tom developed a friendship with Pastor Samuel of Valley. Both Tom and Samuel agreed that the broken relationships between members in their congregations were unhealthy and a poor witness to the community. They began to dream about joining their two fledging congregations for a stronger and more visible ministry to the community. They broached the idea of uniting the two churches to their respective church leadership teams. Both leadership teams approved! Next, Tom and Samuel approached their respective denominational regional boards with a reunion plan. Their plan stated that the churches would reunite under Samuel's denomination because of its original jurisdiction. Tom would transfer his ordination to Samuel's denomination and become the associate pastor.

When Tom brought this idea to the church-planting committee of his regional board, members reprimanded him for being irresponsible. They sternly reminded Tom that he was hired to start a new church and that he should cease and desist in his activities with the other denomination. Tom left the meeting feeling misunderstood and angry. He questioned whether the committee members upheld a biblical ethic on reconciliation and the unity of the church. He wondered if their only interest was the growth of their denomination rather than the kingdom of God. He asked himself whether he could continue planting this church under these circumstances.

Identifying the Stakeholders

The first place to start in any analysis is to identify the stakeholders involved in the story. As a reminder, stakeholders are all participants who have something to gain or to lose as a result of the decisions being considered in the negotiation process. Or, put more simply, stakeholders are those with vested interests.

> The first place to start in any analysis is to identify the stakeholders involved in the story. Stakeholders are those with vested interests.

In Tom's story, consider eight key stakeholder groupings (six of those eight are duplicated in Tom and Samuel's churches). Since many people were involved, there were many possibilities for conflicting interests and unequal power dynamics to affect the negotiations which occurred. There were four stakeholder groups in each congregation:

1. Pastor (and family)
2. Church leadership team (or board)
3. Original church plant team
4. Congregants (apart from the original plant team)

Then there were two stakeholder groups in each denomination:

1. Denominational regional committee
2. Church planting committee (a subset of the denominational regional committee)

Finally, there were two stakeholders often not considered in ministry politics:

1. The broader community
2. God

The first set of stakeholders were each congregation's pastors, Tom and Samuel, and their families (spouse and children and others who live in their households). Note that a ministry leader's family members play a key role in ministry deliberations, although they are not the focus in this analysis.[2]

The next set of stakeholders was the church leadership team. For Samuel, whose church was fully organized and self-sustaining, this was his leadership board. A number of these board members had been in Valley at the time of the split. For Tom, whose church was still in the planting stage, this meant a small group of persons designated by Tom in conjunction with his church-planting committee. Only one of Tom's leaders had been involved in the original church split.

The third group of stakeholders was the initial plant team of each church. On the one hand, because Valley had grown, members of the original plant team were now a minority in the church. Most of the people attending Valley knew little about the split. In Tom's plant, about a third of the plant team had come out of the church split with Valley. The rest had been recruited early in the planting process and knew little of the earlier conflict.

The fourth stakeholder unit was the congregants (members and regular attenders) in each church, apart from the plant teams. These people had no knowledge of the original split and had been attracted to their congregations after it had taken place. At the time of this story, Valley averaged around ninety in attendance, while Tom's plant averaged around forty.

Each denomination had a regional committee made up of pastors and representatives from member churches. These formed a fifth stakeholder group. And each of these regional committees had a smaller church-planting committee, the sixth set of key stakeholders. While Valley no longer officially reported to their regional committee, they continued to look to the smaller group informally for insight and perspective. However, in Tom's case, the regional church-planting committee was his "boss." He was hired by this committee, and they provided oversight and funding for his work.

Two other stakeholder groups are worth noting. One was the broader community where both of these churches were located. Since each congregation began with a small number, most in the broader community were unaware of the early infighting that had taken place. However, most likely some people had shared the issues with friends and family who were not involved in either congregation. Because the expressed purpose of each church was to reach this community with the gospel,

> To help us ground our political reflections on biblical principles, God should be considered the ultimate stakeholder, who is invested in every work done in his name.

it was possible that residual feelings of the original members, or negative stories about the split, hindered the reputation and growth of each congregation.

Finally, to help us ground our political reflections on biblical principles, God should be considered the ultimate stakeholder, who is invested in every work done in his name. Revelation 1–3 reveal that Jesus is aware and concerned with the details of what is happening in each of the seven local churches addressed. The apostle John describes Jesus as being "in the midst" of the seven churches (Revelation 1:13, 20).

Analyzing the Power Dynamics

After identifying the main stakeholders, the next step in analyzing the politics of a situation is to observe the power dynamics between the stakeholders.

> After identifying the main stakeholders, the next step in analyzing the politics of a situation is to observe the power dynamics between the stakeholders.

Reviewing key points about power. First, every ministry context has a complicated relational structure in which people are emotionally connected to one another. People influence and are influenced by the interests and power of others. These relationships fall on a spectrum from solely professional to highly trusted friendships.

Second, power is intricately connected to the people work of ministry, so much so that we define power as the capacity to act and to influence, which comes as a result of specific socially structured relationships. This power develops through interpersonal interactions of all varieties. Formal power is given through the roles and responsibilities vested in official positions. Relational power comes primarily through interpersonal trust developed over time. Relational power will usually prove to be more potent and enduring in the end.

Third, ministry leaders must be sensitive to the broad range of relationships they have with others, including staff, board members, people in their ministry, and others in the community. Effective leaders tend to be acutely aware of the health of these relationships and the overall impact the various relationships have on the ministry. Wise ministry leaders consciously work on developing these relationships.

Fourth, people usually do not enter ministry situations thinking about power. And yet managing dynamics of power is a reality of life. Therefore, it is important for anyone, regardless of their position, to gain perspective by becoming a student of the power dynamics in their ministry organization and in other relationships.

> Every ministry context has a complicated relational structure in which people are emotionally connected to one another. People influence and are influenced by the interests and power of the others.

Finally, power is often unequal. Unequal power does not necessarily mean people are in disagreement or conflict with one another. That depends on the interests of the parties and how those interests are negotiated.

Power dynamics in Tom's story. Although Tom already had two years of ministry leadership experience in an established church, he seems naive about power dynamics. This story covers about a year, suggesting that while Tom had the formal power of an ordained pastor, the relationships he had with most of the stakeholders were neither long-standing nor well-developed. For example, members of his regional organization and regional church-planting committee (his "boss") lived all over the state. So his contact with these members, while cordial, was minimal.

While Tom attended his denomination's theological graduate school, he had not grown up in that denomination. Rather, he had come to faith through a parachurch student ministry and had few relational roots in the denomination itself.

Therefore, while Tom carried some formal power in his congregation because he was the ordained pastor, this formal power did not extend to the regional organization of his denomination. And his relational power with all parties—his initial plant team, the leadership team, his congregants, as well as in his denomination—was not well-established.

Furthermore, while Tom's church leadership and plant team members had developed an initial level of friendship and trust, they had been meeting together for only a year before Tom arrived. Some of the plant team were still reacting to the split from Valley Church. None of them, including new people visiting the church, had deep relational bonds. While everyone seemed interested in seeing a healthy new church develop, deep commitments had yet to be formed.

In stark contrast to Tom, all the members of the denomination's regional organization, including those on the church-planting committee, had been in the denomination for their entire careers. Most had served in that regional organization for five years or more. However, they were not experienced in church planting. Tom's plant was the first attempt in over ten years to start a new church in their region. They were highly invested in seeing this plant work. They had promoted this young pastor and his fledgling congregation in their churches. Each one supported the plant in their missions giving, and many had Tom visit their congregation during his first year on the job.

During his first year pastoring the church plant, Tom had developed a fairly close friendship with Samuel, the pastor of Valley. They had similar backgrounds in student ministries. They both had been married for less than five years and had young children. Both were pastoring new congregations and were learning on the job, with similar challenges. Neither received much mentoring or emotional support from their denominational organizations. So they viewed each other as trusted peers and encouraged each other in their shared ministries.

Tom did not have any relationship with Valley congregants, with the members of Samuel's denomination, or with his church-planting committee. However, Tom did respect Samuel's denomination and had once been a member in one of their churches in another state. He believed that both denominations held a similar theological and missional vision.

To summarize the power dynamics in this case story, Tom had a fair amount of capacity to act in his local congregation, though this was regulated by the congregational leadership team as well as by the church-planting committee. At the same time, his church-planting committee, as well as his regional organization, held greater organizational power. The denominational committee members were all relationally bonded by a shared commitment to their denomination and many years of service in the region. Meanwhile, Tom and Samuel developed a level of trust in their friendship that gave each a freedom to share candidly about their work and family life.

Probable Interests of Key Stakeholders

Previous chapters discussed how people's interests can be difficult to identify. These interests were compared to the branches and roots of a large oak tree. Interests develop from many sources. They are often hidden, even from the individual holding them, and can be contradictory. People rarely recognize all the interests at play in any given situation. Identifying interests requires looking beyond the immediate surface issues and seeking to name the deeper convictions supporting the more easily observable interests.

> Interests develop from many sources. They are often hidden, even from the individual holding them, and can be contradictory.

Remember that interests develop from one's personal uniqueness, organizational culture, or societal cultural concerns. *Personal interests* are individually held convictions and commitments about how life should work or what should be possible. *Organizationally influenced interests* involve the history, orientations, and values of an institution or group. *Societal cultural interests* develop from relational norms rooted in a broader cultural setting, such as a community or city.

> Identifying interests requires looking beyond the immediate surface issues and seeking to name the deeper convictions supporting the more easily observable interests.

Tom's story has many sets of stakeholders, with too many possible interests to focus on here. Instead, consider the interests of the following primary stakeholders listed. Think of how an analysis of the interests informs a broader perspective of the political process in this story.

Interests of Tom's denominational committees. The members of Tom's denomination had significant interest in growing a successful church plant. The regional pastors had endorsed Tom in front of their congregations. So, these leaders had a *personal interest*, having put their own reputations on the line to help Tom and this new church develop. They also had significant *organizationally influenced interests* in the church plant. First, because their churches had financially supported the work, there was an above-ground interest for their investment to pay off with a new congregation. In addition, since their denomination's regional outreach had become stagnant, they had below-ground interests for this new plant to bring new energy into the churches of their region. And, finally, Tom's denomination had a strong culture of valuing a family-like atmosphere and loyalty, which promoted an interest in family (denominational) unity, where success and failure were shared by all involved.

Interests of Samuel's denominational committees. Similarly, the leaders in Samuel's denomination also had a strong *organizational interest* to see a healthy congregation flourish in that region. It turns out the earlier split at Valley Church concerned a former pastor the church-planting committee had deemed ineffective. When this initial pastor was relocated in the midst of the church-planting work, those unhappy with the decision left the church to form the nucleus of Tom's original church-plant team. This nucleus simply assumed the leaders in Samuel's denomination had abandoned the region. But the opposite was true. The denomination's committees poured in more financial resources and brought in Samuel to revitalize Valley. Samuel's denomination exhibited characteristics somewhere between a creative and competitive culture. These committee members tended to be more aggressive, looking to leverage resources for growth, and they expected results.

Tom's interests. There were at least four interests that particularly motivated Tom. First, from an *organizational* perspective, he was angry to learn of his denomination's failure to perform due diligence regarding the history of the church plant. He was unhappily surprised to discover there was a growing congregation of a similar denomination literally across the street from his apartment. Second, Tom believed the broken relationships in both churches were a discredit to the gospel. How could they present the good news to the community while some members remained embittered toward one another? And how could God bless their ministries while such brokenness persisted?

Third, Tom's desire was not just to plant another church. He wanted to influence the entire region. As he and Samuel grew in friendship, they dreamed together of how much more they could accomplish as one larger church than as two smaller congregations. Finally, Tom's personal and more hidden interest focused more on the expansion of God's kingdom than the growth of his denomination. He did not care which denomination benefited as long as the gospel affected the lives of people. With this attitude, he was not inline with the organizational culture and interests of his denomination. Frankly, while Tom and Samuel's denominations held similar theological convictions, Tom's organizational interests were more similar to those of Samuel's denomination's culture than to his own.

During the time frame of the story Tom seemed rather clueless about the power dynamics involved in various relationships. His interests focused his attention on relational reconciliation in the two churches and gospel impact in the community. He seemed to assume the members of his church-planting committee would agree with his analysis and plan for church union.

Both church leadership teams' interests. It is intriguing that while there were still participants of the Valley Church split on both Tom and Samuel's leadership teams, both teams approved of the reunion plan. This was due in large part to how Tom and Samuel had both addressed the split with their teams. They spoke of Christ's mandate for relational reconciliation and unity in the gospel. While the situation did not require organizational union, each pastor felt the advantages of coming together far outweighed those of having two similar congregations. The members of both teams unanimously agreed to take steps toward relational unity, while Tom and Samuel approached their respective boards.

God's interests. Scripture identifies many of God's concerns and values. The calls for unity found in the New Testament encourage and command us to pursue personal and relational unity. When ministry organizations share a similar vision and mission, joining together may be a way to utilize resources more effectively. And the watching world can see shared love and harmony. However, as Francis Schaeffer wrote, there are times when organizational unity is not a wise or realistic goal. Still, God calls Christians to love one another, even when they cannot work together. Indeed, the world will know we are Jesus' disciples by the love we visibly demonstrate toward one another (John 13:34-35; 17:21).[3]

Similarly, God calls all Christians to work out their relational challenges in a manner that reflects the gospel. This does not happen by simply walking away from relationships. Instead, Christians need to express humility toward one another, to confess to one another, and to walk in fellowship with one another by "walking in the light" (1 Peter 5:5; James 5:16; 1 John 1:7). As seen in chapter ten, this should happen by carefully addressing and even rebuking one another in love, followed by repentance and forgiveness (Matthew 18:15-35; Luke 17:3-6).

However, these passages on seeking love and unity seem to assume equal power dynamics between the people in conflict. Perhaps, as New Testament scholar R. T. France suggests, these Bible verses do not apply as easily to people dealing with unequal power dynamics, especially in a toxic or abusive context.[4] In those situations, it seems Scripture would commend a conversation involving two, three, or more persons (Matthew 18:16-17; 1 Timothy 5:19-20).[5] Only when this is not effective should one walk away from the relationship.[6]

Due to the emphases in Scripture, perhaps God's interests in Tom's story focused more on the relational than the organizational concerns. God is as concerned with the manner in which we pursue work and change, and how we treat each other, as he is with what we get accomplished. Jesus will build his church, regardless of the sins and weaknesses of his followers.

Interests Represented During Negotiation

In review, negotiation involves four unique actions. People promote their interests *between* each other, by advocating for their *own specific interests*, with the *power available to them*. And their actions during and after the process *affect the ongoing interests and the power* of those involved. As a result, the capacities of participants to function in the ministry will change. So, with these four principles in mind, consider the following questions for Tom's case story:

1. Who was negotiating with whom?

2. What interests and power did stakeholders bring to the table (that is, in what cells were they negotiating)?

3. And how did these negotiations change Tom's ongoing interests and capacities to work in ministry leadership?

Who was negotiating with whom? Some negotiations had already taken place prior to Tom's meeting with his church-planting committee. Both Tom and Samuel had been regularly consulting with each other, their spouses, and their respective leadership teams. All unanimously agreed to take steps toward relational unity and approved initiating merger conversations with the church-planting committees. Samuel met with his denominational church-planting committee, and they endorsed the idea. After all, they had everything to gain through the merger, since the joined congregation would remain in Samuel's denomination with Samuel as senior pastor.

These negotiations, which occurred before Tom met with his oversight committee, took place in either cell one, where interests were shared and power was equal, or cell two, where interests were shared and power was unequal. The invested parties were collaborating and networking. Note how intriguing it is that Tom's church-leadership team also affirmed steps toward both relational and organizational unity. Based on such a change by committee members who were involved in the church split, Tom might have entered the conversation with his denominational church-planting committee with a hope that everything would go smoothly.

What interests and power did stakeholders bring to the table? Here we focus on the negotiations between Tom and his denominational committees. Tom's actions show that he did not understand the differences in power between himself and the committee members who represented his denomination's regional churches. They were all older than Tom, and each had served as pastors or board members in an established church in the region for many years. For over a year Tom's experience with the committees had been one of cordiality and support. He may have naively assumed that their unity of faith and theology, together with their common organizational status as ordained ministry leaders, meant they also had the same interests and power.

However, there was quite a difference between Tom's interests and those of his church denominational committees. Table 11.1 compares the two sets of interests, listing some previously noted together with other possible variances.

Prior to their meeting, Tom did nothing to prepare his church-planting committee for the merger proposal he brought to the table. He felt that he should make such a proposal in person, where they could discuss what he had learned about the church split, how he and Samuel had begun steps toward relational reconciliation, and how both felt a merger would best accomplish kingdom objectives in their region.

In making this strategic decision about the meeting, Tom probably assumed he would be negotiating either in cell one or two, where interests were shared and power was distributed equally or at least was focused on the same objectives. He would soon learn that his naively hopeful assumptions were wrong.

Table 11.1. Comparing Tom's and his denominational committee's interests

Tom's Interests	Denominational Committee's Interest
Tom was unhappy that the committee failed to investigate church plant team history.	The committee was unaware of the history.
Tom felt broken relationships discredited the gospel and prevented effective witness.	The committee understood relational reconciliation was appropriate but did not believe a merger was required.
Tom shared a vision with Samuel to affect their entire region.	The denomination had not planted a new church in over ten years. Their vision was focused on one new church.
A larger church might be more effective to accomplish the broader vision.	All of the denomination's churches in the region were fairly small and one new church was the goal.
Tom placed priority on expanding God's kingdom. He had no priority of denominational loyalty.	Loyalty to denominational family was a high value.
Tom was entrepreneurial and change oriented, similar to Samuel's denomination.	While desiring growth, there was a risk aversion that approached change cautiously. They also may have been intimidated by the aggressive nature of Samuel's denomination.
Tom did not fully appreciate the efforts his denomination's pastors had made for him.	The pastors put their reputations on the line to support Tom and the new church plant.
Tom did not grasp the level of significance that the region's churches invested financially in him.	The regional churches strongly promoted the church plant and invested financially as a key missions commitment.
Tom did not appreciate the emotional investment the regional pastors and churches had in the plant.	The regional pastors and churches deeply desired their risk of a new church plant to be successful.

As far as the committee members knew, the agenda for the meeting was hearing Tom's report on how the church plant was progressing. After providing basic information about worship attendance and church activities,

Tom shared what he had learned about the history of his plant team. This was news to the committee, and its members were clearly unhappy to learn that their new plant had developed through a church split from a similar denomination. They were also surprised to learn that the other denomination still had a young but growing church in the area. But they were pleased when Tom reported how steps had been taken to initiate relational reconciliation between the churches.

However, the committee was not prepared to hear what Tom said next. Assuming everyone in the room held the same interests, Tom launched into a full presentation on the reunion plan under the jurisdiction of Samuel's denomination. He wanted to explain how such a reunion could demonstrate the unity of the gospel, how shared resources could ignite church growth, and how, in turn, more churches could be planted around the region. He never got beyond the proposal for a merger under Samuel's denomination.

Quickly the conversation shifted to cell four—conflicting interests and unequal power. Tom was a young man, newly ordained, who had been serving with them for barely a year. In the committee members' view, Tom now wanted to jump ship and give their work over to another denomination. Tom discovered that his interests conflicted with the committee and that he had little organizational or relational power to promote his interests in the church merger.

In retrospect, looking at the varied interests represented in table 11.1, it is easy to see how this negotiation quickly devolved into cell four, where emotions run hot and trust is easily broken. Imagine what it would have taken for the committee members to assume a collaborative stance rather than one of command. Consider how naive Tom was to expect the committee members to see the opportunity his way, with a calm and unbiased response to his proposal.

Acts 5 describes a much more heated confrontation than the one Tom faced. The apostles were regularly accomplishing signs and wonders among the people of Jerusalem. As a result, multitudes of men and women were becoming Christians. Responding in jealousy, the high priest and his party arrested the apostles. But an angel of the Lord released them from prison, and they returned to minister in the temple. After rearresting the apostles, the Jewish leaders were enraged and wanted to kill them. But Gamaliel interceded and had the apostles put outside. He spoke calmly to the angry Jewish leaders, reasoning why such action was inappropriate. So the leaders took his advice and let the apostles go, albeit with a beating and warnings to stop proclaiming the good news of Jesus (Acts 5:17-42).

Unfortunately for Tom, there was no Gamaliel in his committee meeting. At first, one member wryly suggested that a merger could happen under *their* supervision. But then the committee united in the *command* mode of cell four, reprimanding Tom for taking initiative outside of his authority. He was firmly told that he was hired to start the new church and he should cease and desist in his activities with the other denomination. If he continued to seek this church merger, he would be fired and another pastor would be brought to the church plant.

How did these negotiations affect Tom's ongoing interests and capacities to work in ministry leadership? Tom intuitively understood he was now in cell four with little power to promote his interests. His response in the committee meeting was to defer to their authority. But he also requested a week to consider their directives and review the situation, which they granted. Still in shock over Tom's news and proposal, the members of the committee also needed time to cool off and to evaluate next actions.

Tom left the meeting feeling misunderstood and angry. He questioned whether the committee members upheld a biblical ethic on reconciliation and the unity of the church. He wondered if their only interest was the growth of their denomination rather than the kingdom of God. He asked himself whether he could continue planting this church under those circumstances.

Similarly, members of Tom's denominational committee must have left the meeting with serious questions about trusting Tom and about his ability to continue the church plant. Tom was a young man with high ideals and good intentions. However, he neither understood nor appreciated the priorities and allegiances of the committee members. Assuming shared interests, and perhaps shared power, he had boldly introduced an innovative plan that cut across all sorts of interests held by the committee members.

Tom had found, in Samuel, a person who dreamed the same ministry dreams he did. And Samuel was easily accessible, more empathetic, and more encouraging than Tom's committee members. Samuel had become a close fellow worker Tom could talk with about the challenges of church planting and the hopes of success. It is not surprising that Tom and Samuel had planned to unite the two fledging congregations.

Key mistakes made in the negotiation process. Due to the denominational power structure, Tom should have first brought his plan to his "boss," the church-planting committee. Tom could have approached the committee with concerns about the original plant team. He also could have tactfully shared his feelings about the committee's failure to understand the history of the situation prior to starting the plant. Tom had failed to learn what mattered most to the committee members. When we do not take account of the interests of those with more power, we risk having our work diminished, dismissed, or even terminated.[7]

At the same time, the committee members failed to respond in a godly manner in order to move the negotiation out of cell four. They could have demonstrated more humility over their failure to learn about the previous church split. They could have acknowledged their lack of research and how that error affected Tom and his ministry. Perhaps they could have empathized with Tom's disappointment over the way people founded the work or the difficulties he faced in planting a church. They could have shown curiosity about Tom's enthusiastic and strategic interest to see gospel growth through the merger of the congregations. Amy Edmondson, a professor at Harvard Business School, summarizes the challenges well.

> The processes and incentives necessary to identify and analyze failure are lacking in most organizations. Add the human desire to avoid the unpleasantness and loss of confidence associated with acknowledging failure, and it's easy to understand why so few organizations have made the shift from a culture of blame to a culture in which the rewards of learning from failure can be fully realized.[8]

Good leadership changes the impact on Tom. In the week following the painful meeting, a calm Gamaliel-like ministry leader with more power intervened. This happened because the chairperson of the regional committee had called the national church-planting director to share the committee's disappointment with Tom. The director assured the chairperson that he would quickly look into the matter. As it turned out, the director knew Tom well.

The director called Tom the next day and asked Tom what had taken place. The director simply listened. With some initial reticence, Tom poured out his heart. He shared about the church split, about the need to demonstrate reconciliation and the unity of the gospel, and about the idea of combining resources with Valley Church. He went on to talk about how lonely he felt and how Samuel shared the same church-planting challenges. And he boldly questioned whether the purpose of the church plant was to extend the kingdom or just grow the denomination.

The director continued to listen, occasionally asking a question for clarification. Then he did something Tom never expected. He apologized. He said that as the director, he had failed to learn the facts or to ask the committee to explore the history thoroughly. He said he understood the loneliness of church planting and had failed to provide Tom with adequate support. And the director said he fully understood why Tom would consider leaving.

Then the director asked Tom, "Knowing what you now know, how do you think things might have gone differently?" They spent time evaluating what had taken place, what assumptions Tom had developed, what decisions he had made, and what happened as a result. Tom identified and acknowledged many of his mistakes.

After talking through these matters, the director shared with Tom that the regional committee was committed to moving forward with the plant. He asked Tom to pray and to consider staying, even with all the mistakes and problems that had happened. He also affirmed Tom, saying the work had made good progress and there were high expectations that the church would become established and thrive. The director ended by sharing something that floored Tom. He said, "Tom, I know you have been disappointed by what has happened. I am as well. But I also know your character and love for the Lord. I want you to stay in Tennessee. But if you decide to leave, I will do everything I can to help you find another ministry opportunity."

A happy ending as a result of moving negotiations out of cell four. After their week of reflection, Tom and his wife came to a conclusion. If the church-planting committee agreed, they would continue the church-planting work, staying with the people they had grown to love. After sharing this with the national director, Tom called the planting-committee chairperson. Tom apologized for his failure to discuss his concerns and ideas with the committee prior to talking with his church leadership team. He shared that he had also gone to the leadership team to acknowledge this blunder. He had asked whether the leadership team would continue to work with him and the denomination. They had agreed to do so. Finally, the chairperson responded, telling Tom how sorry he was that the committee had failed to do their homework or to provide the emotional support he needed. They agreed to continue their partnership.

Tom learned and grew from the experience. He and Samuel remained friends, mutually supporting each other and working together for relational reconciliation between members of their churches. Tom and his wife moved to an apartment further from Samuel's congregation, and each pastor focused on reaching a different part of the community. Tom served a number of other congregations and continues in ministry to this day. The church he planted in Tennessee still has a vital ministry.

An Ethical Review of Tom's Story

To do an ethical review of Tom's story, consider the following questions concerning the negotiation process of stakeholder interests. What were the primary risks involved? How were key interests represented at the planning table? Who would benefit from this planning? Who should benefit from this planning?

> To do an ethical review of a planning table event, consider these important questions: What were the primary risks involved? How were key interests represented at the planning table? Who would benefit from this planning? Who should benefit from this planning?

The primary risks. All of the primary stakeholders had interests at risk. Predominant stakeholders taking the most direct risks were Pastors Tom and Samuel (and their families) as well as Tom's church-planting committee and the regional committees. Tom could have lost his job and occupational status. Tom's church-planting committee could have lost their new church plant. Members of Tom's regional organization might have lost face since they had personally promoted the plant and encouraged investment in it. However, Samuel (and his team and regional committee) might have benefited if the merger had gone through. And of course God's interests for the visible unity of his church and for healthy, sustainable relationships were also at stake.

Key interests represented at the planning table. The conversation in Tom's committee meeting quickly moved from cell two (where there was a difference in power but each assumed they shared the other's interests) to cell four (where interests conflicted and the committee held more power than Tom). Using cell-four spectrum terms, the committee reacted to Tom with a response of *command*. Tom, in turn, *deferred* to the committee but considered *counteracting* by resigning. The national director of church planting mediated the situation, humbly taking a stance of *collaboration*. This moved the negotiation into cell three, where Tom had more power to consider alternatives through gracious *bargaining*. By eventually owning their own failures, both Tom and the committee (through the chairperson) were able to move back into cell two and continue *networking* together to establish the church plant.

Planning benefits. At first, Tom's church-planting committee was determined to benefit regardless of Tom's decision. When they shifted into *command* mode, they disregarded all other interests. Fortunately, when the national director interceded, he encourage members to bring almost all other interests back to the planning table. Only Tom and Samuel's plans for a merger were no longer considered.

While the interests of both church-planting committees and denominations were important, so were the interests of the people forming each local congregation. And Tom's concern over the formation of his original church-plant team also needed to be addressed. The strategic wisdom of having two theologically similar churches so close together also needed to be reviewed.

Perhaps least considered but most important were the interests of God in this story. The apostle Paul's commented on church-member conflicts to the Philippians: "They all seek their own interests, not those of Jesus Christ" (Philippians 2:21). When all of the varied interests in this story are reviewed, it is worth pondering how many were motivated by personal and organizational interests over those of Christ. It is far too easy for all of us to place our own interests above those of Christ during intense negotiations at the planning table.

The gentleness and humility of the national director created an atmosphere of understanding and repentance for all involved. His actions moved the negotiation from cell four back to cell two, where the stakeholders could work together with mutual respect. But such a happy outcome is not often the case.

Concluding Thoughts

People usually enter ministry because they want to participate in God's work of helping people come into a relationship with Jesus and grow in their faith. However, far too often, as in many of the stories in this book, people in ministry assume they will be working in cells one and two, only to discover they are laboring in cell three and struggling in cell four, with less power and conflicting interests than others at the table. Ministry leaders need to learn that working with people requires the diagnosis of interests, an understanding of power dynamics, and the ability to select negotiation options that will advance God's kingdom, all while staying connected to God's interests throughout the process.

This book provides ways to learn the politics of ministry by naming, illustrating, and analyzing true ministry case stories. These descriptions and tools can help us identify and understand our own experiences of past, present, and future ministry work with others. Using these terms and tools can bring much clarity to our ministry leadership and help equip God's people to work together more fruitfully for God's kingdom.

> For too often, people in ministry assume they will be working in cells one and two, only to discover they are laboring in cell three and struggling in cell four, with less power and conflicting interests than others at the table.

Applying the contents of these chapters is not easy. It is simpler to read and to discuss the elements of the politics of ministry than to practice them. Even people who have a significant understanding of interests, power, and negotiation can find themselves caught up on the dance floor and unable to gain perspective on what is happening to themselves and others in the midst of the action. Often, it is only in retrospect, in reflection-on-action, that we gain understanding of the interests and power dynamics of the situation.

Ministry takes place in a broken world with and through broken people. But, by God's grace, Jesus decided to use broken people for his eternal purposes and glory in redeeming his creation. May our understanding of the politics of ministry allow us to speak the truth in love and to further our growth in every way into Christ, while being kind to one another, tenderhearted, forgiving each other, as God in Christ has forgiven us (Ephesians 4:15, 32).

Postscript

How People Learn the Politics of Ministry

How do ministry leaders learn the politics of ministry? Do they learn it in a classroom? Do they read about it in a book like this one? Or are there other ways to learn and grow in these skills?[1]

Over many years we have had the privilege of holding extended conversations with ministry veterans. A number of their stories are in this book. One topic we have listened for in these conversations was the way they learned about power, interests, and negotiation in their work.

It is clear that they valued the formal education they received as students, be it in a Bible college, Christian university, or a theological seminary. They considered these years of pre-professional academic training as an investment in their ministry.

But the fact is, when ministry leaders review their formal education, they often think it was limited in helping them understand what they actually experience in leading ministry work. There is a constant refrain that when they entered vocational ministry, they were naive about what they might face while working with people.

For example, while the pastor of a mid-sized church in the Midwest deeply appreciated his formal seminary training, he said he learned everything about being a pastor from mentors in his congregation. And although he graduated with honors and received the highest award for preaching in his class, he confessed that when he began his ministry, "I did not know what I was doing. All I had was head knowledge." Another pastor of a mid-size Southern church agreed, saying, "I was prepared academically, but in terms of people skills and church dynamics, no. It was a baptism of fire for me."

How People Learn the Politics of Ministry

When these leaders speak of their education, they tend to overlook their own professional experience of day-to-day ministry practice. Most are unaware of the profound knowledge they gain on the job.[2] But our conversations with them have identified at least four ways they have learned in the course of daily ministry. Two of these we have already discussed in this book: reflection-in-action and reflection-on-action. The other two categories are learning from mentors and models and learning from negative experiences.

Reflection-in-Action and on-Action

We discussed these two reflection skills earlier in this book. Unfortunately, few ministry leaders consciously take time to stop and reflect on what they are doing or just did. For all of us, the practice of reflection could greatly enhance our learning in ministry leadership. MIT professor Donald Schön's comments about managers applies to ministry leaders as well:

> Managers do reflect-in-action, but they seldom *reflect on* their reflection-in-action. Hence this crucially important dimension of their art tends to remain private and inaccessible to others. Moreover, because awareness of one's intuitive thinking usually grows out of practice in articulating it to others, managers often have little access to their own reflection-in-action.[3]

As Schön suggests, there is a great need among leaders to make time for such reflection. Ministry leaders grow in their knowledge over time and with reflective time. Therefore congregants and board members would do well to give them time and space to develop, rather than expect ministry leaders to know all they need to know as a result of their formal education or ordination.

Leaders from all types of ministry contexts should consider both planned and spontaneous opportunities for reflection. One encouraging recognition of this need for reflection time is a movement in some evangelical denominations to promote pastoral sabbaticals. Encouragement to take sabbaticals has been a long-standing practice in mainline denominations such as the United Church of Christ, the Lutheran Church—Missouri Synod, the Presbyterian Church (USA), the Reformed Church of America, and the United Methodist Church. And for many years the Lilly Endowment has provided pastoral renewal grants for church leaders to take time off to pursue learning and growth.

At the same time, more consideration needs to be given to ways ministry leaders practice Sabbath or take a day off. For example, should pastors consider their busiest day of the week as their Sabbath? Are leaders faithfully taking time each week to disengage from their normal activities and to rest? And is reflection a structured part of these days?

Ministry leaders need to schedule regular times for retreat and reflection. While this occasionally happens on staff retreats, most of these retreats are focused on future planning. As important as planning is, taking time to reflect on past activities and interactions can provide rich lessons for future ministry and greatly enhance a later planning session.

Mentors and Models

A *mentor* is a wise and trusted person who acts as a guide for one's career journey.[4] In contrast, a *model* is an individual, ministry, or church that serves as an example for imitation or comparison. Mentors and models had an important place in the learning of the ministry leaders we have interviewed. This was evident in a story shared by a pastor, where older church-board members served as mentors in helping him learn how to do ministry. He explained, "The grasp they had of what it meant to lead people was just something that was overwhelming to me. I would say the majority of what I've learned about being in the ministry has come from that experience of working with those board members."

When another pastor was trying to make sense of his trauma after being fired from his first pastorate, he called older, experienced pastors for insight and advice. When he left that church, he went "straight into working very closely with one of the most effective leaders in the American church today." That individual had an indelible influence on this pastor. "I took everything I could from that leader, and by watching him I contrasted what he did with the mistakes I had made in my previous church."

Another ministry leader experienced a unique model of ministry when she visited a fruitful church in a different part of the country. "That weekend visit blew me away. It was just amazing. Overwhelming. I realized, I want to be part of a ministry that is able to take people from coming to faith, to growing, and then to have all of their relationships affected. That church, it almost ruined me."

A number of church models also influenced this minority pastor, who explained:

> While attending [my first seminary], I went to a black, inner-city church. And while I was at [my second seminary], I'd moved from going to an inner-city black church to a very upper-class white church. My wife and I were probably the only black people in the whole place. And it was a huge church. At the same time, I was working in an inner-city ministry. This whole time it was kind of building in me a very cross-cultural, crazy kind of mixed-up involvement in all kinds of stuff from the poorest of the poor to the most wealthy, from folks that were white and black. I mean just the whole experience really shaped the way I think about people in ministry.

Ministries that can serve as positive models of fruitfulness have a vital role in the political education of leaders. Professional education researcher Barbara Daley points out that the learning process involves looking at past experiences and new experiences, and reflecting on these for the purpose of making meaning of these events.[5] Exposure to model ministries moves developing leaders through a process of thinking about the information and comparing and contrasting new experiences with their existing perspectives.

It is highly valuable for fruitful churches and organizations to share what they have learned through years of ministry. More time for this sharing of best practices would serve the body of Christ well. However, in doing so, there is always the trap of assuming that ministry solutions are found in the reproduction of programs. This quick-fix default disregards unique contextual issues and fails to address the specific needs facing local ministries. At the same time, rich lessons in ministry practice gained from model ministries could promote healthy evaluation and enlightened political planning for any leader. The already-mentioned ministry leader provided an example of healthy modeling when she added, "That church raised the bar to what we should be. I wasn't trying to duplicate them, but it was the way in which they expected God to see something happen."

Few of the people we talked with were consciously involved in mentoring others. This is a great loss to the work of God's kingdom. All of the mentoring that took place among the leaders we interviewed came as a byproduct of work commitments. For example, the first pastor mentioned earlier was mentored by board members he was fortunate enough to inherit when he became pastor of their church. The second viewed the senior pastor he worked with as a mentor, but this was not a reciprocal understanding. And while the third ministry leader described the pastor she first worked with as a mentor, this relationship grew as a result of being called to work together. Again, it was fortunate that such a rapport developed. But, unfortunately, it was not planned.

The health and growth of the church needs seasoned ministry leaders to plan purposefully to pass on to younger leaders their political knowledge of how to work with people in the midst of negotiating power and interests. Consciously structured mentoring relationships should be established and nurtured. Seasoned ministry leaders need to explore models for mentoring in order to pass on the explicit political knowledge gained through years of experience. This would promote informed practice over a lifetime of ministry. There is much work for us all to do toward this ongoing professional and continuing education of our ministry leaders.

Learning from Negative Experiences

Every one of the conversations we had with ministry leaders included stories of learning through pain and disillusionment—what we call hardships. These stories involved personal rejection, physical trauma, false accusations, and even church splits. For many, over time a positive and growth-producing outcome was the result. But a number of ministry leaders carried significant scars that produced defensiveness and a level of cynicism about the ministry and the people they worked with. The mantra, expressed one way or another by almost everyone, was, "I learned the hard way."

One pastor experienced weeks of pain after some of his board members disagreed with the extent of his newly instituted crosscultural worship service.

> I was a defeated man. I went home, stood in front of my refrigerator in my kitchen, and broke down crying. I was messed up. And for two weeks, I thought of quitting. I started to shut down. Then three board members came to me and said, "We are behind you 100 percent." When the fourth one returned from a business trip, he'd moved to *wanting* a crosscultural church. Now I have a board that is committed. And something in that crisis period did this.

Learning through hardships is heightened by the fact that most people are idealistic when they enter into ministry. We heard this in Brian's story when he shared that his experience of the senior pastor being asked to resign "was sort of a wake-up call. I had never personally experienced any negative stuff in church. My assumption was rather naive. That church life was more pleasant, more idyllic, that people more or less loved each other, after a fashion anyway . . . It made me less trusting. It scared me to death."

Another pastor also affirmed this initial idealism about the ministry. He said, "I was naive. Here I came into this Christian environment and I thought, *I can trust all these people.* Now, I'm still very trusting, but when I don't get that trust in return, I'll say to myself, *They're going to get me. They're going to burn me. It's just a matter of time.*"

How can we respond to hardships more fruitfully?[6] Here are two suggestions. First, we can view our hardships through the lens of Scripture. In Romans 15:4 Paul says, "For whatever was written in former days was written for our instruction, that through endurance and through the encouragement of the Scriptures we might have hope." God designs our hardships to shape our character and strengthen our faith. This is seen in Paul's experience of a thorn in the flesh, which God used to keep him humble and to strengthen Paul in Christ's power and grace. Similar examples are found throughout the pages of the Old and New Testament.

A second way to respond is to do an audit of past and current experiences. Pondering and praying about these lessons can teach us how God is forming our character and faith. Journaling is a helpful method to do this, recording thoughts and reflections on difficult experiences, and remembering how God was faithful while we went through them. This kind of reflective introspection can be difficult. We need safety and support to learn well. Talking with friends, sharing with a mentor, and meeting with a professional counselor can provide the needed encouragement and insight to help us better understand our experiences and the implications of our experiences in our lives.

In our previous coauthored book *Resilient Ministry*, we refer a number of times to the work of Russ Moxley, an ordained Methodist pastor and former Senior Fellow at the Center for Creative Leadership. He states that hardships—coupled with support and reflection—are the most important method of leadership development.[7]

The first ministry experiences ministry leaders have are critical in forming their perspective and attitudes. A majority of the life-shaping stories we heard came from circumstances encountered early in their professional experiences. The research literature on the pastorate confirms this finding. E. W. Mills and J. P. Koval discovered that nearly half of all the highest stress periods of pastors were in the first five years of ministry, and half of those periods were in years one to three.[8] And pastoral leadership researcher Roy Oswald cited the first five years as critical experiences for setting patterns for future ministry leadership.[9]

Born a slave, Josiah Henson became a lay preacher and abolitionist leader. In 1851 he traveled to London, where he continued his fight against slavery. After one lecture, the Archbishop of Canterbury asked Henson where he had attended university. The former slave simply replied, "Sir, I attended the university of adversity." God doesn't waste pain. He uses difficulties as a course of graduate study for our leadership and character development toward Christ. Hardships, and even great adversity, are part of our continuing education in learning the politics of ministry.

Learning Happens over Time

Learning in ministry is cumulative. We mature over time through different levels of proficiency. The friends and research participants who shared their stories for this book generally entered vocational ministry with a good bit of what might be called "book learning," but very little understanding of the politics of ministry. Pastor Brian said that he was equipped academically but ill-prepared for the people skills and relational dynamics he would face in the church. Another pastor also described being a beginner in ministry politics. In his first church, he selected people for board membership who turned on him immediately after they joined the board. When asked why, he stated, "I was not experienced enough to realize where they were coming from." And another ministry leader explained, when he shared his difficulties in a parachurch organization, "I was young. I was just out of seminary. I just didn't know anything about how things worked."

Although most of the people who participated in the research for this book were naive about how to get things done early in their ministries, today their years of experience help them understand ministry politics. When asked how he would use what he learned at his first church to teach young church planters, one pastor shared,

Well, it's hard for me to just look at that one experience, because there are more lenses I am looking through today. There is the lens of that first experience. And then there is the lens of the experience of working with a great pastoral leader while on the staff of his church. And finally there is the lens of things going well in this church now for six years.

Each new stage of ministry requires new learning. Brian is now serving in his fifth pastorate and has been in the ministry for twenty-three years. He explained that every new ministry context creates a different learning experience. "You never know the full story (about a particular ministry) until you're swimming in the pond."

The wisdom of the oldest person we spoke with puts this developmental nature of learning into perspective. He shared that it takes time and patience to grow and learn. This is hard when young men and women receive a degree and believe they are ready to fulfill their dreams. When asked what he would say to a group of graduates going into vocational ministry, this retired pastor shared,

> I think you need to make peace with reality. I think a lot of people just can't do that. They can't make peace with what *is* and what *should be*. That frustrates a lot of young people. I find they come out of school and have got this very idealistic idea of how people in a church *should* be, how board members *should* be, and so forth. And when these people in their ministry don't measure up to that, they start hammering at them. And that really causes problems. Make peace with reality, where you look at what *is*, and what you *want* to have happen, and figure out, *All right, how am I going to get from the way things are to what I think they should be?* Without pounding on the people. Because that won't work.

Conclusion

The political education that took place in the lives of ministry leaders after the completion of their formal education was cumulative in nature; they matured and grew in leadership and political skills over time. These leaders reported that while their formal education was helpful, it was limited in providing an understanding of the political challenges of working with people to get things done.

Ministry leaders conduct their ministries in a relational swamp that presents messy, confusing problems that defy technical, efficient solutions.

Through learning in practice by reflection-in-action, reflection-on-action, mentors and models, and negative experiences, these leaders demonstrated ways they learned how to navigate the politics of ministry explained in this book. May we all grow in mastering this art of getting things done with others in the politics of ministry.

Acknowledgments

The three of us would like to thank University of Georgia professor Ron Cervero and his coauthor Arthur Wilson for the ways they developed the theoretical framework of daily political activity in the workplace. Donald and Bob have also benefited from Ron's mentorship in their doctoral studies, for which they will always be grateful.

We would also like to thank all of the ministry leaders, congregants, pastors, and seminary students we have worked with over the years. We shared many of their stories in this book. In each context, we were learning and often failing forward in the work of the politics of ministry, while seeking to bring the hope of the gospel into the lives of others.

Thanks to our friend Steve Garber for writing the foreword. In the midst of his busy transition into full-time teaching at Regent College, he took the time to read, reflect, and comment on our work. He is a cherished partner in our shared mission of seeking to bring gospel health into vocation and culture.

Of course, the primary place we have learned the politics of working with people has been in our homes. Love and gratitude go to our parents, siblings, spouses, children, and grandchildren for their trust, forgiveness, and acceptance as we have stumbled along, learning how to accomplish work and pursue change in truth, love, grace, and community.

Bob would like to thank all of the churches and pastors he has worked with over the years, as well as the faculty and staff of Covenant Theological Seminary. He is particularly grateful to Randy Pope, John Purcell, and the elders of Perimeter Church in John's Creek, Georgia, who supported him throughout his doctoral studies.

Tasha would like to thank all the saints she has partnered with during years of ministry, as well as the board of Covenant Theological Seminary for granting her a sabbatical to work on this book. She is especially grateful to both of the women named Leela in her life for meticulously editing drafts.

Donald is especially thankful for his colleagues at Covenant Theological Seminary and Trinity Evangelical Divinity School with whom he has shared the fruit of gospel partnership.

Appendix 1:
Emotions Checklist

Reviewing a checklist of adjectives describing varied emotions can be helpful in learning to accurately identify emotions.[1] When we better identify emotions, it deepens our understanding of ourselves and others. Try using this list at the end of the day, considering your circumstances and how you felt. Or keep the list in your journal so that you can identify feelings as you write. Or use it as a test and retest, exploring how your feelings may have changed from one point of time to another.

Place a check next to all the adjectives that describe how you feel right now.

❏ Ambivalent	❏ Defeated	❏ Grateful
❏ Amused	❏ Dejected	❏ Guilty
❏ Angry	❏ Delighted	❏ Happy
❏ Annoyed	❏ Depressed	❏ Hateful
❏ Anxious	❏ Detached	❏ Helpful
❏ Apathetic	❏ Different	❏ Helpless
❏ Ashamed	❏ Discouraged	❏ Hesitant
❏ Attractive	❏ Disgusted	❏ Hopeful
❏ Bitter	❏ Disinterested	❏ Hurt
❏ Bored	❏ Empty	❏ Impatient
❏ Brave	❏ Engaged	❏ Independent
❏ Bright	❏ Excited	❏ Indifferent
❏ Calm	❏ Exhausted	❏ Inferior
❏ Cheated	❏ Foolish	❏ Insecure
❏ Collected	❏ Fulfilled	❏ Inspired
❏ Confident	❏ Funny	❏ Interested
❏ Confused	❏ Glad	❏ Involved
❏ Contented	❏ Glib	❏ Irritated

❑ Jealous

❑ Joyful

❑ Jubilant

❑ Judged

❑ Lonely

❑ Loved

❑ Loyal

❑ Miserable

❑ Misguided

❑ Misunderstood

❑ Needy

❑ Neglected

❑ Nervous

❑ Neutral

❑ Optimistic

❑ Overjoyed

❑ Overwhelmed

❑ Peaceful

❑ Pessimistic

❑ Phony

❑ Pleased

❑ Powerful

❑ Preoccupied

❑ Puzzled

❑ Questioning

❑ Quiet

❑ Rejected

❑ Relieved

❑ Reluctant

❑ Resentful

❑ Resilient

❑ Respectful

❑ Restless

❑ Romantic

❑ Sad

❑ Satisfied

❑ Secure

❑ Selfish

❑ Sexual

❑ Sexy

❑ Shy

❑ Silly

❑ Smart

❑ Sorry

❑ Strong

❑ Stupid

❑ Suicidal

❑ Supported

❑ Surprised

❑ Tense

❑ Terrible

❑ Thankful

❑ Touched

❑ Tough

❑ Trusting

❑ Ugly

❑ Unappreciated

❑ Unhappy

❑ Unsure

❑ Upset

❑ Useful

❑ Violent

❑ Weary

❑ Welcome

❑ Well

❑ Whole

❑ Willing

❑ Wise

❑ Worried

Appendix 2: Constructing and Exploring a Family Diagram

A genogram is a visual description of behavioral systems in a family over the course of three or more generations.[1] It serves as a helpful tool for leaders to see the family system they belong to and how their family of origin has influenced their leadership, both positively and negatively. Families do not ultimately determine us. God's grace, gifting, and sovereign purposes can shape and even override the influences of our family. At the same time, God ordained our family of origin as one means of his divine design for our lives. Therefore, one way for us to "number our days that we may get a heart of wisdom" is to review how we were shaped by our family of origin (Psalm 90:12).

Steps to Creating and Exploring Your Genogram

1. Draw a family tree with three generations: you and your family, your family of origin (parents and siblings), and your parents' families of origin (your grandparents, aunts, and uncles). Use a circle to represent females and a square to represent males. To the best of your ability, place the year of birth and, if applicable, the year of death for each person.

2. Use the following Genogram Symbols Guide (fig. A2.1) to illustrate the types of relationships that existed between key persons in the genogram.

3. To provide insights for reflection on a particular theme, mark each person with a symbol to represent their typical behavior on a particular issue. For example, for each person, note how they responded to success or to failure.

4. Make observations on any patterns, contrasts, or spectrums that you discover in behaviors across the genogram. Note patterns of gospel health or of sinfulness.

5. Reflect on your observations in light of your own behavior.

   - How have you superimposed unhealthy patterns of behavior on God?

   - How have you continued the family patterns in your home?

   - How have you continued the family patterns in your ministry leadership?

   - How do your strengths and struggles correlate to family patterns?

   - What can you do to strengthen the healthy patterns?

   - How can you leverage your strengths to correct the sinful patterns?

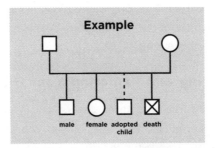

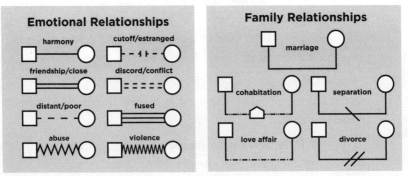

Figure A2.1. Genogram symbols guide

Additional Genogram Questions

Foundational Genogram Questions

1. Who was the dominant person in your family?[2] How did you learn to relate to that person? Who taught you to relate to that dominant person in that manner? Who was the dominant person in your parents' family of origin? If you have heard, how did your parents (and their siblings) relate to that person?

2. What were the major life-altering events and crises in your family of origin? In previous and subsequent generations? How did individuals and families respond and react to these events? What were some of the long-term effects of these events on individuals and families as a whole?

3. The following presents a spectrum of emotions one might feel: sad, glad, mad, strong, afraid, weak, confused, anxious, calm. Using these descriptors, identify the dominant feelings for each member of your family system. What was the predominant feeling describing your entire family of origin? What influence has this emotional environment had on your ministry leadership?

Leadership Models and Methods

Ken Blanchard has identified four styles of situational leadership.[3] The patterns form around two types of specific leader behaviors with individuals: support and direction.

- ❑ high supportive, low directive (Supportive)
- ❑ high supportive, high directive (Coaching)
- ❑ low supportive, low directive (Delegating)
- ❑ low supportive, high directive (Directive)

1. To the best of your ability, label the leadership pattern exhibited most often by your parents and grandparents. How would you describe your natural pattern?

2. Who were your models growing up? What influence did these models have on your expectations for yourself as a leader?

3. Using words or short phrases, describe your father as a leader. Describe your mother as a leader. Describe your grandparents as leaders.

4. Identify the three key leaders in your congregation (elders or otherwise) or your business.

- What criteria did you use to identify these three leaders?
- What do you know about the family of origin of these three leaders?
- How do you think your family of origin has shaped who you consider these three leaders to be?

Emotional Experience and Expression

1. Describe any hobbies or sports family members participated in, as well as the level of their involvement.

2. How did your parents respond to you when you were in a highly reactive emotional state? How do you respond to your children when they are highly emotional? Comment on any similarities between these family patterns and the way you respond to the emotions of your elders or others in the congregation or to your employees in your business.

3. *The Leader's Journey* defines acute anxiety as "our reaction to a threat that is real and time-limited. We react to the threat, respond to it, and then eventually return to a normal state of mind and body. . . . With chronic anxiety, however, the threat is imagined or distorted, rather than real. Consequently, it is not time-limited; it does not simply go away."[4] Every emotional system sustains some level of chronic anxiety.[5]

- How would you describe the family system in which you grew up with regard to the level of chronic anxiety? Were you led to think of the world as basically secure or basically threatening? What did people in your family fret over? What difference has growing up in this environment had on the way you lead? Consider an anxious time in your current family. How has your training in your family of origin affected the way you handled that situation?
- How would you describe the ministry system you are engaged in with regard to the level of chronic anxiety? Do leaders in the system see the world about them as threatening? How does

this manifest itself? Are there frequent emergencies and crises? When a crisis occurs, does the leadership take it in stride and solve the problem, or are they likely to develop symptoms? Review a difficult or crisis situation you have faced as a ministry in light of these questions.

- How do you think your three key leaders would describe the chronic anxiety of the congregation? How do they respond when a crisis occurs?

Relational Connectivity

1. What is your place in the constellation of your family of origin: oldest, youngest, middle? Were you a brother with younger sisters? Younger brothers? Older sisters? Older brothers?

   - How did your unique spot in the family shape you in learning to relate to others?

   - How did it shape you in the way you lead and the way you respond to others' leadership?

2. Describe the kind of community and social involvement reflected in the members of your family system. What roles did your family members play in this involvement?

3. In *The Leader's Journey,* the authors identify four symptoms of chronic anxiety that are indicative of an anxious system: *conflict* (often identified with all-or-nothing thinking), *distance* (keeping the peace by maintaining superficial or no contact), *overfunctioning* and *underfunctioning* (compensation of an individual or group within a system to take on too much responsibility for another person or group), and *projection* (projecting anxiety onto an individual or a part of the system).

   - Which of these four symptoms do you most typically see in your congregation? How about in your own family?

   - How do you, as a leader in the system, participate in this? How do your elders or staff participate in this?

   - How do key leaders in the congregation participate in these four symptoms of an anxious system?

4. God has created us as unique individuals. The complexity of the human DNA makes each of us distinguishable from others (Psalm 139:1-14). Yet God calls us to community (Ephesians 4:1-3). In this context, we are called to be sensitive to the needs of others, serve others, and fit in with each other.

- How would you describe your family of origin with regard to individuality and togetherness?

- How would you describe your family with regard to individuality and togetherness?

- How would you describe your three key leaders with regard to individuality and togetherness?

- How would you describe your church with regard to individuality and togetherness?

Metrics and Means of Success

1. Describe the level that each family member completed in school.

2. Identify the job experience of those in your genogram. Describe the employment and career patterns that you see (including homemaking). What types of leadership responsibilities are evident in those job roles?

3. When it came to education, career, sports, hobbies, and social involvement, what were the expectations placed on you within your family system? What was the response when you succeeded or failed to succeed in these areas?

4. Describe how your family of origin planned and accomplished goals. Were plans and goals ever made? If so, where did these goals fall on a spectrum between individual goals versus family goals? Did the family plan these together, were they imposed, or did everyone make up their own goals when they wanted? How were goals accomplished (individually, in partnerships, or as a group)?

5. Who were the heroes and heroines in your family? Why or for what were they honored?

6. What was applauded in your family? How and for what were you applauded in your family?

Failure, Loss, and Pain

1. Who were the unrecognized or disregarded members of your family? Why were they treated this way?

2. How was failure viewed in the family? How have you superimposed these standards on God? How have you reflected these in your leadership of others?

3. What was criticized in your family? How and for what were you criticized in your family?

4. What secrets are in your family tree? What are you not allowed or supposed to talk about?

Spiritual Influences and Experiences

1. What were the views of God in your family of origin? What did it mean to be religious? What did it mean to be a Christian?

2. What events formed your view of God and humanity?

3. What events informed your understanding of Jesus?

4. What spiritual understandings were formed in your childhood that you now consider helpful and significant?

5. What spiritual understandings or beliefs were formed in your childhood that you now consider dangerous or destructive?

Application Questions

1. How would you relate your sense of call into ministry to your family of origin? To your extended family?

2. Dissociating from the emotional anxiety of your system while staying connected to people is hard work.

   - Identify three methods you use to manage your feelings during times of anxiety. Where, how, or from whom did you learn these methods? Do you consider these methods healthy or an avoidance method? Why?

   - How well do your three key leaders dissociate from anxiety yet stay relationally connected to people? Explain.

3. Who in your congregation do you struggle to connect with? In other words, when you leave their presence you think, *This person just doesn't get me?*

- What characteristics of this person triggers such an emotionally allergic reaction?

- Can you think of anyone in your history you had a similar response to?

Notes

1 Three Ministry Stories

[1]This is gleaned from a quick online survey and is not based on a definitive research study.

[2]Dean R. Hoge and Jacqueline E. Wenger, *Pastors in Transition: Why Clergy Leave Local Church Ministry* (Grand Rapids: Eerdmans, 2005).

[3]We are consciously not using the term to refer to political issues of, or with, national or state government organizations. This is how the term *politics* was used in an earlier time. Its usage and meaning in the United States has changed a great deal. For example, see *Webster's New Twentieth Century Dictionary*, 2nd ed.

[4]Mark summarized this with Jesus saying, "The time is fulfilled, and the kingdom of God is at hand; repent and believe in the gospel" (Mark 1:15; see also Mark 1:38-39). Jesus' authority was acknowledged in Mark 1:27 and Mark 2:12, and was seen in his teaching on fasting (Mark 2:18-22) and the Sabbath (Mark 2:23-27). The semantic range of meaning for the Greek term Mark uses for "authority" largely overlaps with the range of meaning for how we use the phrase "power and authority" today.

[5]By the time of our story he had already called Simon, Andrew, James, John, and Levi (Mark 1:16-20; 2:13-4).

[6]People with unclean spirits (Mark 1:23-26, 32, 39), a leper (Mark 1:40-44), a paralytic (Mark 2:1-11), Simon's mother-in-law, who was suffering with a fever (Mark 1:30-31), and others who were sick (Mark 1:32).

2 The Four Dynamics of Politics

[1]Donald C. Guthrie and Ronald M. Cervero, "The Politics of Moving Continuing Education to the Center of the Institutional Mission," in *A Lifelong Call to Learn*, ed. Robert E. Reber and D. Bruce Roberts (Nashville: Abingdon Press, 2000), 182.

[2]John Forester, *Planning in the Face of Power* (Berkeley: University of California Press, 1989), 75.

[3]Ronald M. Cervero and Arthur L. Wilson, *Planning Responsibly for Adult Education: A Guide to Negotiating Power and Interests* (San Francisco: Jossey-Bass, 1994), 29-32.

[4]Bob Burns, Tasha D. Chapman, and Donald C. Guthrie, *Resilient Ministry: What Pastors Told Us About Surviving and Thriving* (Downers Grove, IL: InterVarsity Press, 2013), 211.

[5]See also Luke 4:14, 37, 42; 5:26; 7:11; 8:4, 19; 11:52–12:1; 13:17; 20:26; 21:37–22:2.

[6]Bob Burns, Tasha D. Chapman, and Donald C. Guthrie, *Resilient Ministry: What Pastors Told Us About Surviving and Thriving* (Downers Grove, IL: InterVarsity Press, 2013), 211.

[7]Ronald M. Cervero and Arthur L. Wilson, *Planning Responsibly for Adult Education: A Guide to Negotiating Power and Interests* (San Francisco: Jossey-Bass, 1994); Roger Fisher and William Ury, *Getting to Yes* (New York: Penguin, 1981); and Gareth Morgan, *Images of Organization* (Thousand Oaks, CA: Sage, 1998).

[8]Quoted in R. C. Sproul, *Chosen by God* (Wheaton, IL: Tyndale House, 1986).

[9]M. Newman, *Defining the Enemy* (Sydney: Stewart Victor, 1994), 153.

[10]Ronald M. Cervero and Arthur L. Wilson, *Working the Planning Table* (San Francisco: Jossey-Bass, 2006), 124-25.

3 Power in Ministry Politics

[1]Paul G. Hiebert, *Anthropological Insights for Missionaries* (Grand Rapids: Baker, 1985), 111.

[2]Andy Crouch, *Playing God: Redeeming the Gift of Power* (Downers Grove, IL: InterVarsity Press, 2013), 187.

[3]We have developed this from the broader framework of educational planning given in Ronald M. Cervero and Arthur L. Wilson, *Working the Planning Table* (San Francisco: Jossey-Bass, 2006), 85.

[4]The three ways formal power is authorized is adapted from categories used by Mary Ellen Stortz, *PastorPower* (Nashville: Abingdon Press, 1993).

[5]D. A. Hagner, "Pharisees," in *The Zondervan Pictorial Encyclopedia of the Bible,* ed. Merrill C. Tenney (Grand Rapids: Zondervan, 1976), 4:747.

[6]Crouch, *Playing God,* 184.

[7]Crouch, *Playing God,* 185.

[8]Mike Bonem and Roger Patterson, *Leading from the Second Chair* (San Francisco: Jossey-Bass, 2005), 8.

[9]Crouch, *Playing God,* 13.

[10]Cervero and Wilson, *Working the Planning Table,* 127.

¹¹Ronald A. Heifetz and Marty Linsky, *Leadership on the Line: Staying Alive Through the Dangers of Leading* (Boston: Harvard Business Review Press), 53.

¹²Heifetz and Linsky, *Leadership on the Line*, 53.

¹³Heifetz and Linsky, *Leadership on the Line*, 53.

4 The Branches and Roots of Interests

¹Jim Herrington, R. Robert Creech, and Trisha Taylor, *The Leader's Journey: Accepting the Call to Personal and Congregational Transformation* (San Francisco: Jossey-Bass, 2003), 52-53.

²Ronald M. Cervero and Arthur L. Wilson, *Working the Planning Table* (San Francisco: Jossey-Bass, 2006), 89.

³Donald A. Schön, *The Reflective Practitioner: How Professionals Think in Action* (New York: Basic Books, 1983). This is groundbreaking work from the late MIT professor. Others who have worked in this area of identifying professional learning include Ronald Cervero, Peter Jarvis, and Chris Argyris.

5 Personal Interests

¹A number of these categories have been adapted from material found in our book *Resilient Ministry* (Downers Grove, IL: InterVarsity Press, 2013).

²Saul McLeod, "Maslow's Hierarchy of Needs," *Simply Psychology*, updated 2016, www.simplypsychology.org/maslow.html.

³Daniel Goleman, *Working with Emotional Intelligence* (New York: Bantam Books, 1998), 4; and Daniel Goleman, Richard Boyatzis, and Annie McKee, *Primal Leadership: Realizing the Power of Emotional Intelligence* (Boston: Harvard Business School Press, 2002), 12.

⁴David R. Caruso and Peter Salovey, *The Emotionally Intelligent Manager* (San Francisco: Jossey-Bass, 2004), xxi.

⁵D. A. Carson posits that the negative attitude among Christians toward emotions comes from the influence of certain strands of Greek metaphysical thought. These views "insist that emotion is dangerous, treacherous, and often evil. Reason must be set against emotion, and vulnerability is a sign of weakness" (D. A. Carson, *Divine Sovereignty and Human Responsibility* [Atlanta: John Knox Press, 1981], 215). Wayne Grudem implies that a negative view of emotions may stem from a tripartite view of anthropology (Wayne Grudem, *Systematic Theology: An Introduction to Biblical Doctrine* [Grand Rapids: Zondervan, 1994], 482).

⁶Wayne Grudem states, "In the area of emotions, our likeness to God is seen in a large difference in degree and complexity of emotions" (Grudem, *Systematic Theology*, 447). And John Frame explains, "Theologians have sometimes thought that emotions are unworthy of God. . . . Scripture ascribes many attitudes to God that are generally regarded as emotions . . . [such as] God's compassion, tender

mercy, patience, rejoicing, delight, pleasure, pity, love, wrath, and jealousy. . . . God, speaking in Scripture, regularly expresses emotion and appeals to the emotions of his hearers" (John Frame, *The Doctrine of God* [Phillipsburg: P&R, 2002], 609, 611). And B. B. Warfield expressed similar sentiments in his "On the Emotional Life of Our Lord," in *The Person and Work of Christ*, ed. Samuel G. Craig (Phillipsburg, NJ: P&R, 1950).

[7] Peter Scazzero, *Emotionally Healthy Spirituality: Unleash a Revolution in Your Life in Christ* (Nashville: Thomas Nelson, 2006), 12.

[8] Caruso and Salovey, *Emotionally Intelligent Manager*, 11.

[9] See also John 13:34; Acts 2:42; Ephesians 4:2, 3; Philippians 1:7; Colossians 3:16; Hebrews 10:24-25; 1 John 1:3, 6-7.

[10] See also Philippians 4:8-9; 2 Peter 3:1.

[11] Peter Scazzero, *Emotionally Healthy Spirituality: Unleash a Revolution in Your Life in Christ* (Nashville: Thomas Nelson, 2006), 95-96.

[12] For more information on RightPath Resources see www.rightpath.com.

6 Organizational Interests

[1] For those not familiar with these strategic planning frameworks, please consult Randy Pope, *Intentional Church* (Chicago: Moody Press, 2006), particularly chapters 3-5.

[2] Michael Jinkins and Deborah Bradshaw Jinkins, *The Character of Leadership* (San Francisco: Jossey-Bass, 1998), 86.

[3] Robert Goffee and Gareth Jones, *The Character of a Corporation* (New York: Harper Business, 1998), 9.

[4] David Livermore, *Cultural Intelligence* (Grand Rapids: Baker Academic, 2009), 98.

[5] See, for example, Edgar Shein, *Organizational Culture and Leadership* (Boston: Sloan School of Management, 1985); William Bridges, *The Character of Organizations* (Palo Alto, CA: Consulting Psychologists Press, 1992); and Richard L. Daft, *Understanding the Theory and Design of Organizations* (Andover, MA: Cengage Learning, 2013).

[6] Philip D. Douglass, *What Is Your Church's Personality?* (Phillipsburg, NJ: P&R, 2008).

[7] Kim S. Cameron and Robert E. Quinn, *Diagnosing and Changing Organizational Culture* (San Francisco: Jossey-Bass, 2011). See chap. 2, "The Organizational Culture Assessment Instrument" and chap. 3, "The Competing Values Framework," 27-72.

[8] Cameron and Quinn, *Diagnosing and Changing Organizational Culture*, 18.

[9] Cameron and Quinn call the creative culture an "adhocracy." "The root of the word is *ad hoc*, implying something temporary, specialized, and dynamic. . . .

The major goal of an adhocracy is to foster adaptability, flexibility, and creativity"
(Cameron and Quinn, *Diagnosing and Changing Organizational Culture*, 49).

[10]Cameron and Quinn, *Diagnosing and Changing Organizational Culture*, 65.

[11]Cameron and Quinn, *Diagnosing and Changing Organizational Culture*, 20.

[12]Again, we thank our friend Jerry Mabe of RightPath Resources who originally
developed these terms without reference to the work of Goffee and Jones. In
their study Goffee and Jones use the words *sociability* for relationships and *soli-
darity* for results. Note that Randy Pope of Perimeter Church has adapted a
similar nomenclature, using *home* for relationships and *mission* for results.

[13]Ronald Heifetz, Alexander Grashow, and Marty Linsky, "Diagnose the System,"
in *The Practice of Adaptive Leadership* (Boston: Harvard Business Press, 2009),
49-68.

[14]Heifetz, Grashow, and Linsky, "Diagnose the System," 50.

[15]Heifetz, Grashow, and Linsky, "Diagnose the System," 57-63.

[16]Heifetz, Grashow, and Linsky, "Diagnose the System," 58.

[17]Heifetz, Grashow, and Linsky, "Diagnose the System," 60.

[18]Heifetz, Grashow, and Linsky, "Diagnose the System," 61.

[19]Heifetz, Grashow, and Linsky, "Diagnose the System," 62.

[20]The meeting protocols questions are adapted from Heifetz, Grashow, and Linsky,
"Diagnose the System," 62.

[21]Heifetz, Grashow, and Linsky, "Diagnose the System," 64.

[22]Heifetz, Grashow, and Linsky, "Diagnose the System," 65.

7 Societal Interests

[1]David Livermore, *Cultural Intelligence* (Grand Rapids: Baker Academic, 2009),
102-8.

[2]"Generational Differences Chart," West Midland Family Center, accessed April
9, 2018, www.wmfc.org/uploads/GenerationalDifferencesChart.pdf. This chart
does not indicate the sources for their information. Therefore, it should be
considered observation based rather than research based. As with all materials
it will express the biases of the developers.

[3]James Plueddemann, *Leading Across Cultures* (Downers Grove, IL: InterVarsity
Press, 2009), 43.

[4]Andy Crouch, "It's Time to Talk About Power," *Christianity Today*, October
2013, 33.

[5]Andy Crouch, *Strong and Weak* (Downers Grove, IL: InterVarsity Press, 2016),
125-26.

[6]James Plueddemann, *Leading Across Cultures* (Downers Grove, IL: InterVarsity
Press, 2009), 103.

[7]Crouch, "It's Time to Talk About Power," 34.

[8]Ronald M. Cervero and Arthur L. Wilson, *Working the Planning Table* (San Francisco: Jossey-Bass, 2006), 18.

[9]Michael Jinkins and Deborah Bradshaw Jinkins, *The Character of Leadership* (San Francisco: Jossey-Bass, 1998), 15.

8 Negotiation, Power, and Interests

[1]Michael Newman, *Defining the Enemy: Adult Education in Social Action* (Sydney: Stewart Victor, 1994), 153.

[2]Robert W. Burns and Ronald M. Cervero, "Issues Framing the Politics of Pastoral Ministry Practice," *Review of Religious Research* 43, no. 3 (2004): 235.

[3]Roger Fisher and William Ury, *Getting to Yes* (New York: Penguin, 1981).

[4]Ronald M. Cervero and Arthur L. Wilson, *Working the Planning Table* (San Francisco: Jossey-Bass, 2006), 6

[5]J. C. Isaac, *Power and Marxist Theory: A Realist View* (Ithaca, NY: Cornell University Press, 1987).

[6]Cervero and Wilson assert, "Planners' actions are always reconstructing the power relationships and interests of everyone involved in planning the program. The process of negotiation affects people's interests and power relationships. It maintains, strengthens, or weakens them. Power relationships and interests always BOTH structure negotiations and are reconstructed by these same practices" (Ronald M. Cervero and Arthur L. Wilson, *Planning Responsibly for Adult Education* [San Francisco: Jossey-Bass, 1994], 30; see also their *Working the Planning Table*, 87). Similarly, John Forester states, "Every organizational interaction or practical communication (including the nonverbal) not only produces a result, it also reproduces, strengthening or weakening, the specific social working relationships of those who interact" (John Forester, *Planning in the Face of Power* [Berkeley: University of California Press, 1989], 71).

[7]Cervero and Wilson, *Planning Responsibly*; and *Working the Planning Table*, 94.

[8]We have adapted and enhanced this four-cell matrix from the work originally presented by Cervero and Wilson in *Planning Responsibly; What Really Matters in Adult Education Program Planning: Lessons in Negotiating Power and Interests* (San Francisco: Jossey-Bass, 1996); "Working the Planning Table: The Political Practice of Adult Education," in *Studies in Continuing Education* 20 (1998): 5-21, and modified by Donald C. Guthrie and Ronald M. Cervero, "The Politics of Moving Continuing Education to the Center of the Institutional Mission," in *A Lifelong Call to Learn*, ed. Robert E. Reber and D. Bruce Roberts (Nashville: Abingdon Press, 2000).

[9]Guthrie and Cervero, *Lifelong Call to Learn*, 184.

[10]Cervero and Wilson, *Working the Planning Table*, 94.

[11]Cervero and Wilson, *Planning Responsibly*, 132-33.

[12]Cervero and Wilson, *Working the Planning Table*, 156.

[13]Cervero and Wilson, *Working the Planning Table*, 95.

[14]Cervero and Wilson, *Planning Responsibly*, 133-34.

9 Negotiation in Cell Four

[1]We have adapted and enhanced this four-cell matrix from the work originally presented by Ronald M. Cervero and Arthur L. Wilson in *Planning Responsibly for Adult Education* (San Francisco: Jossey-Bass, 1994); *What Really Matters in Adult Education Program Planning: Lessons in Negotiating Power and Interests* (San Francisco: Jossey-Bass, 1996); "Working the Planning Table: The Political Practice of Adult Education" in *Studies in Continuing Education*, 20, (1998): 5-21 and modified by Donald C. Guthrie and Ronald M. Cervero, "The Politics of Moving Continuing Education to the Center of the Institutional Mission" in *A Lifelong Call to Learn*, ed. Robert E. Reber and D. Bruce Roberts (Nashville: Abingdon Press, 2000).

[2]Guthrie and Cervero, *Lifelong Call to Learn*, 184.

[3]"Subversion," *Wikipedia*, accessed April 9, 2018, https://en.wikipedia.org/wiki/Subversion.

[4]Cervero and Wilson, *Planning Responsibly for Adult Education*, 135.

[5]Andy Crouch, *Playing God: Redeeming the Gift of Power* (Downers Grove, IL: InterVarsity Press, 2013), 147.

[6]See Peter's extended discussion in 1 Peter 2:13-25; 3:8-18.

[7]David C. Jones, *Biblical Christian Ethics* (Grand Rapids: Baker, 1994), 16.

[8]"Martyrdom of Polycarp" 9, in *The Apostolic Fathers*, trans. J. B. Lightfoot and J. R. Harmer, ed. Michael W. Holmes, 2nd ed. (Grand Rapids: Baker, 1989), 139.

[9]Scripture passages dealing with God's care for the weak, vulnerable, widows, and orphans, and God's judgment on his people when they oppress them: Deuteronomy 10:17-19; Isaiah 1:12-23; 42:1-4; Amos 2:6-16; Micah 2:1-5; 3; 6:1-8; Luke 11:42-44; 20:45-47; 1 Timothy 5:3; James 1:27.

[10]Cervero and Wilson, *Working the Planning Table*, 140.

10 Ethical Issues in the Politics of Ministry

[1]David C. Jones, *Biblical Christian Ethics* (Grand Rapids: Baker, 1994), 16.

[2]Ronald M. Cervero and Arthur L. Wilson, *Working the Planning Table* (San Francisco: Jossey-Bass, 2006), 92; and Ronald M. Cervero and Arthur L. Wilson, *Planning Responsibly for Adult Education* (San Francisco: Jossey-Bass, 1994), 122.

[3]A great deal of the theological reflection in this section is drawn from J. I. Packer, *Concise Theology* (Wheaton, IL: Tyndale House, 1993).

[4]Packer, *Concise Theology*, 83.

[5]Packer, *Concise Theology*, 171.

[6]Paul references lifestyle characteristics such as marital fidelity, being self-controlled, respectable, hospitable, not a drunkard, not violent, but gentle, not quarrelsome, not a lover of money, not double-tongued, not slanderers, sober-minded, self-controlled and disciplined (see 1 Timothy 3:1-13; Titus 1:5-9).

[7]Peter Scazzero, *Emotionally Healthy Spirituality* (Nashville: Integrity, 2006), 11-12.

[8]Scazzero, *Emotionally Healthy Spirituality*, 15.

[9]David A. Livermore, *Cultural Intelligence* (Grand Rapids: Baker Academic, 2009), 94.

[10]Robert Goffee and Gareth Jones, *The Character of a Corporation* (New York: Harper Business, 1998), 9.

[11]Richard L. Daft, *Understanding the Theory and Design of Organizations* (Andover, MA: Cengage Learning, 2013), 389-91.

[12]Daft, *Understanding the Theory*, 390

[13]Daft, *Understanding the Theory*, 390.

[14]Amy C. Edmondson, *Teaming: How Organizations Learn, Innovate, and Compete in the Knowledge Economy* (San Francisco: Jossey-Bass, 2012), 131. See also pages 131-35.

[15]Frank J. Barrett, *Yes to the Mess* (Boston: Harvard Business Review Press, 2012), 42.

[16]The hierarchy structure is one of five organizational types discussed by Jacob Morgan in his book *The Future of Work* (New York: Wiley, 2014) and outlined in a series of articles in *Forbes*, www.forbes.com/sites/jacobmorgan/2015/07/22 /the-complete-guide-5-types-of-organizational-structures-for-the-future -of-work/#2fdd81b27705.

[17]Jacob Morgan, "The 5 Types of Organizational Structures: Part 1, The Hierarchy," *Forbes*, accessed August 8, 2018, www.forbes.com/sites/jacobmorgan/2015/07/06 /the-5-types-of-organizational-structures-part-1-the-hierarchy/#1c8b0cad5252.

[18]Andy Crouch, *Playing God: Redeeming the Gift of Power* (Downers Grove, IL: InterVarsity Press, 2013), 185; emphasis added.

[19]Preston Ni, "14 Signs of Psychological and Emotional Manipulation," *Psychology Today*, October 11, 2015, www.psychologytoday.com/blog/communication -success/201510/14-signs-psychological-and-emotional-manipulation.

[20]"Social Influence," *Wikipedia*, accessed April 9, 2016, https://en.wikipedia.org /wiki/Social_influence.

[21]Jim Fogarty, *Emotional Manipulation: Understanding Manipulators and Helping Their Victims* (Brentwood, TN: Cross Country Education, 2014), 2.

[22]Chamorro-Premuzic describes these traits as follows: "Psychopathic individuals are generally more dishonest, egocentric, reckless, and cruel than the population average. Machiavellianism is somewhat more related to superficial charm, inter-personal manipulation, deceit, ruthlessness, and impulsivity. People who score highly on this trait are morally feeble and likely to endorse the idea that 'the end justifies the means' or agree that 'it is hard to get ahead without cutting

corners here and there.' Narcissism relates to unrealistic feelings of grandiosity, an inflated—though often unstable and insecure—sense of self-worth, and a selfish sense of entitlement coupled with little consideration for others. As the term, and the legend of Narcissus, suggests, narcissistic individuals are so self-indulged that they may end up drowning in their own self-love—this makes it harder for them to focus on others. Narcissists are often charming, and charisma is often the socially desirable side of narcissism: Silvio Berlusconi, Jim Jones, and Steve Jobs personified this" (Tomas Chamorro-Premuzic, "Why Bad Guys Win at Work," *Harvard Business Review*, November 2, 2015, https://hbr.org/2015/11 /why-bad-guys-win-at-work).

[23]Chamorro-Premuzic, "Why Bad Guys Win at Work."

[24]George K. Simon Jr., *Character Disturbance: The Phenomenon of Our Age* (Little Rock: Parkhurst, 2011), 30.

[25]Simon, *Character Disturbance*, 15.

[26]Manfred F. R. Kets de Vries, *Reflections on Character and Leadership* (San Francisco: Jossey-Bass, 2009), 126.

[27]Francis A. Schaeffer, *True Spirituality* (Wheaton, IL: Tyndale House, 1971), 134.

[28]Chamorro-Premuzic asserts, "There is clearly a bright side to the dark side [of these traits of psychopathology, narcissism, and Machiavellianism]. As found in a study examining the overlap between positive and negative personality characteristics, extraversion, openness to new experience, curiosity, and self-esteem, these traits are generally higher among dark triad personalities. In addition, dark triad traits tend to enhance competitiveness, if only by inhibiting cooperation and altruistic behaviors at work. In addition, studies have shown that psychopathic and Machiavellian tendencies facilitate both the seduction and intimidation tactics that frighten potential competitors and captivate bosses" (Chamorro-Premuzic, "Why Bad Guys Win at Work").

[29]Manfred Kets de Vries and Danny Miller, *Unstable at the Top* (New York: New American Library, 1987), 8.

[30]Daft, *Understanding the Theory*, 392.

[31]Diane Mandt Langberg, *In Our Lives First: Meditations for Counselors* (Jenkintown, PA: Diane Langberg, 2014), 112-13.

[32]See the final story in this chapter as an example of firing with grace.

[33]A great deal of insight for this section was gleaned from the literature review in Kelly H. Dehnert, *Serving the Toxic Leader: Self-Differentiation in the Christian Organization*, DMin diss. (St. Louis: Covenant Theological Seminary, 2017).

[34]R. T. France, *The Gospel of Matthew*, New International Commentary on the New Testament (Grand Rapids: Eerdmans, 2007), 691.

[35]Mary Alice Chrnalogar, *Twisted Scriptures* (Grand Rapids: Zondervan, 1997), 65. This conclusion is affirmed in Jean Lipman-Blumen, *The Allure of Toxic Leaders*

(Oxford: Oxford University Press, 2005), 149; and Ken Sande, *The Peacemaker* (Grand Rapids: Baker, 2004), 156.

[36]Dehnert, "Chapter Two: Literature Review," *Serving the Toxic Leader*, 59.

[37]Kelly O'Donnell, "Wise as Doves and Innocent as Serpents? Doing Conflict Resolution Better," *Missio Nexus*, January 2007, https://missionexus.org /wise-as-doves-and-innocent-as-serpents-doing-conflict-resolution-better.

[38]Kets de Vries and Miller, *Unstable at the Top*, xii.

[39]Manfred Kets de Vries and Danny Miller, *The Neurotic Organization* (San Francisco: Jossey-Bass, 1985), 209-10.

[40]Steven Garber, "When we choose against grace, we choose for an eye-for-an -eye," Facebook, December 31, 2016, www.facebook.com/steven.garber.16 /posts/1363365850361077.

11 Tom Moves into a Political Struggle: A Final Case Study

[1]Ronald A. Heifetz and Marty Linsky, *Leadership on the Line: Staying Alive Through the Dangers of Leading* (Boston: Harvard Business Review Press, 2002), 53.

[2]Bob Burns, Tasha D. Chapman, and Donald C. Guthrie, *Resilient Ministry: What Pastors Told Us About Surviving and Thriving* (Downers Grove, IL: InterVarsity Press, 2013), 170, 174.

[3]Francis A. Schaeffer, *The Church Before the Watching World* (Downers Grove, IL: InterVarsity Press, 1971); see especially chapter three, "Practicing Purity in the Visible Church." See also Francis A. Schaeffer, *The Mark of the Christian* (Downers Grove, IL: InterVarsity Press, 1970).

[4]R. T. France, *The Gospel of Matthew*, New International Commentary on the New Testament (Grand Rapids: Eerdmans, 2007), 691. While France's comments are made directly in reference to Matthew 18:15-20, we believe the power dynamics reflected in Luke 17 show a similar equality, thus applying the same principle.

[5]See Mary Alice Chrnalogar, *Twisted Scriptures* (Grand Rapids: Zondervan, 1997), 65. This conclusion is affirmed by Jean Lipman-Blumen, *The Allure of Toxic Leaders* (Oxford: Oxford University Press, 2005), 149; and Ken Sande, *The Peacemaker* (Grand Rapids: Baker, 2004), 156.

[6]Matthew 18:17 seems to imply that only after significant attempts for reconciliation and understanding should a person be treated "as a Gentile and a tax collector."

[7]Ronald M. Cervero and Arthur L. Wilson, *Working the Planning Table* (San Francisco: Jossey-Bass, 2006), 231.

[8]Amy Edmondson, *Teaming: How Organizations Learn, Innovate, and Compete in the Knowledge Economy* (San Francisco: Jossey-Bass 2012), 182.

Postscript: How People Learn the Politics of Ministry

[1]This postscript is adapted from Robert W. Burns and Ronald M. Cervero, "How Pastors Learn the Politics of Ministry Practice," *Religious Education* 97, no. 4 (Fall 2002): 304-21.

[2]R. M. Cervero, *Effective Continuing Education for Professionals* (San Francisco: Jossey-Bass, 1988); R. M. Cervero, "A Model of Professionals as Learners," in *Visions for the Future of Continuing Professional Education*, ed. R. M. Cervero and J. F. Azzaretto et al. (Athens: Georgia Center for Continuing Education, 1990), 161-81; G. Kuhne, *Needs Assessment in Continuing Professional Education: Applying the Word Context Triad Approach with Evangelical Protestant Clergy* (State College: Pennsylvania State University, 1991); M. Eraut, "Knowledge Creation and Knowledge Use in Professional Contexts," *Studies in Higher Education* 10, no. 2 (1985): 117-33; M. Eraut, *Developing Professional Knowledge and Competence* (London: Falmer Press, 1994); V. J. Marsick and K. E. Watkins, *Informal and Incidental Learning in the Workplace* (London: Routledge, 1990); Donald A. Schön, *The Reflective Practitioner: How Professionals Think in Action* (New York: Basic Books, 1983); and Donald A. Schön, *Educating the Reflective Practitioner: Toward a New Design for Teaching and Learning in the Professions* (San Francisco: Jossey-Bass, 1987).

[3]Donald A. Schön, *The Reflective Practitioner: How Professionals Think in Action* (New York: Basic Books, 1983), 243.

[4]L. A. Daloz, *Mentor* (San Francisco: Jossey-Bass, 1999).

[5]Barbara J. Daley, "Creating Mosaics: The Interrelationships of Knowledge and Context," *The Journal of Continuing Education in Nursing* 28, no. 3 (1997): 133-47.

[6]The remainder of this section was adapted for use from Bob Burns, "Survive and Thrive," *Online Pulpit*, http://onlinepulpit.ivpress.com/2013/03/survive_and_thrive.php.

[7]Russ Moxley, "Hardships," in *The Handbook of Leadership Development* (San Francisco: Jossey-Bass, 1998), 196.

[8]E. W. Mills and J. P. Koval, *Stress in the Ministry* (Washington, DC: Ministry Studies Board, 1971).

[9]Roy M. Oswald, *Crossing the Boundary Between Seminary and Parish* (Washington, DC: Alban Institute, 1980).

Appendix 1: Emotions Checklist

[1]The emotions checklist is adapted from Bob Burns and Tom Whiteman, *The Fresh Start Divorce Recovery Workbook: A Step-by-Step Program for Those Who Are Divorced or Separated* (Nashville: Thomas Nelson, 1998).

Appendix 2: Constructing and Exploring a Family Diagram

[1]This appendix was originally presented in Bob Burns, Tasha D. Chapman, and Donald C. Guthrie, *Resilient Ministry* (Downers Grove, IL: InterVarsity Press, 2013), 275-81.

[2]The following books and tools were used to develop these questions: Jim Herrington, R. Robert Creech, and Trisha Taylor, *The Leader's Journey: Accepting the Call to Personal and Congregational Transformation* (San Francisco: Jossey-Bass, 2003); Rita DeMaria, Gerald Weeks, and Larry Hof, *Focused Genograms: Intergenerational Assessment of Individuals, Couples, and Families* (Philadelphia: Brunner/Mazel, 1999); Peter Scazzero, *The Emotionally Healthy Church: A Strategy for Discipleship That Actually Changes Lives* (Grand Rapids: Zondervan, 2003); Peter Scazzero, *Emotionally Healthy Spirituality: Unleash a Revolution in Your Life* (Nashville: Thomas Nelson, 2006); and *RightPath Leadership 360 Manual* by RightPath Resources. For more information on RightPath Resources see www.rightpath.com.

[3]Ken Blanchard uses this model in his leadership profile assessments. See Kenneth H. Blanchard, "SLII: A Situational Approach to Managing People," University of Wisconsin, Madison, www.talent.wisc.edu/download/supervisor/pdf/BLANCHARD-A%20Situational%20Approach.pdf.

[4]Herrington, Creech, and Taylor, *Leader's Journey*, 35.

[5]The following questions were previously published in Bob Burns, Tasha D. Chapman, and Donald C. Guthrie, *Resilient Ministry: What Pastors Told Us About Surviving and Thriving* (Downers Grove, IL: InterVarsity Press, 2013).

About the Authors

Bob has been a pastor and teacher for more than forty years, with experiences ranging from church planting to family ministries, and from worship and the arts to youth and singles ministries. For nearly a decade, Bob was dean of lifelong learning, professor of educational ministries, and director of the Center for Ministry Leadership at Covenant Theological Seminary in St. Louis. During this time he led the Lilly Endowment funded research on pastoral sustainability and ministry leadership, in which the three authors pursued the questions and issues for this book and the companion book previously published by InterVarsity Press, *Resilient Ministry*. He currently serves as pastor of spiritual formation at Church of the Good Shepherd in Durham, NC. Bob and Janet have two married sons and eight grandchildren.

Tasha has served in a variety of administrative and teaching positions at Covenant Theological Seminary in St. Louis for the past seventeen years. She currently teaches full-time as professor of educational ministries. Tasha has over thirty years of experience working with diverse ministries in the United States and overseas. These include university campus ministry, church women's ministry, and international women's ministry, as well as consulting for youth, children's, and special needs ministries and elementary schools. She and her husband, David, have two young adult children, who attempt to keep them technologically and culturally savvy.

Donald serves as professor of educational ministries and director of the educational studies PhD program at Trinity Evangelical Divinity School. He also serves as executive director of Trinity's Center for Transformational Churches. Prior to joining the TEDS faculty, Donald worked in campus ministry with the Coalition for Christian Outreach in Pittsburgh, PA, and served on the faculty and administration of Covenant Theological Seminary in St. Louis. He has enjoyed serving as an elder in several local churches and is a frequent teacher at conferences and retreats. Donald and Mary have two young adult children and one wonderful daughter-in-law.

IVP PRAXIS

EQUIPPING LEADERS FOR MINISTRY

"...TO EQUIP HIS PEOPLE FOR WORKS OF SERVICE,

SO THAT THE BODY OF CHRIST MAY BE BUILT UP."

EPHESIANS 4:12

God has called us to ministry. But it's not enough to have a vision for ministry if you don't have the practical skills for it. Nor is it enough to do the work of ministry if what you do is headed in the wrong direction. We need both vision *and* expertise for effective ministry. We need *praxis*.

Praxis puts theory into practice. It brings cutting-edge ministry expertise from visionary practitioners. You'll find sound biblical and theological foundations for ministry in the real world, with concrete examples for effective action and pastoral ministry. Praxis books are more than the "how to" – they're also the "why to." And because *being* is every bit as important as *doing*, Praxis attends to the inner life of the leader as well as the outer work of ministry. Feed your soul, and feed your ministry.

If you are called to ministry, you know you can't do it on your own. Let Praxis provide the companions you need to equip God's people for life in the kingdom.

www.ivpress.com/praxis